TEACHING AND CHRISTIAN PRACTICES

Teaching and Christian Practices

Reshaping Faith and Learning

Edited by

David I. Smith and James K. A. Smith

WILLIAM B. EERDMANS PUBLISHING COMPANY
GRAND RAPIDS, MICHIGAN / CAMBRIDGE, U.K.

© 2011 Wm B. Eerdmans Publishing Co.

Published 2011 by
Wm. B. Eerdmans Publishing Co.
2140 Oak Industrial Drive N.E., Grand Rapids, Michigan 49505 /
P.O. Box 163, Cambridge CB3 9PU U.K.

Printed in the United States of America

17 16 15 14 13 12 11   7 6 5 4 3 2 1

Library of Congress Cataloging-in-Publication Data

Teaching and Christian practices : reshaping faith and learning /
    edited by David I. Smith and James K.A. Smith.
        p.   cm.
    ISBN 978-0-8028-6685-1 (pbk.: alk. paper)
    1. Universities and colleges — Religion. 2. Teaching — Religious aspects —
    Christianity 3. College teaching. 4. Spirituality — Study and teaching (Higher)
    5. Christian education — Teaching methods   I. Smith, David, 1966-
    II. Smith, James K. A., 1970-

    BV1610.T43   2011
    378'.071 — dc23

                                                             2011020582

www.eerdmans.com

Contents

Contents

Foreword

If you want to see great teaching in action, read this book. If you believe that college classes can be communities of learning where knowledge of self, others, and the world is sought in response to God's call and the world's need, read this book. If you yearn for pedagogical wisdom capable of sustaining resistance to consumerist and instrumentalist pressures on teaching and learning, read this book.

Here, ten college teachers tell what happened when they rethought and re-enacted specific courses in ways that incorporate Christian practices. After accepting the invitation of colleagues David Smith and James Smith to discuss recent philosophical, sociological, and theological literature on social practices, each of these teachers reshaped a course in light of this literature's claim that human beings become who we are in large part through embodied participation in shared activities sustained by traditioned communities and oriented toward specific goods. One outcome was a batch of new courses that turned out to be remarkably engaging for students and teachers alike. Another outcome is this excellent book, one of the best we have ever read on the subject of pedagogy. It is also one of the best we know on the subject of Christian practices.

Teaching and Christian Practices both makes a case for a certain approach to pedagogy and offers multiple illuminating examples of this approach. The editors' brilliant introductory chapter, which analyzes recent work on practices and lifts up its implications for Christian higher education, lays the conceptual groundwork for practice-shaped experiments in teaching and learning. (This chapter clarifies themes in Alasdair MacIntyre and Etienne Wenger, as well as in our own work, that will also be helpful to practitioners in other fields.) Building on this foundation, most of the later chapters portray pedagogical interventions that invite students into learning communities whose *telos* is well-articulated, whose approach is not limited to that which is rational or discursive, and whose acknowledged source and end is God. That practices are not mere techniques for eliciting student engagement and participation is clear on every page. Instead, practices help to create social spaces that have a certain character, spaces graced by regard for human beings as embodied, imaginative members of God's beloved creation. Practices also help students and teachers understand their place in time by disclosing connections between the teaching and learning going on today and the educational aspirations and pedagogical wisdom of historic Christian communities, thereby extending their legacy. Further, the teleological orientation of practices encourages clarity about the guiding purposes of a given course, both within a field of study and as a potential source of personal and social transformation.

Nudged out of accustomed ruts in well-worn pedagogical roads, teachers try something new. They engage in well-informed conversation with colleagues about purposes and pedagogies. They design specific pedagogical moves — assignments, conversations, experiences — while also negotiating student and institutional expectations. They explain innovations to students and try to help them imagine, name, and embrace learning experiences some may find unsettling. They teach, evaluate, listen, converse, and teach again, asking how a specific repertoire of moves relates to how they imagine a given course, its content, and its relation to God's purposes.

Reading the narratives of course development, success, and disappointment that comprise most of this book, we encounter reflective practice at its best. All who read this book will appreciate the humility and honesty of these accounts. We hope that the teachers who read it will also be inspired to undertake similar pedagogical experiments with colleagues in their own settings. If they do, they will soon recognize (as did some of the authors) that they have taken on work that is both rewarding and difficult. This kind of teaching is difficult because Christian practices make not only students but also teachers vulnerable to unpredictable encounters with God and others, and it is rewarding for that very same reason.

Christian faith impels these authors' pedagogical embrace of the shared, concrete life of practices. As the work of faculty members in Christian colleges where integrating faith and learning has typically entailed encounters with theological ideas and the development of a Christian worldview, this book will be seen by some in that setting as a countercultural summons to change. What is even more remarkable to us, however, is that it directly addresses and resists many of the debilitating assumptions that beset teachers across the contemporary academy. In our view, this book represents a countercultural proposal for the wider context as well.

We hope that this book will be read by the teachers from whose ranks we ourselves have come. Seminary and divinity school professors from every curricular area will discover here ideas for deepening the communities of learning over which they preside and ultimately the communities of worship, learning, and practice that their students will someday serve. How might the slow, attentive reading of *lectio divina* open students to comprehend difficult theological texts more fully? How might deliberate attention to the details of classroom hospitality, such as arrangements of space and gestures of greeting and farewell, prepare students to be hospitable pastors and teachers in congregations? How might sharing meals disclose a sacramental dimension in the conversation that takes place around a seminar table, within a specific course, or in the multiple meetings that shape seminary life? How might understanding lectures, discussions, and various forms of student speaking and writing as part of the Christian practice of testimony help to shape a mutually accountable community of learning? And how might attention to the *telos* of abundant life in and for the world, toward which theological education presses, be woven more fully into the awareness and experience of students?

Moreover, although this book was written by and explicitly addressed to Christian teachers, we believe that the pedagogical wisdom gathered here will resonate for faculty members of other faiths or none. In a time when many professors believe that university structures and student demand are deformed by consumerism and economic instrumentalism, education in Christian practices requires that the ends of learning be articulated in terms of specific and transcendent goods and that teaching be enacted, as far as possible, in congruence with those goods. In such education, the formative dimensions of learning are acknowledged, strengthened, and oriented to these same goods. Further, participation in practices opens the educational process to forms of knowledge that are locked out of academic settings focused only on abstract ideas or technical skill. Wisdom becomes something learners can investigate and pursue. Imagination — not as fantasy but as what David I. Smith calls "a particular way of making sense of the world, a construal of what it is that we are doing together and why" — attains its rightful place as a feature of teaching and learning and as a component of abundant living in and beyond the classroom.

Foreword

Rarely does a book so generatively engage the dynamic tension between the particular, concrete moves of teaching and the all-encompassing horizon of faith toward which the finite but hopeful efforts of Christian teachers are oriented. We heartily commend *Teaching and Christian Practices* to all who teach. Reading it will stir their imagination, encourage their faithfulness, and renew their pedagogy.

CRAIG DYKSTRA
Lilly Endowment Inc.

DOROTHY C. BASS
Valparaiso University

Easter 2011

Acknowledgments

As with any substantial project, gratitude is due in a number of directions. We are grateful to the Valparaiso Project on the Education and Formation of People in Faith for funding, to Dorothy Bass for her enthusiasm and support, and to John Witvliet for helping forge that key connection. We would like to thank Jeff Bouman and Rebecca Flietstra for their participation in and contributions to the discussions that shaped these essays. The offices of the Seminars in Christian Scholarship and the Kuyers Institute for Christian Teaching and Learning, both at Calvin College, made the logistics of multiple team meetings and a national conference painless. We are thankful to all of the students whose efforts at Christian learning and patience with our efforts at Christian teaching are represented in what follows. Our thanks also to Jon Pott at Eerdmans for his confidence in this book before it was written. Many others, of course, have nourished our bodies, minds, and spirits in ways that surely leave some trace in what follows; we are grateful to them also.

Introduction: Practices, Faith, and Pedagogy

David I. Smith and James K. A. Smith

Over the past twenty years we have witnessed a ferment of reflection on Christian higher education, Christian scholarship, and the "integration of faith and learning." There were multiple catalysts for such a conversation. On the one hand, though Christians (both Protestant and Catholic) had a long legacy of building colleges and universities, the recent history of these institutions was largely one of decline: from intentionally religious institutions to institutions with a basically secular ethos where Christian faith mattered little, if at all.[1] On the other hand, for a long time the constellation of Christian colleges and universities that continue to exist (and grow) in the United States often operated with a dualistic conception of the relationship between faith and learning — which is just to say that they had little sense of any integral relationship between the two. Instead, what made a college "Christian" was the presence of a chapel, the prescription of certain mores in the dorms, and a blanket of prayer over the whole project. On this model, the classroom, laboratory, and scholarship were still considered "neutral." Furthermore, Christianity in the United States has long exemplified a pervasive American anti-intellectualism, intensified in evan-

---

1. There are both Protestant and Catholic versions of this story. On the Protestant side, see George Marsden, *The Soul of the American University: From Protestant Establishment to Established Nonbelief* (New York: Oxford University Press, 1994). For a history of American Catholic universities' slide toward secularization, see James Tunstead Burtchaell, *The Dying of the Light* (Grand Rapids: Wm. B. Eerdmans, 1998). See also Christian Smith, "Secularizing American Higher Education: The Case of Early American Sociology," in *The Secular Revolution: Power, Interests, and Conflict in the Secularization of American Public Life,* ed. Christian Smith (Berkeley and Los Angeles: University of California Press, 2003), pp. 97-158.

gelical spirituality, which required a special apologetic to justify the work of scholarship and the value of higher education.

It was into this milieu of challenges that several important books spoke. Mark Noll's *The Scandal of the Evangelical Mind* challenged the latent anti-intellectualism and lingering dualism that plagued evangelical higher education, calling for a more integral understanding of the relationship between Christian faith and scholarship.[2] While Noll's analysis was something of a jeremiad, he also constructively called for a robust vision of explicitly Christian scholarship, echoing (and tipping his hat to) Abraham Kuyper as a source and model. In a similar vein, George Marsden — building on his historical analysis in *The Soul of the American University* — pushed back on the latent orthodoxy of the secular academy by pointing out the "confessional" starting points of any and all scholarship, opening room at the table for explicitly Christian scholarship and encouraging "explicit discussion of the relationship of religious faith to learning."[3]

This emerging paradigm, which stressed the "integration" of faith and learning, called into question the very idea of "secular" or "neutral" learning, emphasized a faith-inspired affirmation of intellectual pursuits, and refused to settle for models that positioned faith and learning as merely complementary or parallel. The classroom was as "holy" as the chapel; the laboratory was an arena for faith as much as the sanctuary; all of life was to be considered "from a Christian perspective." And while this (largely Reformed) conversation about "the integration of faith and learning" also generated critique,[4] even the alternatives continued to be concerned about the perspectival role of faith in informing scholarship.

But a funny thing happened on the way to the Christian university: the central task of *teaching* almost completely dropped off the scholarly radar. While the conversation was commonly billed as a consideration of "the integration of faith and *learning*," the focus tended to be the role of faith in research and scholarship. In other words, the debate seemed to forget that Christian higher education has two main concerns. Of course, on

---

2. Mark A. Noll, *The Scandal of the Evangelical Mind* (Grand Rapids: Wm. B. Eerdmans, 1994).

3. George Marsden, *The Outrageous Idea of Christian Scholarship* (New York: Oxford University Press, 1997), p. 3.

4. See most notably Douglas Jacobsen and Rhonda Hustedt Jacobsen, eds., *Scholarship and Christian Faith: Enlarging the Conversation* (New York: Oxford University Press, 2004).

the one hand, Christian colleges and universities rightly serve as centers for the scholarly varieties of Christian engagement with the life of the mind, the issues of the day, and the needs of the world. Under the banner of "integrating faith and learning" (or some alternative nomenclature), Christian faculty engage in research, advocacy, and service rooted in Christian intellectual perspectives. But on the other hand, Christian colleges and universities tend for the most part to be primarily teaching institutions, concerned with educating those students who choose a Christian education. To judge by the mission statements typical of Christian institutions of higher education, this is generally felt to involve more than the transmission of information — the spiritual and moral as well as the intellectual formation of students is in some sense at stake.

While both of these two broad endeavors absorb the best energies of faculty on Christian campuses, it seems fair to observe that our commitment to Christian scholarship has been significantly more articulate than our commitment to Christian pedagogy. Complex and continuing debates about the dynamics of worldviews, presuppositions, perspectives, science and religion, and various "isms" have made space for the emergence of nuanced understandings of the relationship of faith to scholarly work. However, only a tiny percentage of the scholarly writing that emerges from Christian higher education is devoted to the development of equally nuanced accounts of how teaching and learning are supposed to work in a Christian setting.[5]

Even conversations that bill themselves as concerned with pedagogy exhibit two problematic tendencies. A significant portion of these conversations focuses on the question of *content* — which Christian ideas and perspectives will be taught — implying that Christian teaching simply means teaching that contains or propounds Christian ideas and perspectives. It is common to find that even when the announced focus is teaching and learning, the emphasis is ultimately on epistemology or theology, and the discussion remains distanced from what happens in classrooms. While

---

5. An ongoing survey conducted by the Kuyers Institute for Christian Teaching and Learning of about 11,000 articles published in the past four decades in Christian scholarly journals has identified less than 500 articles that deal with teaching and learning as opposed to disciplinary concepts and theories. It is also interesting to note that some of the disciplines that have had a somewhat less obvious relationship to the "integration of faith and learning" discussion in terms of Christian scholarship have devoted relatively more attention to pedagogy, while disciplines central to the faith and learning debate (notably philosophy and history) have produced virtually no Christian scholarly writing on pedagogy.

the choice of individual examples may have a degree of arbitrariness, consider, for instance, Mark Noll's essay titled "Teaching History as a Christian." Noll opens with questions about how a Christian view of persons might affect history pedagogy, but after a few paragraphs his essay is dominated by a discussion of how a Christian epistemology views the knowability of historical facts. Harry Huebner's essay on the kind of learning needed for a Christian university — "Learning Made Strange: Can a University Be Christian?" — similarly sets out to address the shallowness of "Christian pedagogy" but spends most of its energies discussing theological and philosophical frameworks before closing with some very apt but rather general reflections on theological content and teacherly virtues. Both of these are interesting essays in their own right; if one is concerned specifically with pedagogical questions, however, their reach is limited.[6] This is not an uncommon state of affairs. It seems remarkably difficult for Christian scholars to focus on the classroom for very long, or perhaps it would be more fitting to say that it seems hard for them to get the classroom into focus. Theological and epistemological frameworks abound, but it is distressingly rare for the resulting pedagogical advice to get beyond broad exhortations to, say, try team teaching, or model humility, or use self-disclosing stories. Such pedagogical suggestions are not wrong, but rarely achieve any significant degree of texture that might allow us, for instance, to begin to see the differences between more and less helpful instantiations of them.

Another subset of published work about Christian teaching focuses more on the personal character or inner self of the teacher — perhaps in terms of the individual modeling of virtues or a spirituality of teaching.[7] Christian teaching here means teaching in which a certain character is displayed or a certain kind of "heart" or ethos sustains the process. This, too, is clearly an important train of thought — Christian education does indeed need more than the fruits of Christian inquiry and should be suffused with a Christian spirit. But it turns out on closer examination that a

---

6. See Noll's essay in *Religion, Scholarship, and Higher Education: Perspectives, Models, and Future Prospects*, ed. Andrea Sterk (Notre Dame: University of Notre Dame Press, 2002), pp. 161-71; this volume seeks to offer a state-of-the-art overview of faith and higher education discussions. See Huebner's essay in *God, Truth, and Witness: Engaging Stanley Hauerwas*, ed. L. Gregory Jones, Reinhard Hütter, and C. Rosalee Velloso Ewell (Grand Rapids: Brazos Press, 2005), pp. 280-308.

7. See, for example, Parker J. Palmer, *The Courage to Teach: Exploring the Inner Landscape of a Teacher's Life* (San Francisco: Jossey-Bass, 1998).

great deal of the available writing in either of these two veins has remarkably little to say about the concrete practices of teaching and learning and the rich texture of embodied pedagogical encounters. Christian scholarship has by and large (with, of course, some helpful exceptions) mirrored the commonly lamented lack in the wider academy of a substantial "scholarship of teaching and learning."[8]

In short, when talk is of "the integration of faith and learning," it seems that "learning" has most often meant primarily the kind of learning that makes faculty learned, rather than learning understood as the pedagogical experiences of students. When conversations about pedagogy do occur among Christian faculty, it is all too common to find them uncritically reflecting tired dichotomies (such as lecturing versus group work) or currently fashionable slogans (such as brain-based or student-centered learning) rather than being informed by explicitly Christian reflection. As a result, the typical pedagogical practices of the modern university often remain largely unrevised as the default medium within which attempts to think, speak, and educate Christianly are conducted. This book aims to signal a game-change in these conversations. Building on a generation of contributions on the integration of faith and learning, we aim to focus more explicitly on *learning,* and specifically on the practices involved in teaching and learning. In other words, we hope to broaden the conversation from a focus on scholarship to include more explicit concern with pedagogy. In order to do so in an explicitly Christian frame, the essays that follow propose that we take a closer look at the possible relationship between historic Christian practices and the practices that characterize courses and classrooms. Such an undertaking opens up potential for articulating more fully what might be Christian about pedagogy in ways that push beyond the spirituality of the individual teacher or the status of the ideas communicated. Such a shift also gives needed

8. On the wider discussion of the scholarship of teaching and learning, see Ernest L. Boyer, *Scholarship Reconsidered: Priorities of the Professoriate* (Princeton, N.J.: The Carnegie Foundation for the Advancement of Teaching, 1990); and Mary Taylor Huber and Pat Hutchings, *The Advancement of Learning: Building the Teaching Commons* (San Francisco: Jossey-Bass, 2005). For examples of recent Christian efforts to address teaching and learning, see, for instance, *Teaching as an Act of Faith: Theory and Practice in Church-Related Higher Education,* ed. Anthony C. Migliazzo (New York: Fordham University Press, 2002); Chris Anderson, *Teaching as Believing: Faith in the University* (Waco, Tex.: Baylor University Press, 2004); and Perry L. Glanzer and Todd C. Ream, *Christianity and Moral Identity in Higher Education* (New York: Palgrave Macmillan, 2009).

weight to the ways in which we are formed by the practices in which we participate, and not merely by the ideas we exchange. We suggest that Christian practices offer a kind of pedagogical wisdom that could reshape and redirect our classroom choices and strategies in surprising yet fruitful ways.

The ideas explored in this volume are at times countercultural, but they do not stand in eccentric isolation; that is, we don't think our intuitions are idiosyncratic. Rather, the project draws together the wisdom to be gleaned from three substantial and important scholarly discussions, three streams of contemporary thought that we will outline further in the remainder of this introduction:

- first, a body of literature in philosophy and sociology that has explored the formative nature of social practices;
- second, discussions among educators and philosophers of education regarding how concepts of practice developed in philosophy and sociology can be used to characterize what happens in teaching and learning;
- and third, a specifically theological literature that connects this recent concern with social practices back to the Christian church's more ancient commitment to formation through practices and disciplines that embody the Christian way of being in the world — practices such as prayer, hospitality, testimony, community, and Sabbath-keeping.

These scholarly conversations represent, among other things, a move away from the notion that rational deliberation on ideas is the primary shaper of the self, and toward a more contextual and embodied understanding of how what we do with and among others shapes who we become.[9] Our concern here is to take these existing discussions — concerning the nature of social practices, of education as a set of practices, and of the role of practices in Christian formation — and explore how they might offer a matrix for re-imagining Christian teaching and learning. We will therefore offer here a little more exposition of these background ideas to provide a

---

9. As Paul Griffiths puts it in his chapter in this volume, "Offering an account of what one does as a learned or would-be learned person is much less formative of and intimate with the modes of knowing one performs than are the practices into which one is catechized as a neophyte of a particular form of learning." See p. 111n.9 below.

frame for understanding the particular projects represented in the chapters that follow.

Learning as Formation: Virtues, Habits, and Practices

Much of the current discussion about the role of "practices" in formation owes a debt to Alasdair MacIntyre's now-classic work *After Virtue*, in which he introduces an oft-cited definition of "practice."[10] But before attending to his definition, we should first contextualize it in his larger project.[11] Diagnosing the demise of the Enlightenment project (and decrying its aims), MacIntyre notes that what doomed the Enlightenment project from the start was its loss of the concept of *telos* (the end of a goal-oriented process).[12] Emphasizing the autonomy of individuals to determine their own ends, and thus rejecting any specified *telos* as an imposition on libertarian freedom, the Enlightenment project underestimated the significance of moral *formation*. Instead, its picture of the moral agent assumed a kind of natural, untutored rationality that would simply "choose" what was right because it was rational. In short, by rejecting the notion of a shared human *telos* and extolling individual rationality, the Enlightenment project had to reject any notion of *virtue* — for virtue language makes sense only where one recognizes the formative role of communities of practice that *create* ethical agents.[13] Enlightenment models of ethical action are allegedly born; virtuous actors are always and only *made*.

So, as MacIntyre argues, there can be talk of virtue only where there is a teleology in place, for virtues are those habits and dispositions that incline one toward the *telos* specified as "the good." Thus MacIntyre also emphasizes that what counts as a virtue is always relative to the *specification* of

10. Alasdair MacIntyre, *After Virtue*, 3rd ed. (Notre Dame: University of Notre Dame Press, 2007).

11. For helpful accounts, see Brad J. Kallenberg, "The Master Argument of MacIntyre's *After Virtue*," in *Virtues and Practices in the Christian Tradition*, ed. Nancey Murphy, Brad J. Kallenberg, and Mark Thiessen Nation (Notre Dame: University of Notre Dame Press, 2003), pp. 7-29; and Jonathan R. Wilson, *Living Faithfully in a Fragmented World: Lessons for the Church from MacIntyre's* After Virtue (Harrisburg, Pa.: Trinity Press International, 1997).

12. MacIntyre, *After Virtue*, pp. 195, 203.

13. It should be noted that Charles Taylor offers a similar diagnosis and critique of the Enlightenment model on this point. See Taylor, *Modern Social Imaginaries* (Durham, N.C.: Duke University Press, 2004), pp. 79-80.

"the good," and such specifications of the good are communicated to us through the narratives of particular traditions.[14]

Such habits and dispositions are not "natural" in the sense of being inborn capacities or abilities; rather, they are "second nature": acquired dispositions and inclinations that are absorbed over time by participating in the routines and rituals of a tradition, as well as by imitating the models upheld as "exemplars" by the tradition. On this account, a moral "education" is not just a matter of getting the right information about my duties, obligations, and responsibilities; rather, moral education becomes a matter of *formation* — the inscription of good habits (virtue) as the construction of character. And such moral formation happens by means of practice. Thus it is that MacIntyre offers his (rather inelegant but influential) definition of a "practice":

> By a "practice" I am going to mean any coherent and complex form of socially established cooperative human activity through which goods internal to that form of activity are realized in the course of trying to achieve those standards of excellence which are appropriate to, and partially definitive of, that form of activity, with the result that human powers to achieve excellence, and human conceptions of the ends and goods involved, are systematically extended.[15]

We should note several of features of this definition of a practice:

- First, a practice is social, communal, and inherited: it is a complex of routines and rituals that is handed down from others.
- Second, not all routines and rituals are "practices" in this sense. MacIntyre draws the distinction by emphasizing that a full-blooded "practice" has "internal goods." These are goals or aims that can be achieved *only* by engaging in the practice. "External" goods can be achieved in any number of ways. For example, chess is a practice with internal goods which are specific to the game (analytic skill, strategic

---

14. MacIntyre means to emphasize the storied character of moral traditions with his use of the term *narrative*. As he later puts it, "I can only answer the question, 'What am I to do?' if I can answer the prior question 'Of what story or stories do I find myself a part?'" (*After Virtue*, p. 216). MacIntyre emphasizes that virtue is, strictly speaking, "relative": that is, what counts as virtue is relative to what a tradition's narrative extols as the *telos* of human flourishing. This is why Homer, Aristotle, Paul, and Jane Austen can all be "virtue theorists" and yet have such significantly different catalogues of virtues. See *After Virtue*, pp. 181-87.

15. MacIntyre, *After Virtue*, p. 187.

imagination, competitive intensity). To really play chess — to be a *practitioner* of the practice — is to seek these internal goods. Now, I might also play chess to become rich and famous; but such goods are "external" to the practice — they could be achieved by any number of strategies.[16] If I merely "instrumentalize" a practice for some other, external end, then I'm not really a practitioner.

- Third, every practice has relevant standards of excellence, determined (but also debated) by the community and tradition that nourishes the practice. Thus "to enter into a practice is to accept the authority of those standards," for the good internal to the practice "can only be achieved by subordinating ourselves within the practice in our relationship to other practitioners."[17]

The upshot of MacIntyre's notion of practice is directly concerned with the nature of education. While his primary concern is the shape of *moral* education, he raises the broader point that any education worthy of the name has to be formative, and that formation happens only through practices which inscribe a *habitus* — an orientation and inclination toward the world, aimed at a specific *telos*.[18]

While MacIntyre's sense of practice has a deeply Aristotelian pedigree, one finds an overlapping sense of practice and formation in the social theory of Pierre Bourdieu, who also invokes the notion of *habitus* to make sense of the formative power of cultural practices. For Bourdieu, this is a matter of honoring the significance of our non- or pre-rational comportment to the world. Contesting both empiricism and intellectualism — that is, both materialist determinisms and overestimations of rational deliberation — Bourdieu is fighting on two fronts, insisting, "contrary to positivist materialism, that the objects of knowledge are

---

16. This is why MacIntyre will claim that "throwing a football" is *not* a practice, whereas the "the game of football is"; or "bricklaying is not a practice," whereas "architecture is" (MacIntyre, *After Virtue*, p. 187). The idea is that bricklaying could never be an end in itself; it would also be subordinate to some grander aim (e.g., building a cathedral). This distinction is germane to the discussion below regarding whether teaching can be a practice.

17. MacIntyre, *After Virtue*, p. 191.

18. Indeed, the claim is that any education is formative in this sense, even if it doesn't own up to the formative power of pedagogy. In short, the question isn't *whether* education forms virtue but rather *which* virtues are being inscribed (and to which *telos* such an education is oriented). For an excellent analysis, see Perry L. Glanzer and Todd C. Ream, *Christianity and Moral Identity in Higher Education* (New York: Palgrave Macmillan, 2009).

constructed, not passively recorded, and, contrary to intellectualist ideal-ism, that the principle of this construction is the system of structured, structuring dispositions, the *habitus,* which is constituted in practice and is always oriented towards practical functions."[19] On this model, *habitus* is an orientation to and understanding of the world that is absorbed and shaped at the level of practice. Bourdieu is thus interested in "the conditionings associated with a particular class of conditions of exis-tence" that "produce *habitus,* systems of durable, transposable disposi-tions, structured structures predisposed to function as structuring struc-tures, that is, as principles which generate and organize practices and representations that can be objectively adapted to their outcomes without presupposing a conscious aiming at ends or an express mastery of the op-erations necessary in order to attain them."[20] Learned and acquired through practice, *habitus* is "embodied history, internalized as a second nature"; it functions as "accumulated capital," and "is a spontaneity with-out consciousness or will, opposed as much to the mechanical necessity of things without history in mechanistic theories as it is to the reflexive freedom of subjects 'without inertia' in rationalist theories."[21] What this generates is a "practical sense" — a kind of know-how that is either un-conscious or preconscious but nonetheless intentional and oriented to some end or *telos.*[22]

Bourdieu wants us to recognize that practice has its own "logic"; to rephrase Pascal, practice has a logic of which logic knows nothing. Or as Bourdieu himself puts it, "Practice has a logic which is not that of the logi-cian."[23] What we're interested in culling from Bourdieu is not only his em-phasis on the formative role of practices and "rites," but also his sense that "practice" has its own logic. It seems to us that this is a fruitful, suggestive lens for considering the irreducible wisdom embedded in pedagogical

---

19. Pierre Bourdieu, *The Logic of Practice,* trans. Richard Nice (Stanford: Stanford University Press, 1990), p. 52.

20. Bourdieu, *The Logic of Practice,* p. 53.

21. Bourdieu, *The Logic of Practice,* p. 56.

22. "Practical sense is a quasi-bodily involvement in the world which presupposes no representation either of the body or of the world, still less of their relationship. It is an im-manence in the world through which the world imposes its imminence, things to be done or said, which directly govern speech and action. It orients 'choices' which, though not deliber-ate, are no less systematic. . . ." An example is "a 'feel for the game.'" See Bourdieu, *The Logic of Practice,* p. 66.

23. Bourdieu, *The Logic of Practice,* p. 86.

practices — not, it should be noted, just because of the content that they transmit but also because of the "logic" that inheres in the practice.

Educational Reflections on Practices

Given the lasting influence of MacIntyre's careful discussion of the criteria that enable a human activity to be identified as a "practice," it is perhaps not surprising that one of the traces of his work in educational discussions is a debate concerning whether teaching is, in the MacIntyrean sense, a practice. MacIntyre himself, somewhat to the consternation of philosophers of education seeking to work with his ideas, offered the view that teaching is not a practice, on the grounds that teaching lacks its own internal good to serve as its *telos,* but instead serves a variety of goods derived from the particular ideas and practices being taught.[24] Others, notably Joseph Dunne, have disagreed, with philosophers of education tending to find MacIntyre's view of teaching somewhat reductive.[25]

Interesting as this debate is, for our present purposes in this volume it is somewhat beside the point, since our focus is not on the status of the act of teaching per se, but rather on what Christian practices can contribute to how teaching and learning are carried out and experienced (more on this below). Once the focus shifts from defining and demarcating practices to the various ways that patterns of Christian practice might inform the practices of the classroom, another influential line of educational discussion becomes relevant and helpful, one rising from the work of Etienne Wenger.[26]

24. Alasdair MacIntyre and Joseph Dunne, "Alasdair MacIntyre on Education: In Dialogue with Joseph Dunne," *Journal of Philosophy of Education* 36 (2002): 1-19.

25. See Joseph Dunne, "What's the Good of Education?" in *The RoutledgeFalmer Reader in Philosophy of Education,* ed. Wilfred Carr (London and New York: Routledge, 2005), pp. 145-60;"Arguing for Teaching as a Practice: A Reply to Alasdair MacIntyre," *Journal of Philosophy of Education* 37 (2003): 353-69. Apropos of this debate, see also David Carr, "Rival Conceptions of Practice in Education and Teaching," *Journal of Philosophy of Education* 37 (2003): 253-66; Pádraig Hogan, "Teaching and Learning as a Way of Life," *Journal of Philosophy of Education* 37 (2003): 207-23; and Nell Noddings, "Is Teaching a Practice?" *Journal of Philosophy of Education* 37 (2003): 241-51.

26. Of course, Bourdieu's work has also been extensively drawn upon in educational research; for the present project, however, his influence was in most cases mediated through Wenger's work, and so we focus on Wenger's contribution to educational discussions of practices here. For a helpful comparison of MacIntyre and Wenger on practices in relation

Wenger is an educational theorist who has written extensively about how "communities of practice" function, an interest that grew out of earlier work on the nature of the learning that takes place in the context of apprenticeship.[27] He defines practice as action "in a historical and social context that gives structure and meaning to what we do" — or, more catchily, as "a shared history of learning that requires some catching up for joining."[28] Groups of people who engage in shared patterns of practice in concrete settings (offices, classrooms, sports fields, etc.) become "communities of practice." People come together on a regular basis and do things together in certain ways in pursuit of certain shared goals, and in doing so, they become a community that is defined and held together by shared practices (rather than, for example, family ties or affectionate attachments).

Wenger sees several basic processes constantly interacting to shape communities of practice. Certain forms of *participation* are available to different members of the community. By this he means the kinds of actions, interactions, and relationships that are available for a given member of the group.[29] For example, in one kind of group I might be able to speak my mind spontaneously and freely, while in another group, speech might be more controlled or even ritualized. In one setting someone asks a question, and I shout out an answer; in another I raise a hand or decide not to speak at all. When I am in the first group, I get to hold the floor and speak as an expert; when I transition to the second group, I get to make the coffee. There may be various forms of participation that are plausible to me in a given group at a given moment. At the same time, there is an accompanying process of *reification,* as ideas at work in the group get turned into things (objects, gestures, sounds) that endure from one session to another.

---

to education, see Terence McLaughlin, "Teaching as a Practice and a Community of Practice: The Limits of Commonality and the Demands of Diversity," *Journal of Philosophy of Education* 37 (2003): 339-52.

27. Jean Lave and Etienne Wenger, *Situated Learning: Legitimate Peripheral Participation* (Cambridge: Cambridge University Press, 1991); *Understanding Practice: Perspectives on Activity and Context,* ed. Seth Chaiklin and Jean Lave (Cambridge: Cambridge University Press, 1993).

28. Etienne Wenger, *Communities of Practice: Learning, Meaning, and Identity* (Cambridge: Cambridge University Press, 1999), pp. 47, 102.

29. Clearly, a wide range of actions is possible in the abstract in any setting (it is always in principle open to a student in class to, say, leap onto the teacher's desk and begin singing); various social constraints, however, including shared imagination (see below), keep a smaller range of behaviors actually available, with variation among participants as to what is available. The issue isn't compulsion, but rather social possibility.

You can't kick an idea — but you can (and might occasionally want to) kick a computer that was installed in the classroom because of someone's conviction that technology helps learning. Reifications in classrooms would include, for example, chairs, desks, textbooks, grades, syllabi, tests, gestures, and so on. Ideas, assumptions, and goals have become reified parts of the shared physical environment, and consequently constrain future actions.

Participation and reification constantly interact as members of the community negotiate the meaning of their actions with one another. If my classroom consists of a large number of chairs fixed in straight rows all facing in the same direction, then certain kinds of participation, such as listening to a lecture and writing notes, become easier. Other kinds, such as group discussion, become more difficult. If the classroom has chairs arranged in circles around larger tables, then the opposite is true. Similarly, some ways of awarding grades (judgments reified as letter-objects) will encourage individually competitive forms of participation; others will encourage cooperation. Some ways of grading will encourage conformity; others, originality. As these choices become reified into stable institutional structures, they may work for or against the intentions of individual instructors or learners the next time around, guiding their choices, whether with or against the grain of their prior preferences. Reification and participation are always at work together, in harmony or in tension.

As they work together and negotiate the meaning of their actions over time, members of a community become aligned to one another and develop a *repertoire* — a set of behaviors having particular meaning for this group. Certain words take on special shades of meaning that are opaque to outsiders. Certain gestures become immediately recognizable. Instructions given explicitly at the beginning of the semester may not need to be repeated later, for everyone in the group comes to know their expected moves. By the end of a semester in which Friday is homework day, if I forget to tell my students to turn in their homework on a Friday, most of them walk forward at the end of class and do it anyway — it has become part of the repertoire, the set of behaviors and meanings shared by this group. Repertoire (like *habitus*) is a way of naming the patterns inscribed in the way we do things together, and helps to define the boundaries that form between the different communities of practice of which any given individual is a part.

Wenger emphasizes that these patterns of practice are informed by a shared *imagination,* a sense of what the community of practice is about, what goods it is pursuing and why. Here *imagination* does not mean "fantasy" or "creativity" (see further the final chapter of this volume); it refers to the ways in which we construe our shared tasks. Sharing this imagination is one way of belonging to the community. Not sharing it is one way of not fitting in. If a group of students imagines that they are fulfilling a boring but necessary task to complete a program requirement, while the professor imagines that the group is engaged in a passionate pursuit of truth, frustrations will emerge. Over time, imagination becomes embodied in repertoire, and repertoire at the same time shapes imagination. Shared imagination is manifest as much in what we do as in what we say.

There is considerably more detail in Wenger's account, but this brief summary will suffice to indicate its relevance. A community of practice, Wenger says, is shaped out of certain forms of participation, an ongoing process of reification that turns intentions into stable objects, the growth of a shared repertoire of meanings and behaviors, and the development of a shared imagination concerning what the group is really aiming for. An account such as Wenger's has value for discussions of Christian practices and Christian learning because it provides a systematic framework for exploring how vision becomes embodied in particular educational behaviors and how learning arises from those behaviors, opening space to examine the relationship of faith not just to ideas, but to pedagogical practices.

Theological Reflections on Practices

The constellation of the MacIntyrean themes of practice, virtue, and formation has also made a significant impact on a generation of discussions in theology, particularly in the area of practical theology concerned with Christian education. In the same way that we want to push back on reducing Christian education to the dissemination of Christian ideas, voices such as Craig Dykstra and Dorothy Bass have contested the reduction of Christian faith to intellectual assent to a set of propositions. This involves a shift from considering Christianity as an intellectual system to (re)emphasizing the church as a community of practice. Thus, as Dykstra summarizes it, "the life of Christian faith is the practice of many practices."[30] Or as Brad Kallenberg summarizes, "Christianity cannot be explained or un-

---

30. Craig Dykstra, *Growing in the Life of Faith: Education and Christian Practices*, 2nd ed. (Louisville: Westminster John Knox Press, 2005), p. 67.

derstood without reference to a distinctive cluster of practices. In order to participate in the tradition called Christianity one must necessarily participate in these practices."[31]

Dykstra's account appreciates MacIntyre's claims regarding the formative power of practices (and this is just returning MacIntyre's model to its originating soil). "The primary point about practices," he emphasizes, "is no longer that they are something we do. Instead, they become arenas in which something is done to us, in us, and through us that we could not of ourselves do, that is beyond what we do."[32] Practices, then, are not just "things we do"; they do something *to* us. Dykstra appropriates the MacIntyrean definition of practice in order to highlight this formative aspect of Christian practices. So, on the one hand, Christian practices are like other practices (like chess and football): they are social, complex, teleological, informed by tradition and narrative, and so on. They fit MacIntyre's definition of "a practice." On the other hand, they're also *more* than that. Thus, while Dykstra often "naturalizes" Christian practices, as it were, in order to help us appreciate their almost mundane formative power, he also emphasizes what is unique or peculiar about Christian practices: they are nothing less than "habitations of the Spirit."[33] One might say that the formative power of Christian practices is never less than natural, but it is also more than natural.

When viewed through this MacIntyrean lens, we begin to appreciate that Christian practices would have implications beyond the confines of "spirituality." If practices form our very comportment to the world and inscribe in us a *habitus* that primes and shapes our action, then Christian practices will do nothing less than configure how we see and act in the world.

But what do we mean by "Christian practices"? What would be included under such a rubric? On one level, the term might refer quite specifically to *worship* practices — the liturgical rites and routines that mark the church.[34] But on another level, the term can refer to a wider set of practices somewhat synonymous with "spiritual disciplines" (and this

---

31. Kallenberg, "The Master Argument of MacIntyre's *After Virtue*," p. 22.

32. Dykstra, *Growing in the Life of Faith*, p. 56.

33. Dykstra, *Growing in the Life of Faith*, p. 63. This is combined with an appreciation for their physicality (p. 71).

34. This seems to be the operative focus behind an important book along these lines: *The Blackwell Companion to Christian Ethics*, ed. Stanley Hauerwas and Samuel Wells (Oxford: Blackwell, 2006). The "practices" considered are generally restricted to those practices that constitute aspects of Christian worship.

wider definition can obviously include the narrower set of Christian worship practices). In this book, our authors generally follow Dykstra and Bass in recognizing a wider set of Christian practices that includes not only baptism and the Eucharist but also hospitality, Sabbath-keeping, testimony, simplicity, and many more.[35] Thus we tend to function with Bass and Dykstra's more generous definition of Christian practices as "things Christian people do together over time in response to and in the light of God's active presence for the life of the world."[36]

While this discussion of Christian practices has been appropriated for thinking about "Christian education" more narrowly (that is, faith formation in the church and in the context of theological education), it has been largely untapped as a resource for thinking about pedagogy in the context of Christian colleges and universities. While there is all sorts of room for discussion regarding how to conceive the relationship between Christian educational institutions and the church more specifically, we are convinced of two things that invite us to see the connection between the two more intimately: On the one hand, we are convinced that Christian education must be *formative* in just the sense that MacIntyre emphasizes. If Christian higher education is going to take seriously its responsibility for education in *virtue*, then it also needs to attend to matters of practice and formation.[37] On the other hand, we are convinced that implicit in the in-

---

35. While there is a conversation to be had regarding the relation (and perhaps priority) between specifically liturgical practices and extra-liturgical Christian practices, we won't distract ourselves with that point here. This project is officially agnostic on the point and has room to absorb models that might prioritize liturgical practices as well as those that do not. Craig Dykstra and Dorothy Bass give a certain priority to liturgical practices as the "consommé" to the "broth" of wider Christian practices ("Times of Yearning, Practices of Faith," in *Practicing Our Faith*, ed. Dorothy C. Bass [San Francisco: Jossey-Bass, 1997], p. 9), whereas Miroslav Volf seems ambivalent about according any priority to specifically liturgical practices (see Volf, "Theology for a Way of Life," in *Practicing Theology: Beliefs and Practices in Christian Life*, ed. Miroslav Volf and Dorothy C. Bass [Grand Rapids: Wm. B. Eerdmans, 2002], pp. 245-63). This stems from Volf's attendant (though contestable) claim that, *de jure*, beliefs "ground" practices (pp. 258-61). For an alternative account of the relation between beliefs and practices, see James K. A. Smith, *Desiring the Kingdom: Worship, Worldview, and Cultural Formation* (Grand Rapids: Baker Academic, 2009), pp. 133-39.

36. Dykstra and Bass, "Times of Yearning, Practices of Faith," p. 5.

37. This is the central argument of Glanzer and Ream in *Christianity and Moral Identity in Higher Education*. Christian colleges also broadcast claims about "virtue" formation. See, for example, the "Core Virtues" included as part of the Core Curriculum at Calvin College (discussed in an appendix to Cornelius Plantinga's *Engaging God's World: A Reformed Vision of Faith, Learning, and Living* [Grand Rapids: Wm. B. Eerdmans, 2002], pp. 225-41).

herited practices of the Christian tradition is a kind of pedagogical wisdom on which we can draw for Christian teaching more broadly.

Christian Practices and Christian Learning

Drawing from these philosophical, educational, and theological inquiries into the nature and importance of practices, our goal in the present volume is to extend their insights in ways that speak to the Christian classroom. We propose that various elements of these discussions can help to frame an account of what a Christian pedagogy could look like *in practice,* beyond a focus on whether Christian ideas are being conveyed or Christian character is being individually modeled.

We noted above that the essays in this book are not primarily concerned with the status of teaching per se as a practice, but rather with the various ways that the work on Christian practices just described might inform classrooms across the disciplines. This focus suggests somewhat differently framed questions. It invites exploration of the possible relationships between particular Christian practices and the learning setting. It soon becomes evident that there is more than one possible relationship between Christian practices and educational practices. Questions worth exploring include these:

- When can or should a particular Christian practice become a direct part of what is taught, a straightforward ingredient in the educational experience, whether in order to enhance the achievement of existing learning goals or in order to expand outcomes to include broader kinds of formation? For example, how would learning processes and outcomes be changed if learners were asked to try *lectio divina* as part of their learning how to engage with great literary works, or if they were asked to fast before a discussion on poverty in an ethics course?[38]
- Are there particular Christian practices that can sustain the enterprise of teaching and learning by forming dispositions that both

38. K. Jo-Ann Badley and Ken Badley, "Slow Reading: Reading along *Lectio* Lines," *Journal of Education and Christian Belief* 15, no. 1 (2011): 29-42. Bradford S. Hadaway, "Preparing the Way for Justice: Strategic Dispositional Formation through the Spiritual Disciplines," in *Spirituality, Justice, and Pedagogy,* ed. David I. Smith, John Shortt, and John Sullivan (Nottingham: The Stapleford Centre, 2006), pp. 143-65.

contribute to successful learning and give it a particular cast? If, for example, a certain degree of humility is a precondition of genuine learning (as Mark Schwehn has argued),[39] inclining the learner to be willing to surrender his or her own quick judgments in favor of a presumption of wisdom in the authors of the material studied, then are there particular Christian practices that can help shape or sustain this form of humility?

• Since Christian practices are themselves, at least in part, pedagogical devices to help form the self in particular directions, then are there ways in which they can function as models for, analogies to, or guiding metaphors for educational practices — framing pedagogy by offering a kind of hermeneutical clue to a normative shape for daily educational life? How, for instance, would foreign and second-language learning look different if it were patterned on the practice of hospitality to strangers rather than on the practices more typically associated with tourism or international business?[40]

• Are there present patterns of educational practice that are in tension with the kinds of formation implicitly aimed at by Christian practices, such that we need to consider restructuring teaching and learning lest their rhythms be in competition with Christian formation? Could, for instance, our investment in individual ownership and rapid consumption of knowledge be at odds with the attentiveness and receptivity needed to read Scripture well, or might our focus on individual autonomy create tension with the goal of growth in humility?[41]

39. Mark R. Schwehn, *Exiles from Eden: Religion and the Academic Vocation in America* (New York: Oxford University Press, 2005).

40. See David I. Smith and Barbara Carvill, *The Gift of the Stranger: Faith, Hospitality, and Foreign Language Learning* (Grand Rapids: Wm. B. Eerdmans, 2000); David I. Smith, *Learning from the Stranger: Christian Faith and Cultural Diversity* (Grand Rapids: Wm. B. Eerdmans, 2009).

41. Paul Griffiths argues the former in *The Vice of Curiosity: An Essay on Intellectual Appetite* (Winnipeg: CMU Press, 2006); Susan Mendus argues the latter in her article "Tolerance and Recognition: Education in a Multicultural Society," *Journal of Philosophy of Education* 29, no. 2 (2005): 191-202. The tension could, of course, run in either direction here — it may be that the practices of particular Christian communities undermine learning. For instance, socialization into certain proof-texting strategies as a part of the communal practice of biblical interpretation may make it more difficult for certain students to succeed in writing or speaking tasks framed by other norms of discourse. See, for example, Chris Anderson, "The Description of an Embarrassment: When Students Write about Religion," *ADE Bulletin* 94 (1989): 12-15; and Elizabeth Platt, "'Uh uh no hapana': Intersubjectivity, Meaning, and

- What difference might it make to Christian students' experience and construal of learning if their learning were framed by Christian practices? Can an overt focus on particular Christian practices reframe the imaginations of students and teachers in ways that undermine a utilitarian relationship to learning and enable the making of new connections between previously unconnected ideas? Can an involvement in learning experiences built around Christian practices provide some degree of counter-formation to the secular cultural liturgies that otherwise shape our lives and perceptions?[42]
- In what ways should Christian teaching and learning be "nested" within specific practices of Christian worship? Is there a way that worship in the church, chapel, and elsewhere constitutes a necessary context for Christian education in classrooms, laboratories, and libraries? In what way is the college, as an educational institution, dependent upon the church?[43]

The examples referenced in this brief sketch of possibilities indicate that some work has already been done in this vein. We hope that the essays presented here can provide a more concentrated, sustained, and cohesive indication of the potential of a focus on Christian practices for broadening our understanding of how faith and learning intersect in classrooms, and for remedying the comparative lack of focus on teaching and learning among Christian scholars to date.

The Outline of the Book

The chapters that follow were written in connection with a three-year project conducted by the Kuyers Institute for Christian Teaching and Learning at Calvin College, with funding from the Valparaiso Project on the Education and Formation of People in Faith at Valparaiso University. A team of Christian scholars from various disciplines was charged first with studying key work from the background literatures surveyed above, and then with choosing a course for which they would design a pedagogical intervention

---

the Self," in *Dialogue with Bakhtin on Second and Foreign Language Learning: New Perspectives,* ed. Joan Kelly Hall, Gergana Vitanova, and Ludmila Marchenkova (Mahwah, N.J.: Lawrence Erlbaum, 2005), pp. 119-47.

42. See, further, Smith, *Desiring the Kingdom.*

43. For initial discussion, see Smith, *Desiring the Kingdom,* chapter 6.

based on one or more Christian practices. Most of the chapters that follow describe these interventions, giving an account of how connections were made between Christian practices and teaching in the relevant subject area and reporting on the results. The emphasis is not upon empirical validation, but rather upon "thick" narratives and thoughtful connections between practices and pedagogy — our intentional aim from the outset was to illuminate and explore possibilities and potential rather than to produce generalizable data. Versions of these chapters were presented at a conference called "Teaching, Learning, and Christian Practices" held at Calvin College in October 2009; three further chapters — those by Paul Griffiths and Rebecca Konyndyk DeYoung and the book's closing chapter — were commissioned for and presented as plenary addresses at the conference.

The opening essay by Rebecca Konyndyk DeYoung weaves general reflections on the learning potential of practices together with an account of the particular learning that went on in a philosophy seminar on Aquinas's writings concerning virtues and vices. This leads to a helpful description of "a certain rhythm between practice and reflection on practice" that remains relevant to all of the following chapters. Students' learning included moments of insight resulting on the one hand from discovering new ways of naming their experience, and on the other from experiencing participation in practices from the Christian tradition designed to re-orient the self. Learning the history of philosophical accounts of virtue and vice turns out in this instance to include encounters with the vices of vainglory and pusillanimity, experimentation with vows of silence, and an event involving Reddi-wip and extensive plastic sheeting. A careful discussion of the relationship of practice to reflection and tradition provides the frame that holds such disparate elements together, and sets the stage for much that follows.

David Smith recounts dissatisfactions with a literature class that were grounded not in content or perspectives, but rather in the reading practices that tend to be operative by default, and the way these are sustained by teachers and students. He draws from various Christian accounts of spiritually formative reading to sketch a contrast between charitable and consumerist reading practices, and questions the classroom moves that help sustain the latter. What if those who teach courses that involve engagement with significant texts were to set out intentionally to construct a repertoire that sustained charitable reading — what would that mean for pace, for rhythm, for posture, for assessment? Exploring these questions not only points to a new classroom repertoire, but also offers hints of how the fruits of such endeavor might trickle through into other areas of students' lives.

Carolyne Call takes a cluster of practices — testimony, fellowship, and hospitality — and uses them to transform her approach to a course in adolescent psychology. With stark honesty and insightful attention to detail, she narrates how the specific changes in focus required by the intentional orientation to Christian practices made the course both profoundly demanding and deeply rewarding to teach. Expecting to be refining a teaching stance that was already Christian, she found her past experience of teaching more deeply challenged than she had anticipated. Her account of how particular challenges were met highlights the importance of the teacher's own grounding in Christian practices in order to sustain a Christian presence in the classroom.

Julie Walton, with Matthew Walters, sets out to investigate the relationship between the Christian practice of table fellowship and the specific stresses facing students in a nutrition course taught to pre-nursing students who are anxious about qualifying for a nursing program. Taking the flurry of recent writing offering hospitality as an educational metaphor a step further, Walton introduced a structured program of shared meals into the course, looking for signs that it might help students "become mindful and accepting of the dreams and needs of their neighbor-classmates sharing time and food with them."

These four examples of particular practices being used to reshape specific courses are followed by a chapter in which Paul Griffiths steps back to the bigger picture and offers reflections on how the appetite for learning needs to be catechized and what liturgy has to do with education. Exploring the reasons for Christian ambivalence about the value of learning, Griffiths argues that "to understand and to seek learning as Christians do is very different from understanding and seeking it as pagan academicians do," and suggests that we all too often settle for "a kind of education . . . that pressure-cooks the vices to a well-done turn." We need to attend to the different shapes that the appetite for learning can take, and to how these are formed; this is where Christian practices come in. Griffiths turns to the liturgy as the place where Christian life is most vividly lived and teases out ways in which the movements of Christian worship suggest parameters for the appetite for learning.

Griffiths underlines how liturgy is shot through with lament and stammering gestures in which we confess our incompleteness and falling short. There is some echo of this motif in Ashley Woodiwiss's essay narrating his efforts to re-orient the underlying narrative of a freshman seminar toward the practice of pilgrimage as an antidote to the superficial tourist gaze of instrumentalized learning. Woodiwiss reports limited success, underlining the point echoed in other chapters that applying Christian practices is no quick and easy fix. He explores some possible reasons for this particular project falling short of initial hopes, including a highly individualistic cultural context, a lack of prior encounter with key Christian practices, issues of time and space, and insufficient working through of the chosen practice into daily shared behaviors.

James K. A. Smith's experiment creatively joins a course on Philosophy of the Social Sciences with the practice of fixed-hour prayer and attentiveness to the liturgical calendar. While the connection here might at first seem rather extrinsic, Smith uncovers connections between Christian practices of time-keeping and the sustaining of moral order (a theme discussed in the authors studied in the course). His interest is not only in prayer as potentially opening up space for learning, but also in how bodily participation in Christian time-keeping practices might change and deepen students' learning about how the cultural liturgies to which we are subjected tether our rhythms and imaginations to secularized time. Testimony from students in the course points to insights gained and perspectives shifted.

Glenn Sanders offers a gradually unfolding narrative of how he set about seeding Christian practices into a Western Civilization course. The project was driven by a central concern with how to engage students with history learning in their capacity as moral and spiritual beings. At the same time, continued reflection on the nature of practices as the experiment unfolded led to the realization that it was easier to adopt the language of Christian practices than the practice of Christian practices. Sanders tracks the stages of realization that led to cumulative changes in the course, culminating in a central emphasis on community-building.

Matthew Walhout points out that pedagogical practices can serve various visions of human flourishing. He compares teaching practices with the physical constraints that underlie the designs of roller coasters and prayer labyrinths. Like those constraints, practices are deserving of careful forethought and studious attention. They can succeed in facilitating the desired kind of experience, or they can fail miserably. After considering three different visions that pedagogical practices might serve, Walhout focuses on his own use of the prayer labyrinth image as a guiding metaphor in his physics course. The labyrinth itself has always referred metaphorically to pilgrimages and the Christian walk through life, and here these references take on their traditional resonance in the context of students working their way through a science curriculum.

Kurt Schaefer also addresses an area of the curriculum that might not seem to offer immediately obvious points of contact for Christian practice. He focuses on learning in technical courses, taking as his specific example a course in econometrics, a discipline commonly associated with mathematically driven technique. He makes the case for viewing such a course as involving an apprenticeship in interpreting well, and in this connection moves to a consideration of Christian practices of interpretation. He finds that particular Christian hermeneutical practices developed in relation to interpreting Scripture, together with the interpretive virtues that they imply, can be suggestive of ways in which students need to grow when interpreting economic data, and he offers an account of how this connection can change teaching and learning practices in technically oriented courses.

In the closing chapter, David Smith draws together some threads from various preceding chapters, in particular emphasizing the need to recruit students' imaginations if experiments with Christian practice in the classroom are to be successful. Christian practices, and their pedagogical analogues, are to be understood neither as theoretical principles to be clinically applied nor as efficient techniques practiced upon students; they depend upon the building of a shared imagination in which students acquire new ways of seeing and understanding their own learning as well as new rhythms commensurate with this renewed imagination.

This closing chapter reiterates a concern that frames the whole. We do not intend these exploratory studies to be received as rigid recipes, finished prescriptions, or guarantees of pedagogical bliss. We do, however, hope to help readers to imagine a practice of teaching and learning that is rooted in the long and rich history of Christian practice, and to do so through examples as much as through exhortations. Teaching and learning are both high callings, and both deserve the disciplined attention of those who call themselves Christian educators. We pray that these explorations will offer some glimpses of how we might pursue them more faithfully.

Pedagogical Rhythms:
Practices and Reflections on Practice

Rebecca Konyndyk DeYoung

Some Reflections on Why Practices Are Needed

Imagine that you died today. In the days that follow, your friends and family gather together to mourn you and remember you. Imagine what they would say about you and about your life. There would be things to celebrate, things to regret, things they would miss about you, and no doubt a few things they wouldn't! If you were to listen in on those imaginary conversations and capture them on paper — in other words, to write an honest testimonial of the person you were and the life you lived — how would that speech read? For the sake of this exercise, an honest word is better than a good word, if you have to choose.

Now imagine a second version of the speech. This time, think of the speech you *wish* someone could honestly have given at your funeral — including all the good things you wish were true of you, the way the first speech you wrote *would* have read had you become all that you wanted to be.

Why this imaginative exercise? Funerals are one of the few places we still reflect on and talk about a person's character — not just one's achievements or quirks, but the person one was and the stories that best revealed this and the qualities that marked the character of one's life. It's also one of the few times we take the time to reflect on our lives as a whole — to set aside the tyranny of the daily and the urgent and to measure our life in terms of "big picture" concerns. A funeral is an occasion to try to view the whole package, to think about how the parts of your character and your life fit together — what they added up to and what your life said about the kind of person you were.[1]

In short, this eulogy-writing exercise is a reflective moment of self-examination and a *memento mori* all wrapped up in one. To put it another way, it's one example of a practice of reflecting. It presses the questions that are at the heart of a liberal arts education and a Christian life of discipleship:[2] "Who am I? Is this who I want to be? What goods and virtues are expressed in the way I'm living? What is the human good, the best way to live? And how does my life measure up to that ideal?" The first speech tells us who we are now. The second speech articulates the calling, the mission, the task that still lies ahead: "What sort of person do I hope yet to become? What picture of a good human life should inform my future choices and commitments?"

I teach a philosophy seminar on the medieval philosopher and theologian Thomas Aquinas at Calvin College. In it, we study Aquinas's writings on the virtues and vices.[3] When my students do this eulogy exercise in class, I have them add a second step. Based on the speeches they wrote, I have them write down three character traits that they would like to get rid of (from the first speech) and three character traits that they want to cultivate (from the second speech). My students tend to begin this assignment hesitantly and with furrowed brows. Their lists of virtues often include invented words such as "forgivingness" and "lovingness," descriptive phrases such as "being more positive about myself" and "laughing more" and "being a better friend," as well as items that they're not sure count as virtues, such as "leadership," "assertiveness," and "creativity." When they write "strength" on their list, I ask them what that means. Perseverance — remembering that you can also persevere in sin? Or the motivation to endure even when it's difficult? Or the guts to withstand physical pain or ex-

---

1. See the Epilogue of my *Glittering Vices* (Grand Rapids: Brazos, 2009) for a more extended explanation of this exercise and its rationale.

2. It's true that many consider both types of educational project training for a certain kind of service in the world (for a Christian example, see Nicholas Wolterstorff, *Educating for Responsible Action* [Grand Rapids: CSI/Eerdmans, 1980]). I don't disagree that service is the probable outcome, but in this essay I prefer to think about the ways such service is grounded in character and the practices that form it, and how to cultivate dispositions that enable us to serve most faithfully, remembering with John Milton that "they also serve who only stand and wait" (from "On His Blindness").

3. In particular, we read Aquinas's *Disputed Questions on Evil* and the second part of the second part (IaIIae) of the *Summa theologiae*.

ertion? Or the ability to stand up boldly for their beliefs? Or is it some combination of these? When I ask them, quite often they're not exactly sure what they meant. Likewise, several students might list "being true to themselves" but then disagree about whether this means being sincere even if you are bad, whether there might be differences between merely telling the truth and being honest or sincere, and whether contemporary "authenticity" has anything to do with, say, a Christian idea of faithfulness or moral integrity. Stumbling through this listing exercise after writing their initial speeches thus helps them feel the need for an education about the concepts and vocabulary necessary to do the next step of articulation and analysis.

I had this experience myself in graduate school. Challenged by the demands of a competitive academic program, I struggled with the usual insecurities — finding and securing a place in a new pecking order, fearing the shame that came with offering a naïve or uninformed answer aloud in class, trying to impress erudite and imposing professors who would eventually be helping or hindering my job prospects. My inner emotional landscape was defensive and fearful; my strategy in public was to avoid detection, lest I be exposed for the incompetent fool that I felt I was. (I found out years later that this common experience had a name: "impostor syndrome.")

My epiphany came when I was reading Thomas Aquinas on the virtues and vices. He was describing a vice called pusillanimity. The word *pusillanimity* literally means "smallness of soul." What Aquinas meant was a habit of shrinking back from all that God was calling you to be out of fear of failure, a sense of inadequacy, a feeling of powerlessness or incompetence. His example: Moses at the burning bush. The man whom we know as one of the greatest leaders of Israel hears God's call and says, "Who — *me?* Surely you've got the wrong person! I'm not qualified!" Hearing God's call, Moses panics, finds excuses, tries to pass the buck to his brother Aaron, and cites all his weaknesses and lack of qualifications.

But read on. This is not the end of Moses' story. It is only the beginning. Follow God's call, Moses, relying on *God's* power this time. Stretch yourself to be what God has in mind for you. Forget measuring possibilities by your puny humanly measured talents and your own unaided efforts. Think like Mary at the Annunciation: "I'm just a lowly handmaiden, but overshadowed by the Almighty, God will become incarnate within me, and all nations will call me blessed."

Reading Aquinas on the vice of pusillanimity was my "aha" moment.

I saw myself and my struggles in a whole new light. With this new concept in mind, I could name my own weakness and diagnose its causes. With these pictures of vice and virtue embodied in real human lives, I had the resources to reframe how I was living and why. Later, when I taught this material to my students, I watched as they had the same experience of epiphany: "Now I have a name for it"; "Finally I see what this struggle was really about"; "I had no idea *that* was the problem."[4] I wonder how common it is to find that naming your vices is itself a moment of liberation?

For this diagnostic process of self-examination, the fourth-century Christian John Cassian offers a metaphor for moral malformation — the "tree of vices."[5] Pride is at the root of the tree, and the trunk extends upward from it. The main seven branches are the traditional seven deadly sins — vainglory, envy, sloth, avarice, wrath, lust, and gluttony. From each of the seven branches grows additional "poison fruit," drooping downward. What this image shows us is the obvious mistake of thinking we can pluck off a vice's surface symptoms (its "fruits") and not address its source motivations or "roots." It offers a picture of self-examination that invites us to dig down to deeper causes. The organic metaphor also shows how sin, left unattended, will not sit idly within us but will grow and branch out further. Moreover, the "tree" of vices shows us the twisted inner connections of sin. It leads us to investigate how each of the vices is connected to pride, and why certain "fruits" or offshoot vices spring from the main seven.[6]

4. The language of self-examination, diagnosis, and remedy are all from John Cassian, fourth-century founder of Western monasticism. In many of Cassian's works, Jesus is named the physician of souls, and the vices name variations of spiritual disease (see, for example, *The Institutes,* trans. B. Ramsey, O.P., Ancient Christian Writers 58 [New York: Newman Press, 2000]). We have to translate these concepts carefully in a culture accustomed to contemporary therapeutic metaphors from psychology and a medical model of treatment that may be inconsistent with this ancient tradition.

5. Note: In the tradition, this was guided by a spiritual director, not something one did all by oneself. The tree metaphor is from *The Conferences,* trans. B. Ramsey, O.P., Ancient Christian Writers 57 (New York: Newman Press, 1997), V.x. Gregory the Great later named pride the ultimate root of the other seven, and artists depicted various fruits hanging from the tree, basing their lists of vices and their typical offshoots on Cassian, Gregory, and others. See for example, http://www.bl.uk/catalogues/illuminatedmanuscripts/ILLUMIN.ASP?Size=mid&IllID=6975.

6. There is also a tree of virtues, rooted in either humility (versus pride) or love (versus disordered love), although the parallels between the two lists of seven end there. See http://www.bl.uk/catalogues/illuminatedmanuscripts/ILLUMIN.ASP?Size=mid&IllID=6976.

Teaching the vices and virtues showed me the power of this process of acquiring new names, new pictures and paradigms. For with them comes the ability to recognize and spell out concepts and connections new inquirers intuitively grasp but cannot yet adequately identify. These new concepts and connections help us analyze and reflect on our character.

The main point in the opening exercises I've described is to see the *need* for naming and to experience *why* identifying the virtues and vices can be helpful and important. The eulogy exercise also locates our intellectual inquiry in a larger, personal, and practical project of character formation. The names we learn have meaning and significance in that frame, while that practical project motivates and makes sense of the detailed intellectual work that follows.[7] Through these practices of reflection, my students feel and identify for themselves the gap between what they are and all that they are called to become. From there, they can see how identifying the vices and cultivating the virtues is a natural next step.

The project of learning about the vices in my class is one example of a certain rhythm between practice and reflection on practice. In attending to the ways this rhythm played itself out in our classroom, I'd like first to highlight two things about the diagnostic practice of naming and the "whole life" reflections in which that diagnosis is embedded. The first is what Craig Dykstra calls the problem of "the too big and the too small."[8] The second is the relationship between concepts and concretely embodied experience.

First, Dykstra's point: the problem of the too big and the too small is roughly this. If we give students too big a picture of the moral project, they have difficulty translating that into action-steps, concrete practices, and a way of going forward. In my students' case, the project of "being virtuous" or "developing more Christ-like character" felt fairly vague as a starting point. Turning to lists of particular virtues and specific spiritual disciplines gave that big picture more traction for them in the actual patterns and practices of Christ-like living. The problem of the too small is the opposite one — losing sight of the forest in one's study of a particular tree: for example, trying to define courageous action without a developed sense of what goods need protecting and why, how courage fits into the network

---

7. Later in this essay I'll turn to the ways the intellectual project can motivate, sustain, and enrich practice.

8. See Craig Dykstra, *Growing in the Life of Faith: Education and Christian Practices* (Louisville: Geneva Press, 1999), pp. 66-67.

of other Christian virtues, or how its common cultural expressions might be transformed in a context of Christian sacrificial love. So the key is to keep these connections between the overarching goals and the daily steps, between the vision and motivation behind the larger project and the need to discern what to do now as a student sitting in the dining hall or in a dorm room. For my class, the tree of virtues and vices functioned as a fruitful link between the "big" and the "small."

Closely related to this concern is a second issue — the connection between intellectual inquiry and reflection on the one hand, and concretely embodied daily practices on the other. To put it in terms of my graduate school experience, acquiring a new conceptual category was not the same thing as knowing how to live it. I could understand pusillanimity at some level, but how could I *become* less pusillanimous? How could I live out the paradigm shift from relying on my own puny efforts to trusting God's grace to see me through the challenges of my calling?

One way I discovered (or better: rediscovered) was to practice observance of the Sabbath. I went from working seven days a week — feeling as though even that was never enough to keep up with the overwhelming workload — to stopping what I was doing one day a week in order to *live* God's liberating promises: "He who called you is faithful, and *he* will do it" (2 Thess. 5:24); "Learn from me, for my yoke is easy and my burden is light" (Matt. 11:29-30). Sabbath rest includes meditating on what *God* has done and is doing, being fully attentive and present in worship, being refreshed by God's presence undistracted by anxieties or future plans, sitting still and breathing deeply, sleeping enough.[9] These are patterns of action designed to help us break the bad habits of believing that success depends entirely on our own efforts, fueled by the anxiety that our efforts will never be good enough. Pusillanimous lack of trust in God was the root of my fear of failure. Sabbath-keeping helped me learn to let go of these fears and open myself up to God's call to engage in his work with confidence. Diagnosing pusillanimity as a vice helped me see that I was living as if my feeble efforts were the only resource I had. Sabbath-keeping, for me, showed me that learning to rest was learning to trust in God. Unfortunately, this trust came only through painful practice. Trusting is hard. Practicing Sabbath rest was a *discipline* for me, albeit a discipline in which I discovered grace

---

9. For a similar point regarding our practices of sleeping enough, see Lauren Winner, "Sleep Therapy," *Books and Culture/Christianity Today International* (1/1/2006), http://www.christianitytoday.com/bc/2006/janfeb/2.07.html.

and freedom and joy. So the virtue-vice tradition gave me the initial concepts and reframing insights, but I also found that the practices to which they also pointed gave me specific new ways to live out those concepts, while those ways of life in turn deepened my understanding of the meaning of trust and dependence.

A Tradition as a Natural Place for the Rhythm of Practices-and-Reflection-on-Practices (and a Classroom as a Natural Place for Reflective Practitioners)

My own discovery of the vices and their diagnostic power was just that — my recent discovery of something already in place. From that place of discovery, I had to move in two directions: first, backward into the past. Moral formation and the imitation of Christ are nothing new, even if their challenges must be taken up anew by each of us. The practices, disciplines, and virtues that shape good character have been part of the conversation in the Christian tradition for centuries. On this topic, therefore, we need not start from scratch or re-invent the wheel — most of our discoveries and epiphanies come from listening in on an ancient conversation and tracing the paths of past practitioners. The key is to recognize in this long-standing conversation something *we* still need to hear. We need to recognize a place for *ourselves* within the tradition.

Second, from my place of discovery, I had to move forward — from my personal experience and appropriation of the intellectual and practical resources of the Christian moral tradition to effective pedagogy for others. It's one thing to have the experience and insights yourself; it's quite another task to find ways to give others the opportunity to gain similar experiences and insights for themselves. My pedagogical goal was to afford my students the opportunity to participate in the same movement I had — moving back into the tradition and then bringing it forward.

In moving back into the tradition, my students learned to submit to what the Christian tradition had to teach them through practices, and in moving the tradition forward, they learned to translate the material into something they could call their own. For my students at least, trying certain practices brought home the need for submission, while the translation process disciplined them to take up a more reflective stance.

In both our practicing and our reflecting on practices, therefore, we were working with and within a tradition. And by "tradition," I don't mean a merely intellectual tradition of inquiry about the good.[10] The Desert Fathers, Cassian's and Benedict's monastic communities, and Aquinas's fellow Dominicans — all those who pondered questions about vices and discipleship and offered us their answers — were themselves already living as members of a body of Christ-followers. All of these inquirers were also disciples actively and communally trying to imitate Christ's character even as they reflected on it; and they reflected on it and inquired further about it because they practiced it. They were immersed in these ethical and spiritual practices themselves, trying to articulate what they were doing and becoming from a place within the practice.

So we had a model for this project. Now it was our turn.

In my class on the vices, we inscribed various practices into our classroom work, and we reflected on those practices in ways that anticipated greater engagement in them. In the next two sections, I offer examples of how we did this.[11]

Practices *for* Reflection

One way we engaged the tradition of the vices pedagogically was to engage in practices *for* reflection. Analyzing a particular discipline or virtue described abstractly or theoretically was different than reading a thick, narrative account of how particular people lived it out, and that too was a different way of learning about it than practicing the discipline ourselves. At each level of immersion, there were things we could see from closer inside — things that made our reflections less vicarious and more experientially grounded.[12] In these assignments of practices I had the following (mod-

---

10. For a richer concept of a tradition which encompasses both practices and reflections on practice, I am indebted to Alasdair MacIntyre, *After Virtue,* 2nd ed. (Notre Dame: University of Notre Dame Press, 1984), chapter 15, especially p. 222.

11. I am analyzing practicing and reflecting on practice as conceptually distinct here, but in our classroom experience the two were often not clearly distinguishable.

12. However, not all levels of "insider" experience and "immersion" would necessarily be required to count as genuine practice. Similarly, there might well be different levels and modes of reflection possible (some more spiritually attuned, some more philosophical, for example). I thank David Smith for pressing this point in discussions of an earlier draft of this essay. His example — that of American football — is instructive: what an NFL quarterback practices and knows is different from what an offensive coordinator practices and knows, and this again is different from what the team's lifelong fans practice and know. Nevertheless, each is a member of the practice called "American football," each is formed by

est) pedagogical goal: To provide students with an opportunity to read a text *through* a life experience. So we tried Christian formational practices — spiritual disciplines — for ourselves, albeit usually in modified form.

How did this work? What type of reflections did it yield?

The class was on the seven capital vices — more familiarly known as the seven deadly sins. The number seven is a bit artificial here, since the traditional list began with eight or nine vices and was shortened to seven over the course of several centuries. This shortening means that the list of seven we have today includes the vice of pride but omits the vice of vainglory. Most of us have never even heard the word *vainglory* before. Vainglory is an unfamiliar vice with an equally archaic name. My students certainly found this to be the case. Later I'll give examples of how these lost concepts and vocabulary we have recovered from the vices tradition lead us to inquire about how those concepts might translate (or how they don't). But here I'll show how partial immersion in the practice made this concept come alive for my students.

The definition of *vainglory* is "the disordered desire for attention and approval." The vainglorious person seeks to project an image of herself that will garner attention, approval, and applause from her desired audience. For the vainglorious person, image is everything, and reality quickly blurs into "spin." The Greek word for vainglory *(cenodoxia)* literally means "empty of glory." Vainglory is the sham side of trying to be appropriately acknowledged and honored by others. The vainglorious person just wants the limelight. You're indulging in vainglory if you're posting Facebook photos of yourself looking fabulous, or using just the right erudite vocabulary to impress your academic colleagues, or buying a luxury car to enhance your social status. Vainglory is perhaps America's favorite vice. The advertising industry would be lost without it.

But we are victims of vainglory, too. Before my students studied vainglory formally in class, I assigned them the practice of silence for a week. Or more precisely, a modified version of it, but one still rigorous enough to have the desired effect. The exercise: No talking about yourself. That's all.

Simple, right? But think about it — no talking about yourself means no commenting about your feelings, no offering your opinions or judgments, no wry witticisms or clever criticisms, no long-winded narratives

---

their immersion (at whatever level) in the practice, and each has reflective insights as a result.

about how your day went and what frustrated or elated you, no interrupting with "bigger and better" stories, no fishing for compliments, no calling or texting to share what you're doing, no blogging about your opinions or favorite movies or annoying neighbors or pet peeves, no complaining. And perhaps hardest of all, no defending what you did, no pre-emptive spin to prevent others from getting the wrong impression of what you're doing, no rationalizing, no excuse-making. No nothing. Instead, be still. Listen. Let other people talk. Let your actions speak for themselves.

We had no idea how hard this would be. I knew at the beginning that it would be a challenge, but until we lived with the discipline for a few days in a row (even in this modified form), we had absolutely no idea how much of our lives revolved around managing our reputations and focusing on how others perceived us. In this practicing of the discipline of silence, my students and I grasped something we couldn't grasp through descriptions or reading instructions or observations of others' practice. The new insights about ourselves came through immersion in the practice.

Although verbal silence doesn't get at the half of the vainglory problem in an image-based culture, we quickly got a robust experiential taste of how deeply rooted a vice can be, and how blissfully unaware we were that we even had it. It's important to notice, too, that our apprenticeship required submission: We had to begin by taking the tradition's word for it that there was something to be gained here that we couldn't see from outside the practice.

The sheer shock value of this exercise never ceases to amaze me. I had the students write a journal reflecting on their practice, and it was clear from reading their journals that they, too, had an "aha" moment of moral awakening, somewhat akin to the experience of someone pouring a bucket of ice water over their heads. They came away not only conscious but convicted.

It's not that we can't or shouldn't share ourselves with others, of course. Communication is essential for human community. And speech is a good way to share ourselves. What this engagement in the practice of silence taught us, however, is that more often than not, we were "sharing" in a manipulatively self-aggrandizing, attention-grabbing way. It also gave us a taste of what it might be like to free ourselves of the constant exercise of boosting our own approval ratings. In a culture that values "honest self-expression," we have a lot to learn from a tradition with "vainglory" still in its vocabulary and analytical toolbox. When speech is taken away, the resulting silence shows us how to rely on attentive listening and non-verbal communication, especially good eye contact and touch. But my point is this: After our weeklong practice, I don't have to explain any of these conclusions. My students have already figured it out. Moreover, unlike most of my lectures about it, they also remember it later.

In my class, the practice of silence is only a starting point for reflection and further inquiry into one vice among many. Through this initial practice, students come away convinced that they have something to learn and something to gain from listening to and imitating those who have already practiced a way of life designed to resist vice and cultivate virtue. It bolsters the credibility of this tradition — convincing us that if we are willing to apprentice ourselves, there are masters here from whom we can learn.

There are other benefits, too: this short trial of spiritual disciplines makes real the possibility of a new life. It offers an experiential encounter with the freedom that can be found in new habits and practices. Understanding the vice of vainglory and practicing the discipline of silence are gateways to entering a new way of being more fully human (i.e., more Christ-like), and with it, a new way of envisioning ourselves and our world. Sometimes a taste is enough to lure us in (sometimes not).[13] Who knows whether it will become an ongoing discipline for any of them? Here we encounter the limits of pedagogy; here, too, we see the need for a church community beyond the classroom to provide a place for continuing apprenticeship in such practices.

To sum up, the first way my class engaged this tradition of character formation gave us an opportunity to be *apprentices,* even if only in an exploratory and experimental way. My experience is that the power of the practices speaks for itself and gives the tradition of which they are a part credibility, and that even temporary submission to the wisdom of the tradition invites one to take seriously the possibilities of engaging further in the Christian life and its practices.

---

13. I have often been asked whether one should teach the vices first or the virtues and spiritual disciplines. My answer is that both approaches can work. Some students practice a spiritual discipline and come away from the experience eager to learn more about the vices, because they now take the extent of the vices' distorting power seriously. Others come away from exercises in self-examination associated with the vices eager to learn about the spiritual disciplines because they now have an incentive to take up Christian practices that will help intentionally shape a new life in Christ.

Practices *of* Reflection

The second facet of our learning experience was a "translation" project — that is, student reflections designed to move them back into further practice. I've just talked about submitting ourselves to the tradition as apprentices — trying out various practices in modified form to experience in an engaged and invested way their diagnostic and formative power and to spur further investigation and reflection. Now I want to say something about becoming a *master* — that is, making the tradition your own (to some extent, at least) and coming into a position to teach it to others.[14] Let me say at the outset that just as our apprenticeship was only partial and truncated, so was our experience of trying to be masters.

By the last month of the semester, my students were at the point at which they had at least some grasp of what Cassian and Aquinas had to say about the vices, their remedial disciplines, and the virtues. The final assignment sent them in teams to give presentations on the vices in the campus residence halls — seven nights, seven dorms, seven vices.

One example of how this went comes from the presentation on vainglory. First, the students began with an exercise in which the audience had to list ten celebrities or well-known people in the United States. Then, when that list was compiled, the audience had to list ten people they would consider heroes. The lists looked very different, and there were no overlapping names. Then my students asked what those on the celebrity list were well-known for. Answers: wealth, good looks, athletic talent, and "being famous for being famous" (poor Paris Hilton always takes a hit here). Then came this question: What had the heroes done to earn their place on the list? The answers shifted. Few if any heroes were "famous" or well-known. Audience lists almost always included a grandparent unknown to anyone

---

14. Let me make a distinction between types of mastery here by way of an example. When I was young, my brother received a Rubik's Cube for his birthday. He solved its mystery in a matter of days, whereas I struggled to complete a first layer of the puzzle. While he quickly gained proficiency at solving the puzzle himself, however, he remained hard-pressed to articulate the way he solved it. By contrast, I was able to lay out the step-by-step process of solving the puzzle (or the part of it I eventually learned to solve), but was never as proficient at doing it as he was. So there are at least two types of mastery — one relevant for practicing proficiently, and one for teaching the practice; one for doing it well, and one for explaining what one is doing and why. In this section of the essay, I am referring to the latter; I assumed that proficiency in the practice comes with more time and experience than was available in a single semester's class.

else in the room. What emerged from the comparison was the distinction between being a person given glory and a place in the limelight, and being a person *worthy* of glory and admiration. Note that there is no discussion of celebrities or heroes in the tradition regarding this vice. But this reflective exercise shows that the unfamiliar vice of vainglory still "translates" today, making sense of distinctions between celebrities and heroes already familiar to us.

Take a second example of the work of translation: My students designed a vainglory quiz — that is, more or less, a contemporization of a confessional manual, listing possible manifestations of the vice (based on the traditional offspring vices) and measuring one's susceptibility to it. It included the question, for instance, about whether one had ever exaggerated the truth or lied about something to win a laugh or the approval of one's friends. Lastly, the presentation team showed "Gaston's song" from the film *Beauty and the Beast,* correctly identifying an exemplar of both vainglory — Gaston — and its opposite — the Beast, who learned that his outward appearance would never win him social approval but that greatness of heart made him honorable nonetheless.

I call these reflective exercises "translation projects" because in them students had to take technical concepts from a medieval text and extend them into contemporary life — into actions such as conforming to peer pressure, into exemplars such as Disney characters, into today's vocabulary of celebrities and heroes. To do the translation, my students had to figure out where the tradition made sense of their lives and where they thought it left gaps or missed the mark. Then, as beginner teachers, they had to make these insights come alive for others. In doing this, they also learned how every translation falls short in some ways, and how some of what they meant to teach was missed or misunderstood. Mastery is not an achieved state but an ongoing process.

Did the translations always go this easily? Certainly not. Let me also describe a particularly challenging area for our translation project: the vice of lust. The primary texts we read were from the Desert Fathers and from medieval thinkers who took a vow of celibacy. Especially in the early ascetic tradition, the counsels about lust focus on abolishing sexual desire altogether, renouncing all earthly things and associations with women or family life, and disciplining the body through stringent fasts and all-night vigils.[15] John Cassian's advice to the monk trying to avoid lust and vain-

15. Moreover, the viewpoint of women's struggles with lust is typically not considered

glory? "Flee women and bishops."[16] This advice did not easily transfer into the lives of those students who considered marriage a viable option and who lived in a world where sexually explicit advertising is ubiquitous. There is no desert to flee to, nor would total flight enable legitimate family life. These texts provided the most difficult case of translating the tradition. The project of teaching demanded not only critical reflection[17] but also a challenging case of creative appropriation for a contemporary audience.

Let me highlight one area where this was possible, despite the dissonances. Common cultural portrayals of sex today tend to dissociate our embodied actions from our inner life. Sex is "just physical" — a pleasurable bodily experience from which we can walk away with no aftereffects on our hearts or minds. Even many abstinence programs focus on avoiding physical contact that will count against one's technical virginity, as if this were the whole story of "purity."

On first blush, the tradition seems to echo this superficial view, treating the body as the site of traitorous desires and temptations. On a closer reading, however, the earliest teachers in the tradition emphasize a more holistic understanding of both lust and chastity.[18] They note that while going into the desert to live a solitary life certainly removes many outward occasions for lustful temptation, this merely moves the struggle inward — into one's thought life and fantasies. When we can't physically indulge in lustful acts, we retreat into memory and imagination.[19] This, too, they

---

at all. The texts are predominantly by men and for men; to these "brothers," women are part of the world to be renounced, and even there, they are the property of their husbands and fathers.

16. Cassian, *Institutes,* XI.xviii.

17. Let me be clear: not all of it translated — the early authors' views about women, for example, sometimes just simply needed rejection or correction.

18. So while their anthropology remained dualistic, their holistic understanding of the dynamics of the vices did not lead them to neglect either element of the person when talking about diagnoses and remedies for the vices. In this sense, their moral psychology is more integrated than the implicit dualism of many contemporary evangelical teachings.

19. As Maximus the Confessor put it, "First the memory brings a mere thought to the mind; and when this remains for a while, passion is roused, and when this is not removed, it sways the mind to consent; and when consent is given, sinning in action finally comes about" (*Century* I.84, p. 149); and "The fight against memories is as much the more difficult than the fight against things as sinning in thought is easier than sinning in deed" (*Century* I.63, p. 145). These quotations can be found in St. Maximus the Confessor, *The Ascetic Life and The Four Centuries on Charity,* trans. P. Sherwood, O.S.B., Ancient Christian Writers 21 (Westminster, Md.: Newman Press, 1955).

warn, can be real lust — no less a barrier to love and pure prayer. This insight resonated with my students. The computer may be destroyed, the photo or person far gone from our presence, but the images in the mind remain. The vice of lust is not "merely physical" — it permeates the whole person. Lust is a battle in our hearts and minds as much as in our bodies.

In fact, in their presentation my students concluded that the pleasure of self-gratifying *fantasy* is at the heart of this generation's attraction to pornography. When Cassian speaks of renunciation not only of his former worldly life but also of the thought-life that went with it, this sounded like advice my students could both understand and endorse to others. To those who have experienced the power of pornography, Cassian's advice to "Flee women" became an injunction to flee not from real, human relationships but from virtual, inhuman ones. The translation gave them a way to take the tradition forward.

By way of summary, then, we can say that the students' partial immersion in modified spiritual disciplines gave them incentive to apprentice themselves to the teachers and texts of the tradition, but the opportunity to teach the vices made them reflective translators, critics, and advocates of the tradition themselves.

Some Reflections on the Need for the Rhythm of Practices and Reflection on Practices

While my class fruitfully included practices and reflection on those practices, we might still wonder why we need pedagogies that afford opportunities for *both* immersion in practices and reflective consideration of them.

First, why do we need practices? How do they prompt and feed reflection? The "apprenticeship" approach discussed earlier shows that sometimes character formation begins with being inculcated in practices the goods of which we do not and cannot fully understand from the outset or the outside — as illustrated by my students doing an experiment countering vainglory.[20] Who knows what their initial motives were? The point is to engage in the practice together as a community, and to do so long enough with the right sort of mentors and models that any initial skeptical or mercenary motives could be transformed and new insights forged.

Then why do we need reflection? For those who do become further

20. See note 12.

immersed, immersion in the practice can be insufficient. Aristotle emphasizes that we have to learn *that* certain practices are good by doing them, and we also have to develop a reflective understanding of *why* these practices make a human life good. According to Aristotle, the "why" arguments may not convince us if we are not already morally formed in certain ways.[21] Without characters formed by certain habits, we will be deaf to certain arguments explaining what makes that kind of character worth having. But fitting our initial habits into this larger perspective is *also* essential to maintain our commitment to the full formation and perfection of the virtues.

Let me offer a contemporary example. The high school seniors in my church education class spend a good deal of their time complaining about the lame, old-fashioned hymns we sing over and over in church. They would prefer to switch to a praise-and-worship genre and have that repertoire keep up with the latest hits being written in the Christian music industry. Putting genre considerations aside, what is the point of having a common hymnal and singing the same songs over and over for generations? It's a practice that forms our corporate worship. But while my students were well immersed in it, they didn't see why it was valuable; they didn't understand its significance. My answer to their questions about practice had to address the "why." Here it is.

When I was in college, I worked second shift on the dementia unit at a local nursing home as a nurse's aide. After we fed the residents dinner, we put them to bed. One particularly demanding patient had her call light on constantly, and it got to the point where the other aides were too frustrated to answer it anymore. As the rookie member of the staff, that meant it was my job. Mrs. B, I'll call her, really didn't need anything from me or anyone else — at least, she didn't need our medical assistance. She needed company; she didn't want to be alone in the dark. So I would sit on the edge of her bed, and she would hold my hand and stroke it while in a wobbly voice she sang hymns to me — hymns she knew by heart from years of singing them over and over, hymns she could recall more clearly than what she had for dinner two hours earlier. At first she did all the singing. But it turned out that all of my own training in singing "boring hymns" over and over in church meant that I too happened to know the verses of "Abide with Me" by heart. So I could join in on Mrs. B's favorite: "When other helpers fail, and

---

21. Aristotle, *Nichomachean Ethics*, trans. T. Irwin (Indianapolis: Hackett, 1999), I.3, 1095a1-15, and X.9, 1179b1-1180b25.

comforts flee, help of the helpless, O abide with me." It got to be a thing with the two of us, part of our nighttime routine: I'd put her to bed, and we'd sing that song — all the verses. Like my students, I had the practice; Mrs. B taught me the "why." Why sing the same old boring hymns over and over? Because they give us the language for lament and loneliness that most praise songs don't, and someday we'll need those words. Because those songs bind generations together into a community. Because now Mrs. B and I share a favorite hymn, and through that hymn I learned to see her not merely as a nursing home resident, but as a saint and a sister in Christ.

So we need practices, *and* we need reflection on practices. Practices enhance and expand our reflection, and reflection enriches and sustains our practices. We need immersion in a practice and we need a context of meaning for the practice itself, something that can be gained through reflection.

Ideally our reflective questions should be asked not once, after an assignment or at the end of the semester; rather, they should be repeatedly asked in conversation with a community of practitioners, because what we see ten years into a practice will be different from what we see after a semester, and what we see when we have children that are grown will be different from what we see when those children are infants, and what we see after living through suffering, disappointment, betrayal, and conflict will be different than what we see at idealistic first blush. The point in the classroom is not merely to offer the students a particular insight or conclusion at that moment but to teach them the rhythm of trusting enough to keep practicing and then examining what they've practiced.[22] Perhaps this rhythm could be thought of as one articulation of what the same Christian tradition calls "faith seeking understanding." What the apprentice learns by trusting faith, the master creatively appropriates through fuller understanding.[23] Deepened understanding in turn can deepen practice, and the cycle continues.[24]

---

22. Reflection on practices also kept the process of formation transparent and enabled us to evaluate our formation with an honest, critical eye.

23. Of course, on broader readings of "practice," intellectual reflection itself could be a practice or part of a practice, but then we just get reflection on the practice of reflection (its goals, goods, and methods, etc.). Again, we can think of the process as reciprocal: the trustful imitation of initial apprenticeship yields greater understanding and creative appropriation, which then brings us back to more intentional and informed apprenticeship in practices.

24. Again, the theoretical distinction is appropriate, but the two are not as easy to distinguish in concrete instances. The "why" questions we asked in my philosophy classes on

I am arguing, therefore, for the fruitfulness and in many cases the necessity of pairing the two, the reciprocal rhythm of practice and reflection on practice. Sometimes reflection can be a retrospective evaluation of a practice. Immersing ourselves in practices first can lead us to acknowledge that there are *some* things we can recognize and appreciate only by submitting and doing faithfully even before we can see why. At other times, reflection on the "why" leads to prospective endorsement of a well-lived human life and incentive to begin (or continue) practices that form a part of it.

So the reflection with which we began this essay — namely, "Who do I wish to become? And why?" — may lead to practices that answer the question "How do I become that sort of person?" Within this lived rhythm, the point of reflecting is to be more intentional about how we live as Christians, what sort of character we are called to cultivate, and what practices best enable us to do so.

Conclusion

I'll conclude with one last story. For their final project, three of my students led a presentation on the vice of gluttony for an audience of their peers in the residence halls. In class, they studied the vice and its traditional remedy — the discipline of fasting. Their highly entertaining presentation included a blueberry pie-eating contest and enough Reddi-Wip to require extensive plastic sheeting over the floor. But the high point for me came when this group of three arrived back at my office a year and a half later at the beginning of Lent, wondering if they could come in and talk more about how to fast. What they had learned and taught made them want to come back to the tradition. They had learned to value and trust its

---

the virtues, vices, and spiritual disciplines were not so easily separated from the practices about which and from which we asked them. Practicing silence or fasting for a week introduced a Christian way of life — its insights and internal goods — and these practices also gave us material for reflection. Similarly, our exercise of modifying Aquinas's practice of fasting, even in modified form (we skipped all snacks and reduced our eating to two small meals a day), made for a richer conversation about the differences between dieting and fasting. Spending a week documenting our anger helped us constructively engage the controversy in the tradition about whether anger is a constructive moral response or whether all anger is wrathful and vicious. We may believe in theory that anger can be a right response, but when our personal records reveal that almost every angry response that week was disordered and destructive, we may be more willing to consider respectfully the early tradition's counsel to purge our lives of anger altogether.

resources, and the reflective work they did in class led them back to the practices, together, to claim them as their own. Not every student took this opportunity (in fact, most did not), nor could I force them to, but it seems to me that this particular moment showed me most clearly both the limits of pedagogy and its unlimited potential.

My class on the vices was an experiment in apprenticing ourselves to a tradition and its spiritual disciplines, with the hope that immersing and submitting ourselves to practices would work in tandem with a reflective understanding of them, a reflection that included both critical distance and creative endorsement.

Self-examination through the vices and spiritual formation through graced disciplines was the form my particular class took. No two classes will do this the same way. But the experience helped me grasp how formative practices and reflective theorizing are richly bound up with each other. It affirmed both their individual importance and their inseparability. The rhythm of practice and reflection on practice is thus something I aspire not only to live, but to teach, and not only to teach, but to live.

Reading Practices and Christian Pedagogy: Enacting Charity with Texts

David I. Smith

Questions about Reading

When Christians (or folk in general, for that matter) discuss reading, most of the energy tends to go into judging the acceptability of particular books. Publications on Christianity and literature tend to consist of faith-informed commentary on significant works, or debates about what books should be read by whom, or whether they should be read at all.[1] This is a fine and necessary enterprise. This essay, however, is more concerned with the kinds of readers that we have become or are becoming, and about how much responsibility teachers bear for that process. I will be examining how reading is nested within the practices of teaching and learning, and what this has to do with faith; but first allow me to set the stage with a few points of reference.

There is a long tradition of discussion of what we might call spiritually engaged reading. This includes the development of specific practices that seek to move the reader beyond mere decoding of information and to slow and enhance his or her ingestion of words with a view to personal transformation. Eugene Peterson, in a recent popular contribution to this tradition, has this to say about the "discipline of spiritual reading":

> [It is] the only kind of reading that is congruent with what is written in our Holy Scriptures, but also with all writing that is intended to

1. The majority of the scholarly articles published on Christianity and literature (for instance, in the journal of the same name) have focused on interpreting works or developing literary theory, while more public Christian debates about reading are often of the "should children be allowed to read Harry Potter" variety.

change our lives and not just stuff some information into the cells of our brain. All serious and good writing anticipates precisely this kind of reading — ruminative and leisurely, a dalliance with words in contrast to wolfing down information.[2]

Such distinctions are common, contrasting kinds of reading in which a text is "used" (treated as a means to information or distraction), and reading in which the text is "received" (approached with vulnerability to being changed by it).[3] Paul Griffiths has explored at length the contours of "religious reading."[4] The kind of reading in which religious people become practiced is repeated and ongoing, revisiting texts multiple times. It seeks to be slow and attentive, drinking in the details of the text and approaching it reverentially. The reader comes to the text expecting it to make moral demands, and is willing to submit and be changed. Reading takes place in a communal context with a shared tradition of interpretation, and faithfulness counts for more than creativity. The act of reading seeks personal transformation through attentive encounter with significant texts. The contrasting term for Griffiths is "consumerist reading." This kind of reading values speed and efficiency. It seeks to master the text and control its meanings for purposes of practical application. Texts are often read only once and are disposable after information has been extracted. Individual motives and interpretations are valued, and originality is prized. The main

---

2. Eugene H. Peterson, *Eat This Book: A Conversation in the Art of Spiritual Reading* (Grand Rapids: Wm. B. Eerdmans, 2006), p. 3.

3. These particular terms are drawn from C. S. Lewis, *An Experiment in Criticism* (Cambridge: Cambridge University Press, 1961). There is a secularized echo of such distinctions in Louise Rosenblatt's account of "efferent" and "aesthetic" reading stances; see *The Reader, the Text, the Poem: The Transactional Theory of the Literary Work* (Carbondale: Southern Illinois University Press, 1978). On some tensions between Rosenblatt's account and past Christian ways of making the distinction, see David I. Smith, "The Poet, the Child, and the Blackbird: Aesthetic Reading and Spiritual Development," *International Journal of Children's Spirituality* 9, no. 2 (2004): 143-54.

4. Paul Griffiths, *Religious Reading: The Place of Reading in the Practice of Religion* (New York: Oxford University Press, 1999); and "Reading as a Spiritual Practice," in *The Scope of Our Art: The Vocation of the Theological Teacher*, ed. L. Gregory Jones and Stephanie Paulsell (Grand Rapids: Wm. B. Eerdmans, 2002), pp. 32-47. See also, for example, Roger Newell, "Teaching the Bible along the Devotional/Academic Faultline: An Incarnational Approach to the Quarrel between Love and Knowledge," *Teaching Theology and Religion* 6, no. 4 (2003): 190-97. While such binary distinctions are common, the issues at stake are not identical in each case, pointing to the need ultimately for a more carefully variegated account than a stark division into two kinds of reading.

goal is information or pleasure, and the text should inform rather than transform the reader. Both kinds of reading have their place — some texts and occasions properly demand consumerist reading — though Griffiths suggests a consumerist stance has colonized far more of our reading practices than is good for our spiritual health.

It seems at first as if "religious reading" implies reading a sacred text — in Christian settings, the Bible. However, the boundary lines are not so clear. Christians interact with a wider range of texts in ways that fit Griffiths' description — classic devotionals, commentaries, hymns, confessions, and so on. Recall also Peterson's comment that other "serious and good writing" beside Scripture is "intended to change our lives"; it may not receive the same a priori submission given to core confessional texts, but it calls for some variant on the kind of self-giving reading that Peterson, Griffiths, and others have in view.[5]

Alan Jacobs explores such a variant in his application of a "hermeneutics of love" to literary texts.[6] Here (and Jacobs is far from alone here) the language of virtue comes to the fore. Charity in reading involves avoiding quick dismissal and cheap disdain, resisting the ego satisfaction of allowing a text only to confirm one's prejudices, and seeking the good in a text, choosing its truths over its defects. Humility implies a working assumption that the text may offer wisdom that I lack, and that if the road to grasping it is stony, then the fault may lie at least as much with me as with the text itself. Justice involves reading fairly, working to weigh evidence before making evaluative judgments and seeking to represent the text without distortion, even when distortion would better fit my interests. The act of reading itself (whatever the specific text) becomes an act in which, as in all other acts, Christian virtues ought to be exercised.[7]

---

5. There is no space in this essay to pursue further how the boundaries should be drawn here so that literary texts receive their due but are not positioned as surrogate sacred texts with quasi-biblical authority; for present purposes, it will suffice to note that there are aspects of accounts of "receiving" texts with the goal of personal growth that seem to fit the ways in which a variety of texts may be read.

6. Alan Jacobs, *A Theology of Reading: The Hermeneutics of Love* (Boulder, Colo.: Westview Press, 2001); Alan Jacobs, "Bakhtin and the Hermeneutics of Love," in *Bakhtin and Religion: A Feeling for Faith,* ed. S. M. Felch and P. J. Contino (Evanston, Ill.: Northwestern University Press, 2001), pp. 25-45.

7. There is a clear intersection here with some common ways of articulating the curricular aspirations of Christian colleges. My own college, Calvin College, has a core curriculum explicitly framed in terms of (among other things) the pursuit of a list of virtues that includes several of those listed here. See Cornelius Plantinga Jr., *Engaging God's World: A Re-*

In sum, connections have long been made between Christian identity and how reading is practiced. Talk of reading as a practice, of course, invokes the particular questions framing this volume, questions arising from discussions of the nature of social practices — sustained, complex, cooperative human activities in which goods are pursued and virtues are formed and supported.[8] Alasdair MacIntyre famously argued that "it is always within some particular community with its own specific institutional forms that we learn or fail to learn to exercise the virtues."[9] Etienne Wenger has offered further exploration (described in the introduction to this volume) of how social groups engaged in shared practice develop norms, rhythms, and repertoires that are of consequence to the imaginations and identities of those who participate in them.[10] Others have extended these concepts in Christian terms: we do not grow in faith through ideas alone; we practice our faith by participating in the Eucharist, corporate worship, prayer, forgiveness, Sabbath-keeping, testimony, and, yes, particular practices of reading and attentiveness.[11]

---

formed Vision of Faith, Learning, and Living (Grand Rapids: Wm. B. Eerdmans, 2002), pp. 177-241.

8. See the introduction to this volume.

9. Alasdair C. MacIntyre, *After Virtue: A Study in Moral Theory,* 3rd ed. (Notre Dame: University of Notre Dame Press, 2007), pp. 194-95. Christian accounts of moral formation of course need to find ways of coordinating this focus on community formation with a primary emphasis on grace and gift; on this, see, for example, Craig Dykstra, *Growing in the Life of Faith: Education and Christian Practices,* 2nd ed. (Louisville: Westminster John Knox Press, 2005), pp. 74-78; and Amy Plantinga Pauw, "Attending to the Gaps between Beliefs and Practices," in *Practicing Theology: Beliefs and Practices in Christian Life,* ed. Miroslav Volf and Dorothy C. Bass (Grand Rapids: Wm. B. Eerdmans, 2002), pp. 33-48.

10. Etienne Wenger, *Communities of Practice: Learning, Meaning, and Identity* (Cambridge: Cambridge University Press, 1999). Of course, as soon as one cites more than one protagonist in recent discussions of social practice, the precise meaning of the term *practice* begins to shift. For comparison of Wenger and MacIntyre on practices, see Terence McLaughlin, "Teaching as a Practice and a Community of Practice: The Limits of Commonality and the Demands of Diversity," *Journal of Philosophy of Education* 37, no. 2 (2003): 339-52. For the purposes of this essay, I am using the term *practices* in a sense somewhat looser than MacIntyre's rather stringent definition, and more reminiscent of Wenger's definition.

11. Dykstra, *Growing in the Life of Faith,* pp. 42-43. Miroslav Volf suggests that "Practices . . . are Christian insofar as they are 'resonances' of God's engagement with the world" ("Theology for a Way of Life," in *Practicing Theology,* p. 260). I explore other aspects of Christian reading in relation to pedagogy in David I. Smith, "Misreading through the Eyes of Faith: Christian Students' Reading Strategies as Interlanguage," in *Teaching Spiritually Engaged Reading,* ed. David I. Smith, John Shortt, and John Sullivan (Nottingham: The Stapleford Center, 2007), pp. 53-66.

With these all too briefly sketched coordinates in hand, we can return to students, teachers, and how they read. What if we approached the Christian literature classroom not only in terms of what interpretations change hands, but also in terms of what kinds of practices are shared? Might this shed light not only on how reading can be Christian, but also on the nature of Christian teaching and learning?

Dissatisfactions with Teaching

I will focus here on a particular course, an undergraduate survey of the literature of German-speaking countries since 1945. The course is fourteen weeks long and is an advanced course taught at Calvin College, a Christian liberal arts college in Michigan. The account that follows draws mainly from the Spring 2006 semester, though the practices described have now been in place for several iterations of the course. With the literatures of four countries in play, several Nobel Prize winners to consider, and a backdrop ranging from postwar reconstruction through existentialism, feminism, ecological concern, and the cold war to terrorism, postmodernism, reunification, and multiculturalism, there is pressure to cover content in the limited time available. Since this is the only survey course in our catalog covering this most recent period of writing in German, some attempt at coverage has to be made, producing a temptation to over-ambition on the part of the instructor that will be familiar to anyone who has ever taught survey courses.

First attempts to teach this course left me with a number of frustrations, mainly in connection with the reading practices that it appeared to provoke and promote. How texts are handled, presented, and framed by pedagogical tasks helps determine the modes of reading and the relationship to the text that are adopted by students.[12] Put more bluntly, reading stances are not accidental: we are partly responsible for how our students read. My students, it seemed to me, often failed to display desirable reading practices. "Charitable" or "spiritual" reading is characterized by the authors mentioned above in terms of applying disciplined attentiveness, reading slowly, repeatedly, contextually, and with humble care. When I considered the practices generated and sustained by my course, I saw stu-

---

12. See Louise M. Rosenblatt, *The Reader, the Text, the Poem;* and "What Facts Does This Poem Teach You?" *Language Arts* 57, no. 4 (1980): 386-94.

dents reading more like consumers. They read quickly in order to cover the ground in the midst of the demands of other classes. They read superficially and once only, gaining enough acquaintance with the text to avoid embarrassment in class. They then blithely offered evaluative opinions about complex texts barely mastered.

These observations are not intended to invite a response that involves blaming students. Many disciplines offer survey courses, and while these are an indication that there is a legitimate time and place for reading for broad coverage, they can also exacerbate existing temptations toward pedagogical practices that invite largely consumerist modes of reading. Common classroom practices tend to implicitly communicate that fly-by reading is a sufficient and acceptable basis for expressing judgments concerning complex texts. Western educational culture associates speed of verbal response with intelligence; we all know what it means if a child is "slow" or "quick-witted." Teachers tend to see those who respond the fastest in class as being the brightest (an odd idea, once one comes to think about it).[13] Add this to common ways of managing class discussion, and the tendency to air swift opinions and evaluative conclusions publicly on the basis of cursory acquaintance with the text can end up actively rewarded through positive regard and good participation grades. Put more bluntly, I began to wonder whether leaping to quick and partially informed judgments was a good success strategy for students in my classroom if pulled off with wit and verve. It seemed to me that our reading practices should be blamed at least as much on the professor (that would be me) and on the larger rhythms of the educational institution as on students; both, after all, help to shape the expectations that students bring to such a class. To a considerable degree, we get the reading practices we deserve.[14]

Although I am generalizing for the sake of brevity, I suspect that the caricature is fairly recognizable. My main point here is that my dissatisfaction was not with course content, but with our practices. This became my question: How much could change, given that the course had to be a survey, the class location, timetable, and format were fixed, and the institu-

---

13. See Ron Ritchhart, *Intellectual Character: What It Is, Why It Matters, and How to Get It* (San Francisco: Jossey-Bass, 2004).

14. Compare Nicholas Wolterstorff's broader questioning of our recurring sense as a society that we are not getting the educational outcomes that we deserve in his essay "The Schools We Deserve," in *Schooling Christians: "Holy Experiments" in American Education*, ed. Stanley Hauerwas and John H. Westerhoff (Grand Rapids: Wm. B. Eerdmans, 1992), pp. 3-28.

tional context would remain more or less constant? Can one make headway from within standard parameters?[15]

Interventions in the Classroom

In turning to classroom interventions, my intention is not to make any big claims for individual strategies, but to characterize a community of practice. In Wenger's terms, this involves sketching how shared imagination and relations of accountability develop around a joint enterprise, and how particular forms of participation and reification (turning intentions into objects) grow into particular repertoires of discourse and behavior (see the introduction to this volume). I will describe the changes made to the class in the form of a continuous narrative, not wishing to set too much store by any single intervention taken out of the wider pattern of practice.

The opening class of the semester was the focus of much reflection. The agenda during this hour was to establish the immediate postwar situation and the harsh economic, social, and psychological conditions facing German writers. How was one to write, without paper or a buying public, in a language denatured by years of propaganda, about realities such as Stalingrad and Auschwitz? I was used to dealing with this material in lecture format. Students were engaged, could repeat the main points on a later test, and got good grades; the class was a success by common criteria. Two considerations moved me to attempt a rethink. One concerned the importance of first impressions: I wanted a way of starting the semester that might set the tone. The other had to do with charitable reading. I wanted to orient us in some way to an exploration of the hermeneutics of charity, and reasoned that regular information transfer methods were likely to be limited in addressing goals such as growth in humility and compassion. With these two concerns in mind, I arrived early and set up a looping PowerPoint presentation consisting entirely of black-and-white photographs of rubble and extermination camps against a black background. I also set a piece of dissonant ambient music looping on the computer, blacked out the classroom, and turned off the lights. Finally, I

---

15. Apposite is Alasdair MacIntyre's comment that "it is indeed from within practice that we disengage from its immediacies in order to correct practice." See MacIntyre, "Review of *Philosophical Arguments* by Charles Taylor," *The Philosophical Quarterly* 47, no. 186 (1997): 94-96; the quotation is on page 96.

stacked the chairs in the corners and hung a sign at the door inviting students to enter in silence. Then I left and deliberately returned several minutes after the start of class. Fifteen students sat in silence on the floor; I sat down among them and said, "It's 1945, we are in Germany, and you are a writer: What is it like?" I immediately learned (as my students proceeded to give me most of what had been in my lecture the year before) that one has a different kind of discussion with students when seated with them on the floor in the dark than when standing over their desks under bright lights. In beginning this way, I intended to physically enact a posture of humility for our initial approach to the experience of the Germans whom we were about to read, and to create a more affectively compelling pedagogical context that called for empathy. In doing so, I hoped to take a first step toward reframing my students' approach to the texts assigned.

For the next class session we read Heinrich Böll's "Wanderer, kommst du nach Spa . . . ,"[16] a short story in which a teenage soldier returns wounded to his school, now converted into a field hospital. He is carried on a stretcher past statues and paintings representing classical, humanistic, and militaristic traditions as co-opted by Nazi German education. This story, itself a masterful critique of a twisted educational community of practice, has more than enough layers to occupy us for some considerable time. After a first reading, we spent a class period discussing the story and its cultural references. Then for homework I asked students to read the story again.

I had become uncomfortable with the fact that while it would seem unprofessional to me as a scholar to write a paper focused upon a work that I had skim-read once only, my students were effectively asked to do this on a regular basis. I made some modest sacrifices of previously assigned texts in order to create a little space in the schedule, and then assigned repeat readings of two texts, in the first and last weeks of the semester. I enforced a second reading by two strategies. First, I openly explained my goals and shamelessly pleaded with students to complete the second reading. Second, in case the daily grind should trump my efforts at persuasion, I assigned tasks for the second reading that required a level of analysis that was not achievable from memory. After the second reading of "Wanderer," we counted the works of art and explored how Böll is presenting the school and the imagination it fosters as a sick parody of the stations of the

16. In Heinrich Böll, *Wanderer, kommst du nach Spa . . . : Erzählungen* (Munich: DTV, 1967), pp. 45-56.

cross. Here again I was looking to reify some larger goals and begin to generate a repertoire consistent with charitable reading. I wanted students to read with humility. I reasoned that perhaps one of the ways that humility might be learned in a literature classroom is to experience reading a complex text, forming initial interpretations, discussing them for an hour in competent company, and then going back and discovering whole worlds of meaning that were missed the first time. As long as my students were asked to read texts only once, that particular experience was denied them in favor of an implied ethos of easy mastery. Again I sought to keep our bodies in play: the first time we read the story, we sat in a circle; the second time, I clustered the chairs tightly and concentrically in the center of the classroom, physically hunching us around the text to embody close, intimate attentiveness.

It was not possible to assign multiple readings of some of the larger novels taught in the succeeding weeks, so I sought another way of structuring repeated engagements with texts into our learning. I decided to assign a single poet for the semester. Every week, regardless of what else we were reading, students were assigned one poem by Hans Magnus Enzensberger. The poems were chosen and sequenced so that connections could be found, whether direct or oblique, with the concerns, themes, or imagery of the other texts assigned that week. Students were asked to read the poem before Monday's class, in which a few minutes were taken to elicit some first reactions and give at least some momentum to any who were nonplussed. Before Wednesday's class, students were required to submit a translation by e-mail — this allowed me to further check comprehension. By Friday, they were to write a journal entry about the poem, using a rubric for guidance. In this way I sought to maximize the likelihood of students experiencing repeated engagements with each poem separated by sufficient time for reflection to occur and new insights to emerge, moving away from an instant response mode of reading. Responding to the translations and journals weekly allowed a formative conversation to emerge between students and myself, with the result that the journal interpretations improved markedly over the semester — even though keeping up this regular rhythm of communication demanded a level of discipline from me that sometimes escaped me. By the fourth week I found comments in student journals to the effect that a line in the current poem looked as if it meant such and such, but that couldn't be right, because that's not the kind of thing that Enzensberger would normally say. Such interpretive moves are essential for handling Enzensberger's frequent irony, and yet had not been possible for students to make during previous versions of the course, since they had no extended experience with a single author as a basis for such comparisons.

As will already be apparent, I was thinking during the semester about embodiment, about how learning and spiritual growth might in some way be connected with such mundane matters as posture, lighting, physical distance, and tone of voice. This made me more self-conscious than before about my own presence in class. One day found me thinking about how I entered the classroom. On the one hand, I might stride purposefully into the room, stand at the front of straight rows of chairs, and briskly utter something like this: "Right. Last time we reached page 37, and for today you were to read as far as page 58. Did everyone do that? Good. Now the main themes of this section are . . . Let's begin at the top of page 40. Would someone read aloud for us?" Or, I might start differently. Spurred on by John Cavadini's fascinating study of how humility before the text was reflected in the specific discursive moves that Augustine made when preaching,[17] I walked into class absorbed in an open copy of the assigned book. I wandered to a seat in the circle, sat down, and continued reading without looking up. Eventually, my opening words were something like this: "You know, I've read this novel four times, and this is the third time I've taught it, and I was still, before class, trying to figure out why on earth we get the sudden change of topic on page 40. Did that strike anyone else as strange? Can anyone help me out?" Either way of beginning could be valid; yet each speaks differently.[18]

Later in the semester, there came a day when, contrary to the norm that had developed, most students were not prepared for class. My attempts to open discussion produced unusually halting responses. After a few minutes, one of the students intervened. "I have to confess that I didn't do today's reading," she said, "and I'm guessing that quite a few of us didn't." There were sheepish nods of assent around the room. I thought for a few moments, and then said, calmly and without rancor, "Please go home; class is over. We can't charitably discuss a text that we haven't read.

---

17. See John C. Cavadini, "Simplifying Augustine," in *Educating People of Faith: Exploring the History of Jewish and Christian Communities*, ed. John Van Engen (Grand Rapids: Wm. B. Eerdmans, 2004), pp. 63-84.

18. Each speaks differently, though admittedly not univocally; much depends also on context, tone of voice, student frames of reference, and so on. I am merely seeking to make concrete the attempt in this particular setting to reify a particular relationship to the text in a way that might contribute to a particular classroom repertoire.

We'll make up the extra hour next week." This took a few moments to sink in; then the students left in silence. It still seems to me that to proceed with class at this moment in this particular community of practice would have been to signal a willingness to cover for their lack of engagement with the text by lecturing, thus implicitly abandoning the project of learning to read charitably. I also take this exchange to be a sign of maturing engagement with the class's framing practices. As Wenger puts it:

> Negotiating a joint enterprise gives rise to relations of mutual accountability among those involved. . . . Responsibility with respect to what makes life harder for others, for instance, is something they enforce among themselves, sometimes quite vocally. . . . The regime of accountability becomes an integral part of the practice. . . . Being able to make distinctions between reified standards and competent engagement in practice is an important aspect of becoming an experienced member.[19]

The emergence of such a distinction seems at least incipient in the proactive response from the students to the signs of lack of preparation as the class got underway.

Thinking in terms of social practices need not imply that learners are sufficiently formed simply by engaging in a set of shared behavioral moves. A social practice involves a narrative, a reason why, a mental horizon within which action is experienced as meaningful.[20] Wenger suggests that a successful community of practice needs to be sustained by an "infrastructure of imagination" that gives particular meaning to moves that

---

19. Wenger, *Communities of Practice*, pp. 81-82.

20. MacIntyre (*After Virtue*, p. 193) argues that "a practice, in the sense intended, is never just a set of technical skills, even when directed towards some unified purpose and even if the exercise of those skills can on occasion be valued or enjoyed for their own sake." He adds, "There is no such thing as 'behavior,' to be identified prior to and independently of intentions, beliefs, and settings" (p. 208). Similarly, Wenger asserts, "Practice is, first and foremost, a process by which we can experience the world and our engagement with it as meaningful. . . . It does not address simply the mechanics of getting something done, individually or in groups; it is not a mechanical perspective. It includes not just bodies (or even coordinated bodies) and not just brains (even coordinated ones), but moreover that which gives *meaning* to the motions of bodies and the working of brains" (*Communities of Practice*, p. 51). This need not imply denial that there are formative effects of practice that are not consciously mediated, but merely affirms that a more holistic account of how we are formed within communities of practice needs to take account of the ways in which meaning and action become linked.

could otherwise be read differently.[21] For this reason, I worked at negotiating with students the meaning of our shifts in practice. I adopted two main strategies.

The first had to do with the themes of the works assigned. While variety remained both inevitable and desirable, several works engaged with themes concerning the shape of modern consciousness and the loss of a contemplative relationship with reality. This allowed explicit reflection on the consumer-oriented nature of our contemporary ways of relating to reality. Works such as Hartmut Lange's *Der Himmel über Golgatha (The Sky over Golgotha)* invited us to discuss what it is about our day-to-day formation as (post)modern selves that makes it difficult for us to sustain loving attentiveness toward significant texts. Why are we often the wrong kind of readers for spiritually significant texts, and how would we need to change to become receivers rather than consumers of what we read?[22]

Second, I wove a further longitudinal thread through the semester that surfaced every two weeks. MacIntyre argues that "to enter into a practice is to enter into a relationship not only with its contemporary practitioners, but also with those who have preceded us in the practice, particularly those whose achievements extended the reach of the practice to its present point."[23] Wenger notes more succinctly that "practice is a shared history of learning that requires some catching up for joining."[24] Every second week I assigned a short text in English, no more than a few paragraphs, that dealt in some way with the question of what reading might have to do with Christian charity. Using Mark Pike's typology of different kinds of readers of poetry, students were encouraged to consider what kind of reader they were and how this might help or hinder their access to certain texts or suggest areas in which they needed to grow or learn from others.[25] We read extracts from Alan Jacobs on the hermeneutics of charity and discussed what love might mean in the context of reading. Was loving a book the same as enjoying it? How does charity relate to eros?[26] We discussed

21. Wenger, *Communities of Practice*, p. 238.

22. Hartmut Lange's novellas proved particularly fruitful in this regard. The particular volume that we used was Hartmut Lange, *Schnitzlers Würgeengel: Vier Novellen* (Zürich: Diogenes, 1995).

23. MacIntyre, *After Virtue*, p. 194.

24. Wenger, *Communities of Practice*, pp. 47, 102.

25. Mark A. Pike, "From Personal to Social Transaction: A Model of Aesthetic Reading in the Classroom," *Journal of Aesthetic Education* 37, no. 2 (2003): 61-72.

26. Jacobs, *A Theology of Reading*.

Mikhail Bakhtin's claim that only "loving attentiveness" is capable of slowing down long enough over a text to linger over it and sculpt every detail.[27] We considered Basil the Great's arguments for the spiritual value of Christian meditation on pagan literature.[28] We explored Kierkegaard's contrast between what he calls the "poet," who is lost in the experience of the text for experience's sake, and the "child," who listens to the text for that which should be obeyed.[29] After each reading, a brief time was set aside in class for discussion. Periodic journal entries reflecting directly on these readings were also assigned. The aim was to weave together imagination and repertoire — the reflective pauses focused on these texts were intended to provide what Wenger terms an "infrastructure of imagination."[30] The question of what it might mean to read with Christian love thus became an explicit and ongoing part of the class agenda, enabling an identification of our developing repertoire as a form of Christian practice. Toward the end of the semester, during one of these discussion times, several students began to talk about their other classes. Some expressed a newfound dissatisfaction with their experiences in other college courses, and with aspects of college life that kept them in hurried and harried mode. Having begun to feel their way into another mode of engagement, they wished for more of it across their educational experience. One student changed his plans for the summer. He had intended to read ahead for the following year; now he planned to select the most important books from the past year and reread them.[31]

I worried for most of the semester about how to assess the course. The inherited examination format, consisting of a few short essay questions covering major works and themes from the period, did not seem a fitting conclusion to what we had been doing. The journal entries, a mid-term exam, and class discussions provided some material for evaluation, but I was looking for a way to close the semester that underlined, rather than undermined, the emphasis on charitable reading. In recent iterations

27. Cited in Jacobs, "Bakhtin and the Hermeneutics of Love," p. 27.

28. Cited in Jacobs, *A Theology of Reading*, pp. 141-42.

29. Søren Kierkegaard, *Christian Discourses and The Lilies of the Field and the Birds of the Air and Three Discourses at the Communion on Fridays* (New York: Oxford University Press, 1961).

30. Wenger, *Communities of Practice*, p. 238.

31. This student also followed through further by requesting an independent study the following semester in order to pursue themes in the literature we had discussed.

of the course, I have used varying combinations of assessment tasks selected from the following in place of a final exam:[32]

- Choose any work studied, re-read at least 100 pages, and write a short reflection paper detailing what was learned from the re-reading.
- Find an undisturbed spot and, notebook in hand, meditate in silence for at least an hour on one of the texts studied. Then meet with two other students, discuss what insights were gained, and write up a summary of the conversation.
- Think of a thoughtful Christian friend and write him or her a five-page letter explaining how a close reading of one of the texts studied could positively impact his or her life.
- Write a short reflection paper showing awareness of existing models of what "Christian reading" might entail and explain how you understand and view the notion.
- Choose a poem by Enzensberger not studied during the semester and write a short interpretive essay with the aim of showing how you have matured as a reader of his poems.

The end result was that I still had student writing on which to base grades, but the mode of engagement became part of the focus of the assessment in a way that discouraged relying on a hurried review of course notes.

The Fruits of Our Labor

A community of practice emerges over time from interaction and gradual attunement. It is not a linear implementation of theory. Not all of the above interactions were planned in advance. In describing them retrospectively, I have inevitably lifted them out of a richer context of daily words, gestures, e-mails, ideas, and adjustments that made up the lived texture of the class. I make no strong causative claims for any single change in the course — the aim and, I think, the reality was a pattern of practice oriented toward the realization of charitable reading. The aim of reading with charitable attentiveness was reified in particular assignments, texts, arrangements of light and furniture, images, gestures, and forms of partici-

---

32. What follow are not the exact instructions given to students (these included some more extensive guidance), but only a brief summary of the tasks.

pation. Amid these, we began to forge a repertoire of language and behaviors that could count as engagement with reading Christianly. Signs of a "regime of mutual accountability" began to emerge in the class as this temporary community of readers struggled with how to relate the demands of the shared practice to the constraints and pressures provided by the larger college community and their everyday lives.[33]

Wenger notes that participation in a community of practice fosters an "identity of participation," a sense of self shaped by the forms of participation that define the group as members become attuned to their shared enterprise. This process also gives rise to new boundary configurations, for group members are also members of other groups and so face the task of brokering the tensions that arise from multi-membership in order to sustain a degree of personal coherence.[34] A clear instance of this is the tension set up by the course design between common college student reading practices and the particular conception of reading practices around which this course was built. A focus on practices invites the assumption that deficiencies in student reading behaviors (superficiality, haste, fragmentation) are not simply manifestations of individual vice but rather are related to existing patterns of practice.[35] They will therefore not be easily modifiable by mere exhortation, but may be put under pressure by the creation of a countervailing community of practice. This pressure became visible as students began to express how difficult the practice of charitable reading was proving to be, internalized a sense of accountability for the readings, and eventually began to express a newly dissatisfied perspective on their mode of study in other courses.

One set of student journal responses offers an intriguing glimpse of further negotiation of boundaries between memberships in overlapping communities of practice. Just over halfway through the semester, a student wrote the following in a journal entry:

> After discussing reading lovingly, with love, I've taken that and reflected on the way I read people. As with books, people need time, and

33. This summary recapitulates some key features of communities of practice as detailed by Wenger in *Communities of Practice;* see in particular pp. 67, 81, 83.

34. See Wenger, *Communities of Practice,* chapter 4.

35. Wenger (*Communities of Practice,* p. 98) notes, "Close scrutiny will usually reveal good reasons — functional or dysfunctional — for a practice to be the way it is. . . . It is a mistake to assume that practice is inherently a conservative force, and it is also a mistake to assume that practice is erratic or can be modified by decree."

cannot merely be skimmed over to be thoroughly understood. While at [a local coffee shop] earlier this week, I made the mistake of hastily casting a rather negative judgment on one of our customers. This young, attractive woman, thin as a twig, visited us on St. Patrick's Day to order a drink. I immediately smelled smoke on her person and noticed her seductively clingy attire. Prostitute? I wouldn't put it past her. She was definitely leading a shady life, maybe involved with drugs. But hey, why was I thinking these things? Had I exchanged two words with her yet? No. My fellow Barista, Chris, finished off her drink, made some small talk, and found out that she was on her way to a nursing home for the night to visit a friend. (Journal Entry 5)

A few weeks later, in the final journal entry of the semester, the same student took up this train of thought and pursued it further:

Not long ago, I took reading Christianly and applied it to the way I read people. I noticed myself casting rash judgments on people without understanding them, knowing their backgrounds, or even talking to them. I think especially because of the focus in this class to read Christianly, I tried to change this bad habit. I had an opportunity to practice reading people Christianly only this past weekend. A middle-aged man from out of town came in, in search of a computer. He claimed he had been wandering around Grand Rapids for the past two days in search of his sister, who he only knew lived somewhere near Kentwood. He didn't have her phone number and needed to look it up online (in an e-mail because she was unlisted). [The coffee shop] doesn't have computers, though, only Internet service. My co-worker wanted to get him out; she thought he was off his rocker. But I talked to him for a little while, and upon hearing he hadn't eaten in at least a day, gave him a sandwich and a cup of coffee, and told him he could ask one of our customers to use their computer. One gentleman was kind enough to let him. So he got on, and couldn't find her number, but left a message for her to come and pick him up; he would be waiting.

Having been in a similar situation once myself (lost in Germany), I was sensitive to his needs and feeling of exhaustion and helplessness. I took my own experience and related it to his, and because of my Christianity, I asked myself over and over what the right thing to do would be. Like skimming over a text leave[s] one unsatisfied, and does an injustice to text and author, I was not at peace having briefly met this man, to leave him out on Breton [Road] for the night. I had to go back (with a male friend), if only to keep him company for a short while, but possibly to bring him somewhere to spend the night.

In this way, I believe, allowing time to get to know a work (or person), realizing from what sort of framework we're looking at it, and doing so lovingly, this is how we should read Christianly.[36]

Here the student responds explicitly to the focus on Christian reading, and indicates awareness of development in her own responses as the semester progressed. While it would be folly to assert that this class was the sole source of her spiritual growth (her own prior maturation and other experiences during the semester were surely in play), she clearly perceives the class as having directly provoked further growth in her ability to suspend judgment of others ("because of the focus in this class to read Christianly"). She also shows explicit awareness of the positive and negative roles of prior identity and interpretive frameworks when it comes to making evaluative judgments ("she thought he was off his rocker"; "having been in a similar situation once myself"; "realizing from what sort of framework we're looking at it"). Most strikingly, she offers an unprompted extension of the class theme to other life experiences ("reading people Christianly") and thus to broader Christian growth.

I suggest that it makes sense to view the negotiations described by this student as arising from the tensions of multi-membership. There are tensions between the classroom community of practice and the community of practice in which she participated as a barista. Participation in the latter typically involves polite but limited engagement with customers, a focus on efficiency, avoidance of possible embarrassments to other patrons, and non-engagement with non-customers. Participation in the former entailed slowing down, learning to avoid swift judgments, and suspecting human depths below the surface. Growth occurred as the practice of charity was allowed to trump the practice of customer service where discord arose between the two. These journal entries provide insufficient evidence to reach general conclusions, but they at least invite the question of whether a focus on ideas alone, without the creation of an alternative repertoire of practices that fostered an alternative identity of participation, would have been enough to force the renegotiation of identity that took place at the boundary between the two communities of practice. Wenger points out that

---

36. Student journal, German 308: Twentieth-Century German Literature II, Calvin College, May 2006; this material is quoted with permission.

in the process of sustaining a practice, we become invested in what we do as well as in each other and our shared history. Our identities become anchored in each other and what we do together. As a result, it is not easy to become a radically new person in the same community of practice. Conversely, it is not easy to transform oneself without the support of a community, as reflected by the countless support groups proposed by the self-help industry.[37]

This suggests that Christian learning ought to be approached not as the insertion of Christian ideas into the default social dynamics of the college classroom, but rather as the intentional fostering of communities of counter-practice rooted in the history of Christian practices.

In terms of matters such as ability to read and interpret literary German, and knowledge of literary movements, terminology, and the sociohistorical background to the works studied, the students in this course did at least as well as those in any previous version that I have taught. I am confident that the redesign to accommodate a focus on charitable reading did not result in a diminishment of learning with regard to conventional goals. This was still very much a class in the literature of German-speaking countries; in fact, it was still a survey course. I did, however, see encouraging signs of spiritual growth in the comments and assignments of many of the students. This was neither guaranteed nor uniform, and some students showed signs of business as usual; this was, however, balanced with striking evidence of growth such as that described above.[38] This of course remains a particular class, with its own peculiar parameters, location, and context. I offer it not as a blueprint, but as an example suggestive of the conclusion that the effort to think through Christian pedagogy in the light of the history of Christian practices is worthwhile, and might even fruitfully extend the repertoire of Christian higher education.

---

37. Wenger, *Communities of Practice*, p. 89.

38. That students should show different degrees of appropriation of the underlying Christian practice goals is not only not surprising, but also not necessarily an indication of lack of progress. As Joseph Dunne notes, "There are important practices which, even though they contain possibilities of great virtuosity, are nonetheless available with real integrity at quite modest, even rudimentary, levels of accomplishment." See Joseph Dunne, "What's the Good of Education?" in *The RoutledgeFalmer Reader in Philosophy of Education*, ed. Wilfred Carr (London and New York: Routledge, 2005), p. 154.

The Rough Trail to Authentic Pedagogy: Incorporating Hospitality, Fellowship, and Testimony into the Classroom

Carolyne Call

What does it mean to be a Christian educator? This is a question I ask myself on a regular basis. Besides teaching in a faith-based institution and referring to myself as a religious professional, what would it mean to say that I am an educator who is a Christian? Would my own faith life make any difference in how I practice my craft in a classroom? Should it? I would like to say it would, and was tempted to assume this as a given. But such an assumption turned out to be pedagogical hubris. Considering the impact of Christian practices on pedagogy pushed me to become intentional about the role of faith in the actual practice of teaching. The idea of practicing hospitality in the classroom arose for me out of Parker Palmer's work[1] and seemed to mesh well with my own previous understanding of how I approach teaching. Wanting to be more deliberate about the integration between my faith life and my pedagogical approach, I started to reflect seriously on a question posed by Ellen Marmon: "What would be different about your teaching if you thought of yourself as a *host* and of your students as *guests*?"[2] This chapter explores how I answered this question.

In order to answer the question, I decided to change the format of an annual course I teach to pre-service teachers. The course is titled "Adolescent Psychology" and is a requirement for all students with a secondary education minor. There are typically from twenty to twenty-five students in the class, and majors vary widely. Students usually have had at least an introductory course in psychology or educational psychology, although this

---

1. Parker Palmer, *The Courage to Teach* (San Francisco: Jossey-Bass, 1997).
2. Ellen L. Marmon, "Teaching as Hospitality," *Asbury Theological Journal* 63, no. 2 (Fall 2008): 33-39.

is not required. The class focuses on psychology within an educational setting, and meets on Monday evenings from six until eight-thirty, from mid-January until the first week of May. The course is taught within the Education Department at Saint Mary's College in Notre Dame, Indiana. Saint Mary's is a Roman Catholic women's college in the liberal arts tradition with approximately 1600 students. Founded in 1844 by the Sisters of the Holy Cross, it is one school among eight within the "family of Holy Cross."[3] Professional programs including education, nursing, and social work supplement the liberal arts curriculum. The student body of Saint Mary's is primarily white and middle to upper-middle class, and is almost exclusively residential. Approximately 85 percent of students identify themselves as Roman Catholic.

My approach to teaching psychology has two primary aims. The first is to introduce students to the history, theories, and concepts of psychology as a discipline. The second is to facilitate greater self-reflective capacities in the students. This means helping them to come to understand their own motives, behaviors, choices, and reactions in a more honest and reflective manner. My intent is for this self-insight to translate into greater insight into others with whom they share their lives and thus to engender greater tolerance, mutual understanding, and perhaps even compassion. This fits with my belief in the necessity of educating for dispositions. In the context of this particular psychology class, the focus for my students was on the psychological reality of middle school and high school age students. This course seeks to help them to better understand the hearts and minds of their own students once they begin teaching full-time.

An Experiment in Christian Practice

As I considered incorporating Christian practices into the classroom, I had to face a number of questions. Could I introduce traditional Christian practices into a classroom that had a mix of students from a variety of backgrounds? Could I do this without creating a sense of exclusion? While the majority of students at Saint Mary's identify themselves as Roman Catholic, there is no guarantee that individual students are active in their faith or even profess any faith. Could Christian practices speak to a spiritu-

---

3. Saint Mary's is the sister institution to the University of Notre Dame and Holy Cross College, which are located across and down the street.

ally diverse group? Could they lead to a greater sense of connection and community among the students? Could I do this and also maintain academic rigor? These were questions that helped to focus the project.

In renovating the course with specific practices in mind, I had to begin with an exploration of the concept of practices in general. My understanding came to be shaped by the work of Craig Dykstra, who notes that "practices are those cooperative human activities through which we, as individuals and as communities, grow and develop in moral character and substance."[4] Practices, in this understanding, have both moral goods and standards of excellence inherent in them. These allow us to enhance "our power to achieve what is good."[5] Dykstra is clear that a standard of excellence in the case of Christian practice is not the idea of mastery (as if one could "master" the ability to pray, for example); rather, excellence is, in this case, "trust and grateful receptivity."[6] I also hold to the related idea of a spiritual practice, which "is an action intended to make a change or adjustment in the deepest realm of the self. A spiritual practice is a thing we do that opens a door."[7] While the practices have their own measures of excellence and contain moral goods, they are also meant to bring about a desired end. In agreement with Dorothy Bass, then, "Practices have practical purposes such as healing, shaping community, or discernment."[8]

My focus here will be on using practices to shape the community of the classroom. In this way they are means to rehearsing a way of life and speak to both mind and heart. Etienne Wenger holds that practices can be the source of coherence within a community.[9] The coherence of a community comes about through the inter-relation of three things: joint enterprise (negotiated response to a situation), mutual engagement (people engaged in actions together, negotiating meanings), and shared repertoire (stories, artifacts, language, actions).[10] This means that the students and I

4. Craig Dykstra, *Growing in the Life of Faith: Education and Christian Practices* (Louisville: Westminster John Knox Press, 2005), p. 69.

5. Dykstra, *Growing in the Life of Faith*, p. 69.

6. Dykstra, *Growing in the Life of Faith*, p. 76.

7. Daniel Homan, O.S.B., and Lonni Collins Pratt, *Radical Hospitality: Benedict's Way of Love* (Brewster, Mass.: Paraclete Press, 2002), p. 32.

8. Craig Dykstra and Dorothy C. Bass, "Times of Yearning, Practices of Faith," in *Practicing Our Faith: A Way of Life for a Searching People*, ed. Dorothy C. Bass (San Francisco: Jossey-Bass, 1997), p. 7.

9. Etienne Wenger, *Communities of Practice: Learning, Meaning, and Identity* (Cambridge: Cambridge University Press, 1998).

10. Wenger, *Communities of Parctice*, p. 73.

would enter into the course together and come to determine its meaning and direction, which would be specific to this class and this group of people. We would also engage with one another through practices and come to determine their meanings within the context of the class, developing a shared language or grammar of practice.

Drawing upon these ideas, I committed to incorporating Christian practices into the classroom that I believed would mutually reinforce and support one another. The overarching canopy would be the practice of hospitality, while the practices of fellowship and testimony would be included under the canopy.

The Three Practices

Hospitality

A critical component of historical Christian communities, hospitality "begins with basic physical needs of food and shelter, most powerfully symbolized in table fellowship."[11] Hospitality, as I define it, is the physical manifestation of welcome — the welcoming spirit is demonstrated through specific actions such as inviting someone into one's home, sharing resources or space, setting out a meal, or other activities meant to facilitate comfort and care. It usually includes the expending of resources by the host. Genuine hospitality also involves movement within the interior life of the host, which usually results in a shift in the understanding of relationships: "Hospitality includes meeting social as well as physical needs. An important component of hospitality is helping the outsider or the poor feel welcome, which at times requires more than food and drink — a recasting of relations."[12] The use of resources is important, but it must be combined with something within the host herself: a particular view or orientation. Amy Oden notes, "Taken as a feature of Christian life, hospitality is not so much a singular act of welcome as it is a way, an orientation that attends to otherness, listening and learning, valuing and

---

11. *And You Welcomed Me: A Sourcebook on Hospitality in Early Christian Communities*, ed. Amy G. Oden (Nashville: Abingdon Press, 2001), p. 14. Other recent books on the practice of hospitality include Christine D. Pohl, *Making Room: Recovering Hospitality as a Christian Tradition* (Grand Rapids: Wm. B. Eerdmans, 1999); and Elizabeth Newman, *Untamed Hospitality: Welcoming God and Other Strangers* (Grand Rapids: Brazos Press, 2007).

12. Oden, *And You Welcomed Me*, p. 14.

honoring."[13] The spiritual dynamic of hospitality includes becoming aware of a particular identity of self (as disciple, believer, child of God), recognizing the stranger before us (as Christ or as the image of God), and then providing for the other. Receiving guests is an honor and a gift from God.

Hospitality has a moral dimension because it involves "what it means to be human."[14] Daniel Homan and Lonni Collins Pratt, in reflecting on hospitality in light of St. Benedict's rule, argues "The biggest obstacle to hospitality is not the state of the world. It is the state of our minds and hearts. . . . Hospitality requires not grand gestures, but open hearts."[15] Hospitality has a moral aspect because it relies on our actions and our orientation toward others. Homan and Pratt write, "It is our own failures to love that we have to deal with when we talk about hospitality."[16] This means that hospitality is "more than being nice."[17]

What, then, would hospitality look like in a classroom? Parker Palmer sees hospitality as central to the act of teaching, claiming, "A learning space has three major characteristics, three essential dimensions: openness, boundaries, and an air of hospitality."[18] In the hospitable classroom, this would mean "receiving each other, our struggles, our newborn ideas with openness and care."[19] Further,

> The classroom where truth is central will be a place where every stranger and every strange utterance is met with welcome. This may suggest a classroom lacking in essential rigor, a place in which questions of true and false, right and wrong, are subordinated to making sure everyone "has a nice day." But that would be a false understanding of hospitality. Hospitality is not an end in itself. It is offered for the sake of what it can allow, permit, encourage, and yield.[20]

13. Oden, *And You Welcomed Me*, p. 14.

14. Homan and Pratt, *Radical Hospitality*, p. 5.

15. Homan and Pratt, *Radical Hospitality*, p. 16.

16. Homan and Pratt, *Radical Hospitality*, p. 11.

17. Homan and Pratt, *Radical Hospitality*, p. 21.

18. Parker Palmer, *To Know as We Are Known* (San Francisco: Harper, 1983), p. 71. Other recent discussions of education in terms of hospitality include Elizabeth Newman, "Hospitality and Christian Higher Education," *Christian Scholars Review* 33, no. 1 (Fall 2003): 75-94; and David I. Smith and Barbara Carvill, *The Gift of the Stranger: Faith, Hospitality, and Foreign Language Learning* (Grand Rapids: Wm. B. Eerdmans, 2000).

19. Palmer, *To Know as We Are Known*, p. 73.

20. Palmer, *To Know as We Are Known*, p. 74.

The belief that hospitality "is offered for the sake of what it can allow, permit, encourage, and yield" is at the core of this project for me. Because it should, ideally, create more openness, hospitality can allow for *more* to enter into a classroom. More ideas, more thoughts, more emotions, more insights. This potential to create a space in which *more* can happen is worth the attendant risks around hospitality. However, as I learned, it is not for the faint of heart. It can also allow for more conflict, more outbursts, more politically incorrect comments, and more anxiety.

Hospitality requires an intentional stance on the part of the instructor that goes against some traditional norms for teachers, such as absolute control over and within a classroom. When Ellen Marmon moved toward encouraging her pre-service teachers to adopt a stance of hospitality in their own classrooms, she encountered resistance, noting, "Usually it's not the student-as-guest connection that ruffles feathers. Instead, when considering shifting from teacher to host, students worry about forfeiting their own power."[21] It is crucial to consider what the redemptive, responsible use of power in the classroom means. As Marmon notes, "While Jesus taught with authority, he also taught within the context of respectful relationships."[22] The creation of respectful relationship is possible in a classroom even though there is an imbalance of power. Oden notes that this is possible when the host sees herself as a recipient as much as the guest does.

Just as we must ask who the stranger is, we must ask who the host is. On the face of it, we might think of the host as the moral agent here, the one who acts for, on behalf of, the other. There is no doubt that hosts have resources, whether it is food, shelter, or connections. By definition, a host makes these resources available to the stranger/guest. However, the host also receives by participating in the economy of hospitality whereby God's grace gifts both host and guest. On the one hand, the host has resources. On the other hand, the host identifies with the guest/stranger and chooses not to live out of any privilege those resources offer, but rather to understand himself or herself as a recipient too.[23]

While the classroom cannot offer genuine equality between host and guest (except perhaps in very nontraditional settings), it can offer a place of mutuality and valuable give-and-take. Oden comments further:

21. Marmon, "Teaching as Hospitality," p. 38.
22. Marmon, "Teaching as Hospitality," p. 38.
23. Oden, *And You Welcomed Me*, p. 26.

The inevitable asymmetry of relationship between host and guest does not prevent due honor and respect. Hospitality requires that the host recognize both the need and the full humanity of the stranger. There is a respectful balance in successful hospitality that neither denigrates the guest's neediness nor denies it. The other is fully honored as a child of God, while at the same time genuine needs are met.[24]

The additional practices of testimony and fellowship fit and are enhanced under the umbrella of hospitality. To actually hear and take seriously the testimony of another, for example, requires a hospitable heart within the listener. Fellowship may occur in fits and starts without hospitality, but in the context of a faith community, it cannot be a soul-feeding experience without hospitality from at least some. Thus I hoped that hospitality would be the overarching orientation of the classroom, with testimony and fellowship included underneath its shade.

I approached the creation of a hospitable classroom with specific actions that were intended to become the repertoire for myself and for the class.

I started with my own interior life and my spiritual preparation for the class each week. This related directly to my understanding of the gap between beliefs and practices.[25] I asked myself some pointed questions. Am I actually living out, in the classroom, the things I say I believe, such as holding to the inherent dignity of every person? How do I walk into the classroom? Do I make eye contact? Call people by name? Ask them questions about their own lives? How do I speak to the students? How do I think about them when I'm not in the classroom? How do I talk about my students to colleagues? In response to these questions, I incorporated my students, by name, into my prayer life each week, and meditated on them and their classroom contributions each week as I prepared the food for our break time. I monitored myself with care in terms of how I entered the classroom and greeted them each week. I also instituted specific actions oriented toward sharing food, feelings, and concerns, as described below. I changed the structure of the class from previous semesters, adding a significant time for discussion in the second half of the class and setting this up to be led by the students. This challenged my own need to be in com-

24. Oden, *And You Welcomed Me,* p. 27.

25. See Amy Plantinga Pauw, "Attending to the Gaps between Beliefs and Practices," in *Practicing Theology,* ed. Miroslav Volf and Dorothy C. Bass (Grand Rapids: Wm. B. Eerdmans, 2002).

plete control of the setting and flow of the class. It provided an opportunity for students' contributions, insights, and stories, and encouraged them to assist one another in drawing connections between their own lives and the course material. I knew that opening up the discussion leadership would have its own awkwardness, but I committed to it. Overall I hoped that these actions would create a more open, inclusive, and hospitable atmosphere, a place in which the beginnings of a community could be nurtured. None of these were actions I had ever taken previously with a class. While I had always strived to create an intellectually safe classroom,[26] I had not consciously tried to create a place that might speak to the intellectual, emotional, *and spiritual* aspects of the students.

Fellowship

Larry Rasmussen notes, "The perennial Christian strategy, someone has said, is to gather the folks, break the bread, and tell the stories."[27] Fellowship includes speaking and listening and reflects the practice Dykstra calls "listening and talking attentively to one another about our particular experiences in life."[28] This includes small talk and chatter, yet Christian fellowship as a practice is different from just "hanging out." Its end or purpose is to build community and strengthen the mortar of relationships between persons. Ideally, fellowship is an integral part of a community that rests on mutual accountability and trust. Fellowship also serves to build a narrative identity for a community. Times of fellowship build a collective memory, adding to a multifaceted sense of shared history for a community. In the best situations, this sense of history can create a feeling of ownership, belonging, safety, and security. In college settings in general, times of fellowship form the foundation for some of the most enduring memories and relationships among students.

So how could the practice of intentional fellowship be incorporated into a college classroom? I integrated opportunities for fellowship in three ways: an opening "call-out," the mid-class break with food, and the closing "joys and concerns." My hope was that these would act in concert and help

26. Carolyne Call, "Defining Intellectual Safety in the College Classroom," *Journal of Excellence in College Teaching* 18, no. 3 (2007).

27. Larry Rasmussen, "Shaping Communities," in *Practicing Our Faith*, p. 119.

28. Dykstra, *Growing in the Life of Faith*, p. 43.

to create a loose mortar of care between these students. While the inclusion of these actions was also part of creating a hospitable space for students, participation in them by students would, I hoped, result in the practice of fellowship.

The opening call-out happened at the beginning of each class. I went around the class and asked each student to choose a word or phrase that best described "where they were coming from" that evening. This could be based on their mood, what was on their minds, how they felt physically, and so on. It was designed both to give me an immediate read of the class in terms of how they were feeling (and thus their attention potential), and to allow them to hear how their fellow classmates were doing. The second component (ten minutes of break time) came halfway through the class period and included the welcome appearance of food. I intended to prepare and bring food each week to share. I recognized that preparing food weekly for the class would probably amount to a significant time commitment on my part. However, I considered this my own "growing edge" and the way I would keep myself invested in and conscious of the process. My hope was that we would share the food and engage in general small talk, including conversation about our lives and work. The third aspect of fellowship was the time for voicing joys and concerns at the end of each class. This was a brief time to allow students to express personal prayer requests, good news, items of concern, and the like. We did not pray in unison, but I closed this time with some words of my own and the request that "those who engage in prayer, please remember these requests this week."

Testimony

The third practice, testimony, is usually understood as "speaking the truth" in a given situation: "Testimony occurs in particular settings — a courtroom or a church — where a community expects to hear the truth spoken. Witnesses — those making the testimony — must speak the truth as they have seen, heard, and experienced it."[29] Further, "The practice of testimony requires that there be witnesses to testify and others to receive and evaluate the testimony. It is a deeply shared practice."[30] There are those

---

29. Thomas Hoyt Jr., "Testimony," in *Practicing Our Faith,* ed. Dorothy C. Bass (San Francisco: Jossey-Bass, 1997), p. 92.

30. Hoyt, "Testimony," p. 92.

who speak the truth, and there are those who listen and ask questions or seek clarification of the testimony. Sometimes, too, there are those who speak the truth even though no one is listening. We can (with love) challenge the testimony when it leads to actions that hinder a life of love or that result in unloving actions. Within Christian communities, testimony is used as a means of sharing one's faith, speaking truth to power, and making connections between personal life and public actions.

How did I envision testimony functioning within a classroom? Testimony may work best in classes that are more narrative in scope (e.g., social sciences, humanities). However, the use of narrative testimony can be a powerful teaching device in the sciences and math as well. Learning can be enhanced through the use of autobiographies and biographies, and in the case of pre-service teachers, engaging students in reflecting on their own experiences with math (for example) while they were in school. Testimony can make a subject more real and immediate to students. It also allows for more personal commitment and can assist them in applying abstract concepts to their own lives, and can also open up discussions in new ways that engage them emotionally and personally.

The concepts we explore in Adolescent Psychology are often personally significant to students and are manifested through their life experiences. For example, discussion of theories of moral development can push students to reflect on their own moral choices and the outcomes of those choices. Calling for voluntary testimony from students can enable all of the students to better connect course material and everyday life. I envisioned testimony in the classroom given through personal narratives. This is not identical to testimony as sharing one's faith life or journey. Yet, in approaching psychological issues, the narrative dynamic is very similar in that students share personal experiences that have influenced their psycho-spiritual development. It is also one of the best ways to elicit empathy and move students toward shared concern and compassion — provided it is done within explicit (spoken, written) parameters of respect. I incorporated testimony in two explicit ways. The first involved sharing my own experiences from adolescence as specific illustrations or case studies in the classroom. For example, in the unit on relational aggression among girls, I shared details of a relationship in high school that was characterized by a form of relational aggression, and the effects of that relationship on my own coping styles, self-concept, and self-esteem. Sharing my own testimony in an appropriate way opened the door for greater honesty and sharing from students. The testimony of students may not be sophisticated or show evidence of deep reflective analysis. But often the mere sharing of testimony allows for that reflection and deeper insight to occur — often with help from others in the classroom. While I committed to personal sharing for my own practice, I also incorporated testimony into the discussion time. Each week I asked discussion leaders to approach the topic in a variety of ways. One suggestion was to share personal stories from their own lives of how this topic/concept was part of their adolescent school experience.

From Concept to Implementation

These practices — hospitality, fellowship, and testimony — were designed to mutually reinforce one another. In this way we might build an active community with a strong sense of connection, engagement, and mutual care.

Once I had determined the practices to be used and the accompanying repertoire, I introduced the practices gradually. I started by bringing in food the first week. The second week I began the "opening call-out question" before we addressed the topic of the day. The third week we began the use of testimony in the discussion section, and I also closed the class with expressions of joys and concerns. By the fourth week we were engaging in the full repertoire. As I began this process, I imagined a seamless integration of the practices and envisioned a flourishing, feel-good community of learners who cared for one another and grew as spiritual persons. My romantic imaginings were quickly dashed as I came up against the difficult work of hospitality in action.

Reflection on the Process: What Happened?

This was easily the most difficult class I have ever taught. The difficulty lay not in the course material, concepts, or even my own scheduling and workload. The difficulty came from the surprising emotional strain of being a hospitable person on a day-to-day basis. This probably sounds humorous, especially coming from a person who is trained in Christian ministry. However, my personal reaction to the class was more often one of tears than one of laughter. It was a deeply humbling process. Until I taught this class, I didn't fully realize just how emotionally removed I had been from my previous students and how comfortable this was for me as an instructor. While I had always cared about my students in general and felt that I demonstrated that care in numerous ways, the challenge to view and actually treat students as "guests" was far more involved and difficult. Preparing food for them was time-consuming and anxiety-laden. Holding them in prayer and reflecting on them personally (in conscious, meaningful ways, by name) *on a regular basis* was emotionally and spiritually taxing. There were evenings when I did not feel hospitable in the least and wanted nothing more than to launch into a two-hour lecture with no discussion. I had fears about control over the class and whether I was covering enough material. By allowing students to lead discussions, I knew I was sacrificing class time that could be used for more lectures and traditional means of covering topics. This concern stayed with me during the semester. I was often angry at the students, frustrated by their occasionally glib reactions to deep issues and their inability to read how their own actions affected the rest of the class. All of this was in marked contrast to Palmer's rhapsodic description of the hospitable classroom: "A knowledge that springs from love will implicate us in the web of life; it will wrap the knower and the known in compassion, in a bond of awesome responsibility as well as transforming joy; it will call us to involvement, mutuality, and accountability."[31]

The experience of transforming joy eluded me. However, this class was also the most dynamic course I have ever taught. The growth I experienced was both personal and professional and, at times, quite profound. There were three areas in which I saw significant personal growth and pedagogical success: shared fellowship, individual testimony, and personal hospitality.

Shared Fellowship

The practice of fellowship was the easiest to implement, and the benefits could be seen almost immediately. Fellowship occurred primarily around the food break we took halfway through each class. I provided food for the first two weeks, assuming that I would be making food throughout the semester. However, after the second week, students began to ask if they could bring the food on a rotating basis. This was a complete surprise, and these breaks became a central experience in the class. When we ate together, we also talked together, and each week I witnessed students getting to know

31. Palmer, *To Know as We Are Known*, p. 9.

one another and asking each other questions. Unlike the students in my previous classes in the Education Department, these students did not all know one another before the class. The sharing of food allowed them an easy way to get to know one another better. The power of this interaction was clear when I reviewed the student evaluations at the close of the semester: they indicated that students found the sharing of food to be the central element of a shared sense of community.

The opening call-out and the closing joys and concerns were enlightening in several ways. The call-out was very helpful for allowing me to take the pulse of the class, and often the words shared by students would ignite a discussion. I also believe that the activity, although brief and superficial, allowed them to focus their attention on the class and enter into the process with greater attention. However, this assessment is based on my own intuitive reading of the class and not on their direct evaluative comments. The joys and concerns session at the end of each class was the most interesting in that it was clear that students had never done anything like this in previous classes. By the second week they were bringing specific requests (some humorous, others painful), and they were following up with each other from one week to the next. It was a deeply sobering activity in that it provided me with a window into their personal lives and the kinds of concerns weighing on them from week to week. The sharing of these highs and lows appeared to break down some walls between them and helped to strengthen the mortar of relationship. This activity, more than any other, brought me close to these students in a manner reminiscent of my previous relationship with a congregation in a local church. While the two settings are obviously quite different, some of the emotional dynamics were similar. This was not comfortable for me and was personally challenging. I had the very sobering realization that I had left parish ministry in large part because I could not bear the personal weight of others' pain. As much as I love my students and want the very best for them, I was surprised to realize that I actually did not want too much knowledge about them. I found it too heavy to bear. This realization gave me pause and has led me to re-evaluate some of my own motivations behind my teaching.

Individual Testimony

This practice had both challenges and benefits for the class. The greatest benefit came from the deepened discussion around weekly topics and the level of engagement I saw among the students. For example, our first discussion topic was adolescent physical development. One of the leaders began by sharing her experience with scoliosis as a teenager and the burden of wearing a full-torso brace to school every day. Her testimony included the impact of her physical limitations on her peer relationships, her self-confidence, and her social development. The class paid close attention and asked detailed questions. The discussion moved into how physical development affects adolescents in general and what the role of teachers might be in assisting students during an awkward and uncomfortable time. This included discussion of how teachers might cope with taunting, teasing, and the use of derogatory nicknames. This student's testimony added a deeply personal element to the discussion and made the issue much more charged and immediate for the class.

Another example comes from the time that the discussion topic was social networks (Facebook, Myspace, etc.). During a discussion around whether it was ethical for teachers to look at students' profile pages, one student shared a personal testimonial. Her younger sister had been sexually assaulted at a party during high school. The assault was filmed on a cell phone by a friend of the attacker and uploaded to the Web for public viewing. When a teacher saw the clip, the authorities were called in, resulting in the filing of criminal charges and the expulsion of the boys from the school. This testimony was especially powerful given the emotional nature of the content and the emotional state of the student. Once again, the inclusion of a personal testimony added a gravitas and immediacy to the topic. Such examples show the importance of reiterating the need for confidentiality within the discussion sessions and the importance of listening with respect. While we can never guarantee that students are responding in their hearts with empathy (and not derision, for example), we can set the scene by speaking openly about *how* we listen (maintaining eye contact, not sighing or rolling our eyes) and *what* we do with what we hear (no out-of-classroom repetition). I tried to remind students of this every week.

I have always encouraged student contributions in class as we talked through psychological topics, but I had never previously received this quality of input in terms of depth, emotional content, or personal connection. I perceived it to be a direct outgrowth of the discussion format and the way the students encouraged one another to share openly. By and large, the students upheld respect for one another, and the testimony added a depth to the course content that would not have been there otherwise.

However, there were also challenges in the use of testimony in the classroom. The primary concern was the need to constantly monitor the discussion and step in to redirect or facilitate when necessary. This is a task that is necessary for any discussion, yet the inclusion of testimony gave this a more charged importance, since testimony refers directly to the self and one's own reality. For example, in our discussion around the topic of racial and ethnic identity, the group moved into uncomfortable waters when one student began discussing personal experiences of perceived "reverse racism" toward white students by the Latina students at the college. I was required to encourage discussion and critical questions while also affirming the testimony of the student who had made the remarks. This had been, after all, her truth and her reality. And this is the inherent difficulty with testimony. The instructor must be willing to facilitate difficult discussions or assist the discussion leaders when necessary so that the personal reflections are respected at the same time that some conclusions might be questioned. In the case of the racial identity discussion, the conversation was abruptly reconfigured when one of the students shared that he had always struggled with his own identity because he was half white and half African-American. His testimony created a moment of cognitive dissonance for the other students, since he appeared to be Caucasian. His narratives about his family and his own struggles allowed us to re-engage the original question at hand having to do with how adolescents negotiate their identities and how race, ethnicity, sexuality, and class play into this process. His testimony balanced the discussion and moved it in a more constructive direction.

The questioning of testimony is part of the testimonial process within a community, and at times the questioning had to be done in very direct ways. I felt strongly that testimony should be used as a way to build up, inform, and encourage the students, not as a means to tear down, demonize, or degrade others. For example, in the discussion on sexuality, the leaders talked about how the use of negative labels for women was a way for girls to tear each other down. One student shared how she and her friends referred to another friend as a slut and would say things to her about her sexual behavior in very negative terms. This created a wave of response in the classroom; other students questioned her testimony about her friend, asking questions such as "Aren't you a Christian? Is this how we speak to each other in love?" and "How can you justify calling your friend by names like that?" As pointed as the questions were, they were asked gently and without rancor, leading us more deeply into a discussion about how girls relate to one another and what impact this has on their lives in school. This type of reflection is critical for those who will be working directly with adolescents in an educational setting. In the adolescent's daily life at school, social realities (such as being called names by others) can bear directly on the ability to be intellectually present and receptive in the classroom. In encouraging my college students to search their own motives for their social behaviors, I hope to better prepare them to respond to social situations in their own classrooms. The discussion that day included excellent testimony, but also excellent questions. This can lead to a classroom experience in which students engage not only their minds but also their emotional, spiritual, and moral selves.

The use of testimony was a critical component in creating this class environment. In combination with hospitality and fellowship, it strengthened ties within the small community and helped to make the class a more holistic and integrated experience.

Personal Hospitality

The hospitality aspect of this project was deeply challenging to me on a personal level. I entered into the classroom experiment expecting to find that I already practiced a hospitable pedagogy and that I was merely expanding the repertoire of that pedagogical style. What I found instead is that genuine hospitality requires an orientation of the heart, and that this orientation requires practice and prayer to maintain. As an administrator, I am used to multitasking, and my teaching fit into my workday as one of many tasks. I was used to being able to teach class and then slip back into the administrative mode and focus on other tasks. Practicing conscious hospitality required a full focus of my mental and emotional efforts both in and outside of the classroom. It also required a different level or type of reflection when it came to thinking about my students.

The best example of this, in my perception, was Kathy (not her real name). Kathy was a junior, an art major, and she was easily one of the most opinionated, disruptive, and socially unaware students I have ever had. She had difficulty focusing in class and often carried on side conversations or made sotto-voce comments in response to topics on which I was lecturing. She never took notes. She was active in discussion, yet she shared reflections and thoughts that were often inappropriate, stereotypical, or even racist. She seemed completely unaware of her effect on the other students. She was brash and openly vocal in her renunciation of anything spiritual or religious. This reality was difficult enough to cope with, yet on top of this she also turned in some of the worst written work I had ever seen. There was no doubt that she was one of the most challenging students with whom I had ever worked. Prior to this project, I would have interacted with her as needed, tried to keep her disruptions to a minimum, and been thankful when the class ended. However, in what I considered a tremendous twist of ironic timing, because of this project I needed to approach Kathy through the lens of genuine hospitality. That meant I needed to see her as a guest in my classroom. During the semester I challenged myself to pray for her, to take the extra time to write long responses to her written work, and to focus on her more in the classroom. My hospitable orientation had to do with a change of heart within myself.

This came to a head one Monday evening when I stood preparing for the evening's lesson. Kathy and two friends were there early and were openly sharing their utter disdain for another faculty member. Kathy said, "I mean, he just stands up there, like 'Duh — I'm so boring.'" This actually caused me physical pain as I imagined the unedited comments that students casually share about all of us. They continued to laugh, sharing examples of this teacher's behavior in the classes they had taken with him. By the time the lesson began, I was oscillating between wanting to yell at them for their disrespect and wanting to run away and hide in despair. Instead, I took a deep breath and prayed in silence: "I love these people. I love these people. God help me to love these people." This did not mean that I then felt the warm and woolly affects of love for them. Instead, it was my personal compass-check. I reminded myself that I had committed to teaching these students out of love and hospitality, not duty and irritation.

Let me be clear in noting that this was one of the most difficult transitions I have experienced. The mental and emotional energy it required of me to turn to these students in love was tremendous. Yet in that moment I knew, in a way I had never experienced previously, what it means to teach as a Christian. It has everything to do with how I perceive my students, starting at the very beginning of the semester. My perception has to be colored by trying to perceive them as Christ would have: surely flawed in many ways, yet worthy of love and respect, attention and focus. This realization never meant that in this particular class I ignored the disrespectful behavior by Kathy and her friends (I did eventually respond to their comments by engaging them in a discussion about teaching). But it did mean that I was engaged in a continual process of self-monitoring about my own commitment to love them and how to live that out appropriately. Still, my hospitality toward the class (and toward Kathy in particular) would never have been possible if not for the other practices in which I was participating, such as praying for the students, preparing food for them, hearing their personal stories, and the like.

The process of the class over the semester reinforced the (difficult, for me) truth that hospitality does not happen in single, isolated events, and it is not expressed simply by discrete actions (such as making food). Instead, it flows out from an individual's orientation of heart and requires constant reflection, monitoring, and support. This reflection is a deeper process than merely reminding oneself to "be more attentive and present." After all, as teachers we can remind ourselves of this over and over, but we may find those reminders far from our thoughts when we come up against a difficult or frustrating student. The cognitive reminders are not enough. Instead, the cognitive must be undergirded with personal spiritual practices (especially prayer) that help to move us toward becoming instructors for whom the heart orientation is a deep and consistent reality that influences all of our actions.

I came to understand Homan and Pratt's comment that hospitality "is not something you do as much as it is someone you become."[32] Hospitality is an act of ministry, and to be genuine it required that I see my students as children of God and as loved by God, regardless of how I felt about them at any given moment. While I would have given lip service to this belief in the past, being conscious of it during this project showed me how difficult it can be to genuinely love my students and treat them as guests despite their irritating, all-too-human actions. Engaging in the practices allowed me to live out a commitment to love-in-action that I had not been capable of previously.

There are, of course, some limits to hospitality. There are times when the guests are hurting others, are unwilling to change, and must be asked to leave. And there are times when our own orientation of heart is not up to the task of loving "in spite of." Yet merely considering what it means to teach with hospitality is a step in a direction that can bring us closer to the integration of faith and teaching. Hospitality is a deeply Christian practice. It also may be one of the most difficult practices of our faith. But it brought home, for me, the messy reality of what it means to be a disciple in the classroom.

---

32. Homan and Pratt, *Radical Hospitality,* p. 38.

Concluding Thoughts

Participation in this project marked a turning point in my self-understanding as an educator. The reflection on the role of practices pushed me to consider my pedagogy in a way I never had previously. My prior understanding of myself as a devoted Christian made me think (erroneously) that making the connection between my own faith and the way I approach a classroom would be obvious or at least second nature. But this was not the case. Engaging with the practices in my own life and then bringing them into the classroom stretched my understanding of the moral aims of teaching and reminded me of our deep responsibility for the spiritual and intellectual lives of our students.

My commitment to the practice of hospitality in the classroom remains firm, although I now grasp the depth of investment this requires of any instructor. When I approached the Adolescent Psychology class again this year, I decided to maintain several of the practices. These included the use of testimony, some aspects of fellowship (sharing food, in particular), and a more realistic and humble embrace of hospitality. My hope remains that through active engagement with these practices in the classroom, I can continue on the rough trail toward an authentic pedagogy of discipleship.

Eat This Class: Breaking Bread
in the Undergraduate Classroom

Julie A. P. Walton and Matthew Walters

Food is a basic life element that, along with air, water, and shelter, unites all humanity in the struggle for survival. The relationship between people and food manifests itself in matters as disparate as appetite, satisfaction, empowerment, fellowship, marginalization, and environmental manipulation. Food serves both as a primary outlet for our selfishness and as a basic mark of our interdependence. Accordingly, the many connections that nutrition has with science and faith, with daily choices and behaviors, with creation care, and with hospitality and social justice make it both a joy and a burden to teach. What better place than a nutrition course to see how a particular Christian practice — in this case, the shared meal — might be woven through existing pedagogy to help influence face-to-face engagement in the classroom? Might enacting shared meals among nutrition classmates and their instructor generate mutual engagement and encouragement?

Students Who Hunger and Thirst

Fostering student interdependence has always been my biggest challenge when teaching nutrition.[1] Imagine this: It is the first day of class, and as I look out over sixty expectant faces each fall, I already know that this set of students bears an unusual burden: their classmates are also their competition for admission to the nursing program.[2] A student — we'll call her

1. The first-person pronoun refers to the faculty member in this project, J. Walton.
2. Over 70 percent of each nutrition class consists of sophomore-level (third semester) pre-nursing students who will apply to the very competitive nursing program at semester's end.

Anica — sits in the front row with her notebook open and ready to be filled. She has never wanted to be anything but a nurse. In a reflective writing assignment, she writes of her certainty that God has called her to be a nurse. But her GPA sits on the fence at 3.0, and she is nearly paralyzed by the thought that she might not make it into nursing: last year there were 90 pre-nursing applicants for 60 spots.[3] Anica stops by my office within the week. She wants to know if she'd benefit from having a tutor, and if I will provide a list of what she needs to memorize. She particularly wants me to know that she just *has* to have an A in this course and doesn't like working in groups. I try to explain that doing well in the course is less about that final grade or how much she can memorize in one semester than it is about developing an understanding of nutrition. Can Anica learn in my classroom when anxiety and vulnerability are her constant companions, and her experience with cooperative Problem Based Learning (PBL), and its attendant analysis and reasoning skills, are nascent?

Students like Anica are desperate to raise their GPAs, while those with an adequate GPA fear that working with others will bring it down. What can be done with a class when many students have inhibited enthusiasm for working together in the classroom? Routinely, there is a three-way split of pre-nursing students in the course. Roughly 35 percent of them have a GPA at or below 3.1. Another third have a strong GPA, and the rest fall in the middle with a GPA between 3.1 and 3.4. While nearly all of the top two-thirds of students will be admitted into nursing, the bottom one-third experience undue stress over grades.[4] Under these conditions, can a nutrition class really gather in the spirit of a reconciling and transforming love of God, as co-inheritors of God's promise, sharing the wonderful array of food he provides, all while learning more about that food?[5] What does Christian teaching and learning look like in such a context? What could count as "success" for such a course?

As a way of rethinking Christian teaching and learning in this con-

3. The Calvin nursing program is currently investigating alternative program placement strategies. The minimum GPA for acceptance in 2010 was around 3.1.

4. In the process, they not only endanger their own emotional health but also operate from a paradigm of pure self-preservation at the expense of the needs of others in the class. The goal here was less about influencing learning outcomes per se and more about building a community of learners who could cooperatively engage the learning process.

5. See Brian V. Hill, "Teaching as Reconciliation," *Journal of Education and Christian Belief* 10, no. 1 (2006): 33-41, for a republication of his essay on the ways in which reconciliation is a helpful metaphor for teaching.

text, I experimented with the sharing of meals outside of class as a possible way to nourish classroom engagement through enhanced relationships. Perhaps improved relationships might help ease students into engagement through collaborative PBL without causing them undue anxiety. Put another way, the shared meal as a practice helped shape the course goals — namely, to learn together in the same manner as we eat together, face-to-face, that we might interdependently counter the anxiety, distrust, and ensuing disengagement displayed by students in previous years. What I wanted to know was whether eating together outside of class would (1) build familiarity and trust enough to improve engagement with classmates and faculty, and (2) reduce grade/performance anxiety enough to create a nourishing communal space for peer-peer PBL.

The Shared Meal as a Christian Practice

My college's curriculum attempts to foster particular virtues as part of the moral formation of students, hoping "in the course of the education it offers, to lift [students] above the tyranny of personal problems, beyond the clutches of the imperial self, into an expansive world that invites their best efforts on behalf of God's kingdom of truth, justice, and peace."[6] Not surprisingly, a classroom filled with anxious students is not peaceful. This particular course was often void of the virtues of empathy, charity, and compassion so central for Christians, especially those in the health care professions. Many students suffered under the "tyranny" of personal doubt about their futures. The Christian practice of the shared meal seemed a practical way to foster these reconciling virtues through student-student and student-faculty relationships, because meals have the potential to turn strangers, perhaps even competitors, into friends. Meals move students from looking at the back of the heads in front of them to looking classmates in the eye, and from segregated desk space to shared table and menu. Eating in community is a transcultural practice that can unite its participants, provide hospitality to strangers, and continually nourish, renew, and reconcile those who eat together. When we consider that "we are all practicing together to become more and more the makers of the kingdom that is both under our feet and right around

---

6. *An Engagement with God's World: The Core Curriculum of Calvin College* (1999), 33 (also available at http://www.calvin.edu/admin/provost/core/).

the corner,"[7] the shared meal takes on even more meaning. Perhaps a simple focus on the practice of sharing meals could help create a more engaged and charitable learning community that "nourishes, challenges, and transforms guests [and] hosts" alike.[8]

Consequently, in the fall of 2008, a project named MEALS was incorporated into two fall sections of a 200-level undergraduate nutrition course (HE 254). The MEALS acronym was used to convey that this course was intended to foster *m*indfulness, *e*xpectancy, *a*cceptance, *l*ove, and *s*haring through the practice of eating and learning together. MEALS was intended to help students become mindful and accepting of the dreams and needs of their neighbor-classmates sharing time and food with them. This is a one-semester (14-week), three-credit course designed for students in pre-nursing, exercise science, and health education at Calvin College, an undergraduate Christian liberal arts college in the Reformed tradition. Nutrition is a required course for all enrolled.[9] Two sections with enrollments of 29 and 34 met at eight and nine A.M. on Mondays, Wednesdays, and Fridays. No cross-attendance was allowed. Of the 63 students, 79 percent were pre-nursing sophomores, 83 percent female and 17 percent male.

The course was managed as similarly as possible to that of previous semesters, with two major exceptions. First, there was an added focus on reading of food-related excerpts from outside sources (e.g., Barbara Kingsolver's *Animal, Vegetable, Mineral* and Michael Pollan's *Omnivore's Dilemma*).[10] These readings were used to foster small-group discussion on eight occasions over twelve weeks in class, followed by a class discussion and brief reflective written response. Written responses were collected and graded pass/fail for participation (8 written responses = 1 quiz grade).[11] Second, students were required to attend two meals outside of class on their own time and at their own expense, once in mid-September and again in early November. Each meal was weighted the same as one quiz grade.[12] I

---

7. Nora Gallagher, *The Sacred Meal* (Nashville: Thomas Nelson, 2009), p. 38.

8. Christine Pohl, *Making Room: Recovering Hospitality as a Christian Tradition* (Grand Rapids: Wm. B. Eerdmans, 1999), p. 11.

9. Because of high demand from majors, it is not offered as an elective.

10. Barbara Kingsolver, *Animal, Vegetable, Mineral* (New York: HarperCollins, 2007); Michael Pollan, *The Omnivore's Dilemma* (New York: Penguin, 2006).

11. Total quizzes represented 25 percent of one's grade. Seven quizzes plus two shared meals plus written responses equaled ten quiz grades, so reflective responses constituted approximately 2.5 percent of one's final grade.

12. Attendance at these meals was mandatory, but students received course credit. The

scheduled the 45-minute meals, and students signed up using their student numbers rather than their names, to discourage friends from signing up together. Groups were purposefully kept small (no more than 8), and I attended every meal. Most of the time, we met in the student dining halls for breakfasts, lunches, and dinners.[13] On other occasions, we shared meals in my home, in a student's apartment (if a student volunteered to host), at local ethnic and organic restaurants, at a Calvin Project Neighborhood house,[14] at a local church supper, and at a local homeless shelter.[15] The point was to offer as many diverse dining options as possible to avoid student scheduling conflicts and to attract their interest. For example, some feel too busy to leave campus, preferring to meet in the dining hall, whereas others are grateful for an opportunity to get off campus even for an hour. During the semester, only one student missed one meal. The meals were expressly meant to be simple; there was no overtly prescribed curricular content to any of the meals other than (1) to remind ourselves why we were gathered (i.e., to focus on MEALS — mindfulness, expectancy, acceptance, love, and sharing), (2) to ask students to share how the semester was going, and (3) to pray together to thank God for his providence and for those who had grown, harvested, shipped, sold, and prepared the foods, and to ask him to bless our time together. Talk around the table ranged from the food before us, to one of our recent readings, to what someone told her family last weekend about the nutritional value of her grandmother's Sunday casserole. At other times, conversation turned to students' concerns regarding

20 points earned for participation in two meals (10 points each) constituted 5 percent of one's final grade.

13. As often as possible, I met the students at a dining hall in order to minimize their time and financial commitments; most sophomores carry prepaid meal plans at the dining halls. In all, I attended 22 meals over 5 weeks.

14. Project Neighborhood homes are owned and staffed by the college. Students live together with the mandate to engage and foster community, in both the home and the surrounding neighborhood. The dining room table at the house we visited seats 20. Eight of us were invited one Saturday night for a simple dinner that the residents cooked and served with great hospitality. One of the nutrition students at that meal was so impressed by the communal bonds of the housemates that she successfully applied to live there the following year, and, to return the favor, invited HE 254 students back for dinner in November 2009.

15. I gave rides to students who had no transportation. Talks in the car are another way to foster relationships. In the fall, I regularly serve dinner one Saturday night per month with my church at Dégagé Ministries in inner-city Grand Rapids. For the MEALS project, I invited students to join me. Homeless men, women, and children gather for shelter and a meal of burgers, fries, and desserts. Students both cooked and served the meals, and spent another 90 minutes visiting in pairs with the patrons.

an upcoming exam in another course. Often, pre-nursing students inquired about the nursing program selection process, asking if I knew how many students might be applying this year, and what the anticipated GPA cutoff might be. Not surprisingly, students were curious about my personal life, and to see the kinds of food choices I made.

The working hypothesis was that adding two outside meals and in-class discussion of several short readings would favorably affect student engagement by fostering greater familiarity with classmates and the professor, as well as greater freedom from anxiety. In consequence, students might more readily participate in cooperative PBL activities, easing them from a learned over-reliance on memorization toward a fulfilling participation in a community of learners collaboratively seeking to apply discerning thought to nutrition issues.

The Shared Meal as a Teaching Practice

Before we present the results of this study, it may be helpful to briefly reflect on two specific concerns: (1) if particular Christian practices can shape teaching and learning in general, and (2) if the practice of shared meals could augment the typical pedagogical practices currently used in nutrition education in particular.

Christians have long participated in particular faith-centered practices in, through, and for community. Because Christian practices are means by which believers respond together to God's call to attend to the needs of one another, they might be viewed collectively as a way in which Christians learn the patterns and rhythms of a godly life. For this reason, Christian practices can also be viewed as formative, meaning that their pursuit is an ongoing process in step with seeking after virtue and, ultimately, wisdom while sharing the common human hunger for identity and meaning.

Of course, shared meals as a daily practice are not necessarily Christian. How, then, can a shared meal be construed as a distinctively Christian practice? Ideally, Christians' food practices are distinctive because Christians understand and acknowledge that all food is God's providential gift, that justice demands that we pay attention to our food habits even as we apprehend the needs of the hungry and hurting, and that hospitality and love of neighbor impel us to collectively respond by acknowledging and enriching the lives of the strangers among us. Furthermore, a shared meal can be an exceptional enterprise precisely because embedded within it is a repertoire of related Christian practices, including prayer, testimony, honoring the body, reconciliation, fellowship, and attentive listening. Most importantly, each meal shared among believers prefigures the shared Eucharist, "in which Christians recognize in faith that what they do for the poor, hungry, and homeless, they do for Christ."[16] As a result of breaking bread with one another, believers not only share particular food and faith practices, but experience these practices together as it relates to living out the gospel.

The early church "devoted themselves to the apostles' teaching and to the fellowship, to the breaking of bread and to prayer" (Acts 2:42, NIV), suggesting that they were committed to the breaking of bread, both as Eucharistic practice and as common meals.[17] The practice of hospitality wove itself through these early church activities. In our world, where stranger often connotes danger, we must learn about what it means to be devoted to "affirm[ing] the goodness of taking people in" as opposed to separating ourselves in a way that allows us to "avoid risky encounters."[18] This is true even for students who are not used to allowing classmates into their lives. Ana María Pineda further raises a pressing point about the erosion of our hospitality to one another: "We are short not only of tables that welcome strangers but even of tables that welcome friends. . . . Can we move beyond strangeness and estrangement to learn the skills of welcoming one another and to claim the joy of homecoming?"[19]

Our daily estrangement from one another is demonstrated by the degree to which the shared meal has suffered under a cultural assault of overcommitment and time famine. The family dinner is an endangered way of life, disrupted by meetings, school co-curricular activities, and work schedules. The church family dinner runs up against the same issues. Consequently, today's eating is more isolated and utilitarian. Is it any won-

---

16. Christophe Boureux, J. M. Soskice, and L. C. Susin, *Hunger, Bread, and Eucharist* (London: SCM Press, 2005), p. 67.

17. Scholars disagree about the nature of bread-breaking in Acts 2:42. Some, like Reta Halteman Finger (*Of Widows and Meals: Communal Meals in the Book of Acts* [Grand Rapids: Wm. B. Eerdmans, 2007], pp. 179-82), support the notion that the first-century church shared meals in the style of the pre-messianic Essenes. Others believe that the translation refers only to the Eucharist.

18. Ana María Pineda, "Hospitality," in *Practicing Our Faith*, ed. Dorothy C. Bass (San Francisco: Jossey-Bass, 1997), p. 31.

19. Pineda, "Hospitality," p. 32.

der that the shared meal holds little meaning as either a personal or a Christian practice for so many people? Our collective ability to recognize the shared meal as a healthy human activity for joint respite from the day's work, and a way to regularly and gratefully cultivate interpersonal nourishment, companionship, and acceptance has been eroded.

This is evident everywhere we look, but no more so than on a college campus, where many students sleep in rather than eat breakfast, rush through other meals, and remain committed to eating with only a handful of friends in the dining hall.[20] Randall Collins maintains that it is bodily presence that strengthens the interaction ritual chains that lead to a "common focus of attention and thus a state of intersubjectivity" necessary for confirming an individual's identity as a member of a group.[21] In contrast, today's culture of individualism, our "i" forms of technology, and our classroom architecture and practices often allow students, although bodily co-present with classmates, to cultivate a sense of interpersonal distancing and estrangement. Perhaps simply sharing a meal is a non-threatening way to get these stranger-students to personally connect and learn about their common identity as members of the same class.

Learning together also sometimes means giving up some content in favor of understanding. We would do well to question the role of consumption in the classroom. If our teaching and learning has erred on the side of information gluttony, creating shallow learners with a tenuous understanding,[22] then this is not a nutritious way to learn. A move toward valuing and practicing wholesome student engagement with the material, one another, and faculty is fundamental to what it means to learn, and to what it means to learn in community. So, the formative nature of Christian education may be in need of renewed attention. Church-affiliated undergraduate liberal arts institutions have grappled with two closely related is-

20. One student commented, "It was good for all of us there [at the class meals] to be pushed out of our comfort zone. . . . I've always done meals with the same group that I know. It is good to spend time getting to know and talking to people you might not have."

21. Randall Collins, *Interaction Ritual Chains* (Princeton: Princeton University Press, 2004), pp. 55, 64. An interaction ritual describes a group process in which a specific assembled group (perhaps a class) is closed to outsiders and is influenced by mutual focus of attention and shared mood. Collins asserts that for interactions to chain together into outcomes of group solidarity, individual and collective energy, and social relationship, it is critical that individuals in the group be fully co-present.

22. Doug Blomberg, *Wisdom and Curriculum: Christian Schooling after Postmodernity* (Sioux Center, Ia.: Dordt College Press, 2007), p. 189. Blomberg lays out a good characterization of the deep learner versus the surface learner.

sues: the disengagement of academic guilds from one another (a silo mentality), and what L. Gregory Jones calls "uncritical uses of technology . . . heightening an *in*formational understanding of the purposes of education, rather than an understanding that aims at formation in Christ."[23] Perhaps it is time for Christian higher education to consider how best to cultivate learning in newer, formative ways.

Such a move takes practice and a set of social practices.[24] What Etienne Wenger counts as the repertoire of a community's practices "combines both reificative and participative aspects, [by] which members create meaningful statements about the world."[25] Practices in the classroom, those sustained, cooperative actions that produce mutuality and cohesive community for the development of deep understanding, are essential to student engagement and the learning project. Miroslav Volf and Dorothy Bass suggest a link between the social practices and Christian theology, in that both provide method and motive for uniting thought, actions, society, and generations.[26] This is a crucial way in which the shared meal might contribute to the social and, by extrapolation, the learning vitality of students. To learn in Christian community, then, is to be committed with intentionality, mindfulness, and cooperation to learning, growing, and becoming care-filled people across generations, and shared food and fellowship at mealtime may augment this process.

As a Christian educator, my pedagogy is shaped by a desire to accompany students in learning and knowing who God is. Our common pursuit is fundamental to our ability to take in new knowledge, compare and connect it with what we already know, understand how it fits (or doesn't fit) into our worldview, and begin to identify and articulate how it challenges our assumptions and shapes our behaviors. This is Chris-

23. L. Gregory Jones, "Beliefs, Desires, Practices, and the Ends of Theological Education," in *Practicing Theology: Beliefs and Practices in Christian Life*, ed. Miroslav Volf and Dorothy C. Bass (Grand Rapids: Wm. B. Eerdmans, 2002), p. 192.

24. An account of social practices is given in Alasdair MacIntyre, *After Virtue: A Study in Moral Theory*, 3rd ed. (Notre Dame: University of Notre Dame Press, 2007). See also Alasdair MacIntyre and Joseph Dunne, "Alasdair MacIntyre on Education: In Dialogue with Joseph Dunne," *Journal of Philosophy of Education* 36, no. 1 (2002): 1-19; Joseph Dunne, "Arguing for Teaching as a Practice: A Reply to Alasdair MacIntyre," *Journal of Philosophy of Education* 37, no. 2 (2003): 353-69; and Nel Noddings, "Is Teaching a Practice?" *Journal of Philosophy of Education* 37, no. 2 (2003): 241-51.

25. Etienne Wenger, *Communities of Practice: Learning, Meaning, and Identity* (Cambridge: Cambridge University Press, 1999), p. 83.

26. Volf and Bass, eds., *Practicing Theology*, p. 4.

tian formation.[27] Thus, my goal has been to create a rigorous pedagogy for nutrition that intentionally connects faith and food and encourages students to learn and begin to practice sound nutrition themselves. A second aim is to help younger students begin shifting from being individuals with a learned reliance on memorization to becoming willing constituents of an engaged, mutually accountable learning community in which teacher and students together inform and transform one another. Such an approach demands what Amy Oden characterizes as an "unbending" of oneself,[28] requiring a charitable teacher, open-minded learners, a safe classroom, and, most important of all, a sense of belonging and community.

During the last decade, the trend in the sciences in general, including nutrition education, has been to move away from the traditional low-interdependence, non-cooperative learning model to one of PBL.[29] Pedagogies of engagement heavily stress the need for today's classroom to promote positive interdependence (i.e., cooperation).[30] Moreover, health care increasingly requires practitioners who are resourceful, engaged, and able to work in an interactive, fast-paced environment while maintaining a high level of reasoned thought.[31] As a result, educators should continue to question the validity of what has been called the "banking model" of education, in which a student's empty account (i.e., mind) is filled with faculty-imparted "deposits" of covering rather than communally uncovering material.[32]

The problem is that my nutrition students resisted the unbending

27. My colleague, James K. A. Smith, might argue that this is actually counter-formation. See chapter 2 of his *Desiring the Kingdom: Worship, Worldview, and Cultural Formation* (Grand Rapids: Baker Academic, 2009).

28. *And You Welcomed Me: A Sourcebook on Hospitality in Early Christianity*, ed. Amy G. Oden (Nashville: Abingdon Press, 2001), p. 146.

29. Karl A. Smith, Sheri D. Sheppard, David W. Johnson, and Roger T. Johnson, "Pedagogies of Engagement: Classroom-Based Practices," *Journal of Engineering Education* 94, no. 1 (2005): 1-15; Alfred K. Anderson, "An Assessment of the Perception of Learning Gains of Freshmen Students in an Introductory Course in Nutrition and Food Science," *Journal of Food Science Education* 5 (2006): 25-30.

30. Smith et al., "Pedagogies of Engagement," p. 5. Smith defines negative interdependence as competition.

31. Patricia H. Terry and D. R. Seibels, "Incorporating Problem-Based Learning into an Undergraduate Community Nutrition Class," *Journal of Nutrition Education and Behavior* 38 (2006): 121-22.

32. Paulo Freire, *Pedagogy of the Oppressed* (New York: Continuum, 2002), p. 72.

process so critical for this kind of interdependent learning. Thus, my hope was that sharing meals would make the students more open to group work in the classroom. Although my students have needed help learning the means and reasons for collaborative PBL,[33] they are universally eager to "learn" nutrition, and learning outcomes are routinely robust. This nutrition course uses a case-based and cooperative learning structure under-girded by regular but short intervals of lecture and discussion. Case studies and cooperative learning projects are designed to ease students into team problem-solving and experiential learning.[34] For example, one such case study involves a 30-minute in-class analysis of one young woman's daily diet. This woman has a family history of osteoporosis and a personal history of anorexia. Using a computerized diet analysis that lists the woman's daily food and nutrient intake, teams of students see that she makes healthy food choices. On closer inspection, however, it becomes apparent that her calorie intake is quite low, that her calcium intake is less than half the daily requirement, and that she may actually be a semi-vegetarian who has not completely recovered from her disordered eating. Teams work together through a set of guided questions to think about why this woman's nutrition, while healthy at first blush, is not adequate or balanced, and what needs to be done to correct the deficiencies. The case helps students become aware of issues related to poor calcium consumption and osteoporosis, including vegetarianism, lactose intolerance, low body weight, limited caloric consumption, and family history of the disease.

Still, case-based learning is new for second-year students, who arrive with limited experience in organizing, analyzing, explaining, and summarizing material in cooperative, contextualized, and coherent ways. When stressed, they easily fall back on habits of memorization in the hours leading up to an exam. So, transitioning to a cooperative, case-based paradigm and environment takes imagination, patience, and courage. Regrettably, unfamiliarity breeds anxiety, even more so in an already apprehensive stu-

33. Bette LaSere Erickson, C. Peters, and D. W. Strommer, *Teaching First-Year College Students* (San Francisco: Jossey-Bass, 2006), p. 9. The National Survey of Student Engagement (NSSE) attempts to follow this phenomenon regarding the inexperience of first-year students hampering their ability to evaluate, analyze, synthesize, and make judgments about posed problems. In 2009 (subsequent to this study), our biology department made curricular changes that heavily favor PBL.

34. Students are assigned to a permanent group of 4 members in the second week of the semester. Each group's membership is based on diversity of major, GPA, gender, and hometown.

dent. Since so many of these students fear that change is too unmanageable in this most important of semesters, they instinctively act to own and control their learning in ways which often express little care about the others in the room.[35] They privately admit to feeling uncharitable toward their classmates in nutrition.[36] So, it is possible that the students' distancing from one another is partly explained as a coping mechanism for an inner dissonance which results if they acknowledge an incomplete love for others in the class.

As a result, students reported on evaluations in past semesters that while they enjoyed the course content and perceived that they had learned a good deal about nutrition, they were less than enthusiastic about many cooperative learning activities. When they were required to work together in teams, an ethos of individual disaffection surfaced; students engaged the material, but less so one another, because the reality that a portion of their final grade was dependent on interactive work made them nervous. I believed that without a willingness to promote each other's success, there could be no pervasive sense of cohesive community.

A self-protective, me-only attitude is hostile to the development of a healthy community of practice. Wenger points out that learning "is not just the acquisition of memories, habits, and skills, but the formation of an identity. Our experience and our membership inform each other . . . transform each other."[37] Of course, not all competition is bad, nor does it automatically obviate collaboration — in some ways the competitive nature of the students is a shared practice in itself.[38] But here the high stakes do seem to blunt the interaction so essential to communal learning. While bodily co-present and mutually focused on nutrition, the pre-nursing students failed (year after year) to build group solidarity precisely because the competition among them is energy-draining. Collins has noted that situations

---

35. For more on the dangers of attempts of scholars, particularly Christian ones, to own and control knowledge, see Paul J. Griffiths, *The Vice of Curiosity: An Essay on Intellectual Appetite* (Winnipeg: CMU Press, 2006). The temptation to sequester information (to keep it to oneself, to be reluctant to share or discuss) is antithetical to the notion that all tangible ideas and knowledge belong to and are freely given by God.

36. A student was upset that she scored near the class mean on a midterm, explaining, "I don't care about how the others did, only that my score is higher than theirs. I don't want any of them getting into the nursing program ahead of me." Although many students don't or can't verbalize their feelings, I don't believe this is an unusual mind-set.

37. Wenger, *Communities of Practice*, p. 98.

38. Wenger, *Communities of Practice*, pp. 7, 212.

which drain energy, instead of creating energy, lead to emotional instability.[39] It was time to see if a shared-meal experience could influence students' attitudes about cooperative work, and to see if it might help replenish rather than deplete their energy for learning. Maybe the simple practice of sharing meals would allow students to gather to greet and eat in a non-class setting less charged with anxiety, thereby reducing estrangement, so that once back in the classroom, they might more gladly work to learn together.

The Results of Shared Meals: Ingredients for Optimism

Consenting students completed an anonymous pre- and post-course survey modeled after the National Survey of Student Engagement (NSSE).[40] These surveys were given in an attempt to collect information regarding both student mental activity and student engagement, as illustrated in Table 1 on page 93. Consenting students (n = 63) completed this survey on the first and last days of the course, and, where statistically feasible, the results were compared to the 2009 NSSE scores for Calvin College first-year (FY) and senior (SR) respondents, and to the responses of just the 2006 FY pre-nursing and SR nursing students.[41]

39. Collins, *Interaction Ritual Chains*, p. 53.

40. NSSE survey instruments can be found at http://nsse.iub.edu/html/survey_instruments_2010.cfm. The NSSE quantifies student engagement with academic and other collegiate activities in schools around the country.

41. Calvin College students participate in the NSSE every third year in March of the freshman and senior years. In accordance with IRB requirements, all participants signed an informed consent form. Where possible, data were analyzed using a two-sample t-test, treating the Calvin 2009 data and the HE254 data as samples (as opposed to treating Calvin cohort data as a population). Calvin's data for 2009 were similar to the 2003 and 2006 scores. The 2009 data were used as the comparative sample, since they were collected closest to the time of this study. Nursing student data were not yet available for 2009. Using NSSE data and survey questions inherently resulted in several limitations. First, the two-sample t-test is not the most robust of statistical tests. Even though Table 2 reports levels of significance, these are discussed as trends rather than fact, since, given the nature of the two independent cohorts and the intervening year between responses, conclusions should be conservative. Second, because the surveys were anonymous, subjects could not be matched on the pre- and post-survey items. With only means to compare, a statistical analysis was not possible. Third, only 79 percent of HE254 respondents were sophomore pre-nursing majors, and the anonymity of the surveys precluded isolating pre-nursing responses, meaning that every projected conclusion regarding a pre-nursing student response is confounded with data from non-pre-nursing students. Fourth, because I felt strongly that shared meals could fos-

Table 1: Pre-course Student Survey, MEALS Project 2008

In your experience last year in college,[a] how much did the coursework emphasize the following mental activities?	Very much 4	Quite a bit 3	Some 2	Very little 1
Memorizing facts, ideas, or methods so you could repeat them in pretty much the same form?				
Analyzing the basic elements of an idea, experience, or theory (e.g., examining a particular case or situation)?				
Synthesizing and organizing ideas, information into new, more complex interpretations?				
Making judgments about the value of information, arguments, or methods?				
Applying theory or concepts to practical problems in new situations?				

Mark the box that best represents the quality of your relationships with people at your college LAST YEAR.

Relationships with classmates:

Unfriendly						Friendly
Unsupportive						Supportive
Sense of alienation						Sense of belonging

| ☐ | ☐ | ☐ | ☐ | ☐ | ☐ | ☐ |
| 1 | 2 | 3 | 4 | 5 | 6 | 7 |

Relationships with course instructors/professors:[b]

Unavailable						Available
Unhelpful						Helpful
Unsympathetic						Sympathetic

| ☐ | ☐ | ☐ | ☐ | ☐ | ☐ | ☐ |
| 1 | 2 | 3 | 4 | 5 | 6 | 7 |

a. This question was altered in the 254-post survey to say "in your experience this semester."

b. This question was altered in the 254-post survey to say "Relationship with HE 254 professor."

A Calvin College McGregor student scholar (Walters) coded and analyzed the survey data.[42] Despite the available statistics, the following discussion leans more heavily on qualitative rather than quantitative measures. Table 2 (on p. 95) contains the quantitative results.

Not surprisingly, incoming nutrition students tended to depend on memorization in their studies, being less likely to attempt to evaluate, analyze, synthesize, or apply elements, ideas, or theories in new situations. Post-course, student scores for memorization went down, while their likelihood of using analysis, synthesis, and evaluation of information rose. Levels of student-faculty engagement were low for nutrition students at the start of the semester, but these scores rose to levels comparable to that reported by seniors by the end of the semester.

Discussion: Is There a Place at the Table for These Christian Practices in Teaching?

Because it was hypothesized that peer-peer and faculty-student relationships might positively prompt a shift in acceptance of PBL, it is important to consider what the HE 254 students reported. In contrast to what students have shared with me during office hours and via course evaluations in the past, HE 254 peer-peer engagement scores were both healthy and similar to those of other FY or FY pre-nursing students at the start and the end of the semester. It is possible that this is an artifact of wording of the NSSE question: it asks students to rate their relationship with classmates as "Friendly" or "Unfriendly," "Supportive" or "Unsupportive," and indicate their "Sense of belonging" or "Sense of alienation" in their college experience *last year*. This means that their responses are confounded with their responses to general first-year core (general education) liberal arts classes. The first-year pre-nursing students take some common coursework in bi-

---

ter engagement (and that exclusion could cause anxiety), I did not think it right to implement MEALS in one section and not the other. As a result, there is no control group to use for statistical comparison. Fifth, all answers are self-reported. Thus, statistical power for the results is not robust, nor was it meant to be. The surveys were simply employed to give a broad view of student inclinations. From that perspective, the survey data pointed to some interesting trends.

42. The McGregor Scholar Program at Calvin awards students in the social sciences a summer research stipend to work with a faculty member. The MEALS project was awarded a McGregor scholar in 2009.

Table 2. Student Engagement and Mental Activity Scores

NSSE Item	Group Surveyed	Means[a]	Sample Mean Difference	Standard Error	P-Value[b]
Memorizing facts	2009 CC-FY vs. HE 254 Pre	2.83 vs. 3.27	-0.44	.0999	<.0001[c]
	2009 CC-SR vs. HE 254 Pre	2.67 vs. 3.27	-0.6	0.101	<.0001[d]
	2009 CC-SR vs. HE 254 Post	2.67 vs. 2.77	-.01	0.121	n.s.[e]
	2006 CC FY pre-nursing students vs. HE 254 Pre	3.394 vs. 3.27	0.124	0.140	n.s.[f]
Synthesizing ideas	2009 CC-FY vs. HE 254 Pre	2.97 vs. 2.47	0.50	.096	<.0001
	2009 CC-SR vs. HE 254 Pre	3.23 vs. 2.47	0.76	.094	<.0001
	2009 CC-SR vs. HE 254 Post	3.23 vs. 3.00	0.23	0.110	0.0407
	2006 CC FY pre-nursing students vs. HE 254 Pre	2.939 vs. 2.47	0.469	0.151	0.0028
Evaluating information	2009 CC-FY vs. HE 254 Pre	2.88 vs. 2.42	0.46	0.103	<.0001
	2009 CC-SR vs. HE 254 Pre	3.12 vs. 2.42	0.7	0.095	<.0001
	2009 CC-SR vs. HE 254 Post	3.12 vs. 2.85	0.27	0.110	0.0165
	2006 CC FY pre-nursing students vs. HE 254 Pre	3.000 vs. 2.42	0.58	0.166	0.001

a. 1 = very little; 4 = very much.

b. $P < .05$ is statistically significant, and ns = not significant.

c. At the start of the semester, nutrition students reported being more dependent on memorization and less likely to synthesize and evaluate information compared to FY students. This difference disappeared by the end of the semester for all three of the mental activity variables.

d. HE 254 Pre students are more dependent on memorization than CC seniors. In addition, their levels of synthesis and evaluation were lower than those of CC seniors.

e. There is no difference between HE 254 students at the end of the semester and CC seniors in the use of memorization, indicating that nutrition students report moving toward a more engaged approach to learning over the course of the semester. Still, CC seniors outpaced HE 254 Post nutrition students on synthesis and evaluation variables.

f. There was no difference between FY pre-nursing responses (2006) and the HE 254 Pre sample except for the synthesis variable; pre-nursing students reported a higher use of synthesis than did the HE 254 Pre sample.

ology, psychology, statistics, and chemistry, but the rest of their first year is spread across the entire core curriculum and spent with a mixed first-year and second-year student population. Perhaps it is a good sign that these scores remained steadily healthy on the HE 254 post-survey: the mean scores were 5.56 (pre) and 5.74 (post) out of 7.0 on this item, indicating perceived levels of friendly, supportive peer relationships that tended to improve over the course of the semester. In any case, the fact that students report such high levels of peer support directly conflicts with their private comments about their worries regarding the pecking order triggered by the nursing program admission policies. It illumines the typical cognitive-behavioral dissonance that has been a hallmark of students in this course over the past ten years. In retrospect, what I have observed may be that students project their angst about getting into the nursing program onto their peers in private conversations with me, while publicly masking their anxiety about others' success. So, whether or not the shared meals were successful in improving face-to-face relationships in the classroom is difficult to say on the basis of the quantitative data, although students' anonymous written feedback at semester's end seems to support the hypothesis.[43] One student, typical of most, wrote,

> A significant component of the nutrition class . . . was to approach food as a gift, a privilege, and an opportunity to serve others and be served by them. . . . The idea of getting together with small groups from the class for a meal in the dining hall or someone's own home at first seemed only like a chance to avoid homework and have extra class time. Looking back, I'm so glad that Professor Walton incorporated these opportunities. . . . The meals were a great way to talk to my classmates about our families, our schedules, and our interests. They were not a continuation of class but a bonding of students in a natural and minimal way that brought us together. . . . The meals were never about diet analysis but instead the joy of eating and drinking while experiencing the joys of social community over these blessings of food.

43. Students answered three questions anonymously the last week of the course: (1) Did you find that the focus on engaged reading helped you learn material in a way that gave you confidence in participating in group and class discussions?; (2) How did the focus on MEALS help you view this course and our classroom as a place and time dedicated to learning about nutrition principles?; and (3) What did you think of having to share two meals with classmates over the course of the semester?

Another student wrote,

> What better way to turn those stranger-classmates into friends than to recognize our common interests over a meal? The competitive tension in the classroom was quickly shattered and instead was filled with genuine encouragement and concern for each other.

And a third said,

> I loved having the shared meals. Sometimes you go to class, take down notes and you leave again not even knowing anything about the person that sits beside you. I feel that it made the classroom a warmer and more inviting environment to be in, which also makes it easier to learn.

Only a few students were less than enthusiastic. They wrote,

> I thought that the meals went well and helped me get to know my classmates better. To be completely honest it was kind of a pain and a little bit intimidating, but I never walked away from the meal feeling like it was total waste of time.

> I liked the emphasis on making the class and learning a shared experience. The groups weren't always my favorite, I'm more of an individual worker, but I admit that it did promote more of a community atmosphere.

The short engaged reading/discussion portions were also well received:

> Doing [engaged reading/discussion] in a small group is helpful too, and for me that helped me to feel more confident about my understanding of the subject matter and more confident about participating in class.

> I felt that when I did the readings thoroughly, I had a lot to contribute.

The faculty-student engagement scores revealed interesting trends. The HE 254 Pre students' engagement with faculty was not different from the overall FY scores. These had increased by the end of the semester to look more like what students report in their senior year, trending toward a real improvement in student-faculty engagement. Because pre-nursing and pre–physical therapy exercise science students all need faculty recommendations for their respective professional programs, their relationships with professors become significantly more important as the semester progresses. The shared meals provided a time for students to personalize shared experiences with their professor, and enhance what each knew about the other. Moreover, they allowed me to get to know more students better in less time than if I had tried to meet with each of them one-on-one. Nearly every student comment was positive on this account:

> [Sharing meals] was a nice way for the professor to get to know me so that if I asked her for a nursing recommendation she would know a little bit about me as well.

> I enjoyed . . . the opportunity to meet new people and looked forward to getting to talk to my professor on a more personal and intimate level. Being with a professor in a close-knit setting is a lot less intimidating and leads to the student being more confident in the classroom as well.

> I wouldn't have minded it if we shared even a few more meals together over the semester. I felt more comfortable in that setting with my classmates and professor, and therefore, more liable to converse and actively engage.

One question about the Christian practice of the shared meal was whether it could impact student response to PBL in the classroom. The trends in the data demonstrate a positive move away from individualized, non-participatory memorization toward collaborative, investigative, and shared learning. Of course, other years may have had similar results: introducing more PBL at this level should help students begin to learn together. The question here becomes how these particular students perceived the shift away from an emphasis on individually owned learning toward collaborative problem-solving, and whether the meals practice made any difference. It is not possible to determine here whether the peer-peer and student-faculty engagement results can explain the trend away from memorization. A likely scenario is that carefully and intentionally introducing students to a PBL approach, while being sensitive to their fears of change, helps them learn and begin to accept this new way of learning. Still, it would be interesting in future studies to attempt to determine whether rising engagement scores precede improved attitude toward PBL, or vice versa.

The shared meals and short, engaged readings certainly can do no harm in helping to undergird the collaborative work in the classroom, particularly in a population of students unversed in such an enterprise. Moreover, for those students inhibited in their relationships because of the backdrop of competition, the meals in particular were practical reminders that God provides for each one of us. At the end of the semester, one student wrote,

> The meals were calming, and kept the scientific component of nutrition from overpowering the sheer blessing of having food and drink when we need it. . . . These little times were a gentle reminder of the worldwide need to educate, provide, and serve so many in our world. These points may seem like a stretch to the benefits of eating with a group, yet I truly am thankful for the refreshing teaching experiences that our nutrition class had together.

Another student wrote,

> [Eating together] made me comfortable discussing different topics in class. Not only did it change my attitude towards my classmates, it also changed the way I view the dinner table, and in a broader sense, food in general. The time I spent eating and drinking with my classmates and professor was an irreplaceable part of my education.

While the trends of the NSSE data create room for optimism, the lack of a control group precludes definitive conclusions. Moreover, it is doubtful that the meal experiences in this one course could, by themselves, suffice in helping pre-nursing students find lasting peace amid their understandable anxieties. Still, a majority of the students enjoyed the shared meals and were grateful for a chance to engage faculty and one another outside the classroom. In all, both the student responses and the NSSE trends give grounds for believing that the practice of the shared meal, as a means of reducing alienation, enhancing face-to-face engagement, and creating an atmosphere conducive for collaborative learning, may indeed be a valuable one.

Dessert: A Sweet and Surprising Consequence

This project was undertaken with a sincere desire on my part to rewrite the menu of teaching in a challenging classroom atmosphere in ways that would create a classroom charged with interdependence and engagement. What I did not anticipate was the energy and joy and rightness I myself encountered as a result. Getting to so many meals was not the sacrifice I'd imagined, but an activity I came to look forward to with eagerness. We like to say that relationships take time, and one semester is a very short time. This experience reminded me, in a deeper way, that relationships take care, and that caring is what Jesus modeled for us around the table. Despite the need to attend multiple meals on and off campus and arrange for rides, I found this a most rewarding semester of teaching. Apparently, the students were not the only ones to feel tuned in and engaged. Suffice it to say that when I repeated this project in the fall of 2009, my enthusiasm and that of the students continued to be strong.

Many who sought out Jesus addressed him as "Good Teacher." Perhaps we can learn from the teacher-like qualities Jesus particularly displayed around the table, those of giving undivided attention, access, compassion, instructive discipleship, and even loving confrontation in very personal ways. This is how eating together incorporates more than just physical nourishment, because it also "represents the deeper reality of the Christian whose life is lived in Christ, that is, one always feasts at the table of the kingdom."[44]

In typical fashion, Jesus taught an important lesson to his disciples at supper the night before his death, saying, "A new command I give you: Love one another. As I have loved you, so you must love one another. By this all men will know that you are my disciples, if you love one another" (John 13:34, NIV). It was not the command to love each other that was new on this night. The unique qualifier was to love our neighbor in the same manner Jesus himself loves us. He chose to share this last meal with each of us, and we in turn receive the command to share ourselves in the very same way. This is the last thought I left with the students at semester's end: Christ calls us out of love to come to his table. We are to be mindful of our neighbor and the abundant and sacrificial love of Christ every time we turn, first toward and then away again from the table to go back into the world. Around the table, we see Christ and each other. As we turn away, we learn to see Christ in each other. And so it was with this experimental pedagogy, an attempt to join students around the table as a practice, and through that, to bring to light what a life devoted to God and neighbor looks and feels like. Sharing food, conversation, and companionship was

44. Oden, *And You Welcomed Me*, p. 146.

an endeavor to foster a dawning recognition that one's classmates are also neighbors dearly loved by Jesus.

I was skeptical at first, but now I am convinced that a rewarding first step toward designing and implementing pedagogical change is with and through the framework of a set of Christian practices. On a college campus, a meal is not only easy to organize (everyone has to eat); it moves students and faculty out of their exclusive airspace and seats them around a table filled with grace, food, testimony, and a brief respite from the day's demands. At the table, we can't hide. For a few precious minutes we sit face-to-face as equals, thankful together for God's provision. We not only satisfy our physical hunger; we learn of the dreams, hopes, and concerns of our image-bearing neighbors. This is what a meal at the table affords: the very moment we notice and understand how precious our tablemates are to Jesus, we are free to leave behind our self-indulgent, even tyrannical fears and suspicions.

It is a meal, a feast, a banquet that awaits us in God's new heaven and earth. Until then, we live in anticipation of that time, and our task as educators is to help students learn to navigate a precarious world. Where food is concerned, we have a lot to learn, because "we finished the twentieth century with more people fed and more people hungry than ever before in human history."[45] The shared meal as a practice among believers brings us together in ways that few other practices can as we continue to learn together what it means to love and serve God and neighbor.

---

45. Cathy C. Campbell, *Stations of the Banquet: Faith Foundations for Food Justice* (Collegeville, Minn.: Liturgical Press, 2003), p. 222.

From Curiosity to Studiousness:
Catechizing the Appetite for Learning

Paul J. Griffiths

Learning requires both knowledge and the skills of thought. To have the former without the latter is to be a storage device, capable of being called upon for information but not for thought. That is not learning; it is at best recall and display, activities better performed by computers than human beings. To have the latter without the former is to be capable of distinction, argument, and synthesis, which are the paradigmatic intellectual skills; but to have nothing to which to apply them. That also is not learning; it tends toward sophistry. The learned, ideally, have intimate acquaintance with and love for a body of knowledge, coupled with the ability to think about it, view and present it from different angles, ornament and develop it, and in those and other ways return its embrace. The learned are active lovers of what they know, and like all lovers they need at once to know the bodies of their beloveds and how best to return the embrace given. The appetite for learning, in this full and nuanced sense of the word, needs catechizing, which is to say instruction, direction, and formation. Christians have, or should have, rather particular ideas about all this — about, that is, the nature and value of learning, and about how the appetite for it should be kindled and directed. Those ideas, or some of them, are the topic of this essay; they run counter to a good many of the ortho-

This essay is a descendant of a lecture given at a conference called "Teaching, Learning, and Christian Practices," hosted and sponsored by the Kuyers Institute for Christian Teaching and Learning at Calvin College in Grand Rapids, Michigan, on 29 October 2009. I have removed from it most traces of its oral origins, and expanded it in various ways. I am grateful to David Smith and Jamie Smith for the invitation to participate in that meeting, and for the many useful questions and comments I received when the lecture was delivered.

doxies about the same matter abroad in our academies, whether schools, colleges, or universities.

Christian Ambivalence about Learning

The first of these particularly Christian views about learning and the shaping of appetite for it is a deep ambivalence about the entire enterprise. Some Christians have thought, and some still think, that the best thing to do with appetites for learning is to catechize them out of existence because they are a distraction from or an irrelevance to the Christian life. Such views are possible for Christians because it is evident that being an active member of Christ's body — being, that is, baptized in the Triune name and becoming sanctified by participating in the spousal love the church returns to Jesus — and being learned have no intrinsic connection. Witness the fact that the vast majority of Christians during the last two millennia have been illiterate and without any of the other particular intellectual skills valued and taught by schools, colleges, and universities, Christian or not. It is still the case that a significant proportion of Christians worldwide cannot read and write in any language. They were, and are, in the Lord's eyes, no worse for that; many among them are saints. Learning, then, whether wanting it or having it, is not among the necessary conditions for entering the company of the saints. That is sufficiently obvious that it does not need to be argued.

But I mean more. I mean also that learning as we now ordinarily understand it is as likely to be a hindrance as a help to living virtuously as a Christian and coming to a fuller understanding of the Christian calling. This is because those who seek learning, and even more those who become virtuosos of learning, are very likely to consider the learning they have their own accomplishment, and to judge it more important than any other. Such views and attitudes are sinful: they oppose the Christian life in profound ways, and they are the special temptation and characteristic deformity of the learned. That is one side of Christian ambivalence about learning. When unchecked, it can lead to a deep anti-intellectualism.

There is, however, another side. This is evident in the deep and abiding interest that the church, construed broadly, has taken in the intellectual life and formation of some among its members as scholars and thinkers. The Catholic Church, for example, honors its intellectual exemplars as *doctores ecclesiae,* and takes them to be among the most accomplished and subtle thinkers and writers to have graced the human race. From the great thinkers of late antiquity in the Latin West (Cyprian, Ambrose, Augustine), to the medieval monastics and scholastics (Bernard, Anselm, Aquinas, Scotus), to the Reformers (Calvin, Luther), the church has acknowledged, needed, supported (sometimes), and learned from its learned and thoughtful members. Why this positive evaluation of learning? First, and perhaps most fundamentally, because the church understands itself to have been entrusted with a revelation that it does not fully understand; seeking to understand it more fully involves seeking and finding both knowledge and the tools of thought, which is to say that it requires learning. The church has, then, found ways to provide at least some of its members the learning necessary to further its understanding of the gospel. In addition to this fundamental cause for a positive evaluation of at least some kinds of learning, the church also has occasional concerns that have the same result. These include a need to make the gospel comprehensible to pagans; a need to apprehend and understand the order and beauty of creation (as well as the damage and loss that order has undergone); and a sheer delight in thinking, understood, sometimes, as *vestigium Domini,* a trace of the Lord in us. When unchecked, this side of Christian ambivalence about learning can lead to a single-minded idolatry of the intellect, and to institutions (like our universities) whose structure makes that idolatry evident without check and without shame.

Christians must live with this ambivalence. It is like the ambivalence we have toward death, which is at once an artifact of sin wearing its unacceptability on its sleeve, and the gateway to eternal life through which we are eager to pass. To attend to only one of these two aspects of death's nature is to abandon a properly Christian understanding of it and to replace it with something less. In the case of learning, the quick and easy way to thread the needle is to say that the body as a whole has needs not shared by its every member. That there need to be learned Christians does not mean that every Christian needs to be learned; much less does it mean that being learned has anything properly to do with being a Christian. This, so far as it goes, is true and important.

But something more always needs to be said, something particular to a specific and contingent situation. When anti-intellectualism is everywhere and the book pyres are burning, Christians may need to emphasize the goods proper to learning, and to provide institutions in which these goods can be cultivated. When idolatry of the intellect is everywhere, and the smothering weight of learning seems likely to extinguish the fires of piety — when admission to a good university is cause for greater celebration in Christian families than baptism or first communion — then Christians may need to emphasize the dangers proper to learning, and to withdraw from or adopt a stance of critique toward the regnant institutional forms and practices of learning. Our situation is, at least for the American and European middle classes, more like the latter than the former, which is why I began with emphasis on Christian ambivalence about learning, and why I turn now to emphasizing the various ways in which learning and what must be done to seek it are incompatible with or otherwise detrimental to living as a Christian. One of the directions in which Christians must cate-chize the appetite for learning in a time like ours is toward radical redirec-tion, so radical that it may look like extinction: to understand and to seek learning as Christians do is very different from understanding and seeking it as pagan academicians do — sufficiently different that we approach equivocation in calling both "learning."

Christianity, then, is not gnosticism: we Christians do not deal in distinctions between esoteric and exoteric learning;[1] we do not elevate learning to the status of a condition necessary for salvation, as is evident by the fact that we are, for the most part, happy to baptize and communicate those with deep mental handicaps;[2] we see clearly that the pursuit and at-tainment of learning has nothing, by itself, to do with the pursuit and at-tainment of virtue, and may often be negatively correlated with it;[3] and we acknowledge that becoming learned often comports well with and actively informs vices that stand in opposition to the Christian life. This last is es-

---

1. The closest the tradition comes to affirming an esoteric-exoteric as valuable is in its treatment of the *oikonomia* (Latin: *dispensatio*). On this, see my discussion in *Lying: An Au-gustinian Theology of Duplicity* (Grand Rapids: Brazos Press, 2004), chapters 9-10.

2. Not all Christians agree about this, of course, and there is a large recent literature on the place the mentally handicapped do and should have in Christian worship. See, for ex-ample, Alasdair MacIntyre, *Dependent Rational Animals: Why Human Beings Need the Virtues* (La Salle, Ill.: Open Court, 1999), especially chapters 10-12; David H. Kelsey, *Imag-ining Redemption* (Louisville: Westminster John Knox Press, 2005); Nancy Eisland, *The Dis-abled God: Toward a Liberatory Theology of Disability* (Nashville: Abingdon Press, 1994); and Hans S. Reinders, *Receiving the Gift of Friendship: Profound Disability, Theological Anthropol-ogy, and Ethics* (Grand Rapids: Wm. B. Eerdmans, 2008).

3. John Henry Newman puts this point lyrically: "Quarry the granite rock with razors, or moor the vessel with a thread of silk; then you may hope with such keen and delicate in-struments as human knowledge and human reason to contend against those giants, the pas-sion and the pride of man." See John Henry Newman, *The Idea of a University*, ed. Martin J. Svaglic (Notre Dame: University of Notre Dame Press, 1960), fifth discourse, section 9, p. 91.

pecially true in a culture such as ours, where the proper *telos* of learning is not virtue or contemplation but, rather, material success and the attainment of power. For all these reasons, we are, or should be, reserved in our enthusiasm for the pursuit of learning. That we do not always manage such reserve but become instead cheerleaders for a kind of education (a bloodless word) that pressure-cooks the vices to a well-done turn shows the extent to which we have become subject to what a blood-soaked pagan world teaches us rather than maintaining the capacity to braid love for that world together with a clear-sighted critique of it. The pastoral office of love for a bleeding world cannot be maintained without the prophetical office of teaching that world what it should be about, and this is as true of our thinking about the practices of teaching and learning as of anything else. We too often forget it.

So much for the critique, the prophetical office. It needs to be held together with the affirmation, the pastoral office. What, in more detail, can we say about why we Christians should affirm the good of the intellectual life, the passion for learning? And how might these reasons help us to understand more fully how we should catechize and nurture the appetite motivating that life?

The first and fundamental assumption informing the Christian conviction that the intellectual life is important and beautiful, and that the church has a strong interest in fostering it, is that everything that is is good. All things other than God, the Triune Lord, are creatures, which is to say that they were brought into being by him out of nothing, and are sustained in being from moment to moment by him. This is an axiom of Christian thought, a claim central to its grammar and syntax. It means that every creature is good exactly to the extent that it exists: being and goodness are exchangeable or convertible. If this is right, and for the purposes of this essay I assume without argument that it is,[4] then what follows from it is, among other things, that knowledge of almost any kind about any aspect at all of the created order is good and needed by the church. To know and think about anything — a theorem in mathematics, the features of a galaxy thousands of light years from here, the face of your beloved, the grammar of Sanskrit — is to know something of what the Lord has made, which is to say that it is to know a good. To know something is to become intimate

---

4. On participation and convertibility, see my discussion in *Intellectual Appetite: A Theological Grammar* (Washington, D.C.: Catholic University of America Press, 2009), chapter 6.

with it; and since to become intimate with a good is itself a good, the conclusion is, unavoidable and delightful in itself, that all knowledge and all thinking are goods. That is why the church is interested in learning. It is not that every Christian, every member of Christ's body should seek learning; neither is it that seeking learning is the church's principal task (that is worship of the one who makes learning possible); but it is the case that in becoming learned, the Lord's gesture of love in bringing what is knowable and thinkable into existence is returned in an intimate way.

Two Kinds of Appetite for Learning

But the appetite for learning is not all of one kind. It, like all appetites, needs to be formed by catechesis before it can become effective. And that catechesis, that process of formation, can go well or badly: we can become good knowers or bad ones, and which we become depends very largely upon how the process of formation goes. Awareness of this led the church to attend closely to the various ways in which the appetite for learning may be formed, and to discriminate better from worse instances of that catechized and formed appetite.

For example, late-antique Christian thinkers writing in Latin distinguished two kinds of catechized intellectual appetite, calling one *curiositas,* which I suppose has to be Englished as "curiosity," even though it is more than a little misleading to do so; and calling the other *studiositas,* which I render as "studiousness," even though that too is misleading, conjuring as it perhaps does images of a bespectacled schoolchild with his or her nose in a book — which is very far from what the fathers of the church meant by it.

Following the Latin fathers, and especially Augustine, we can briefly define *curiosity* as "appetite for the ownership of new knowledge." This appetite the fathers judged a vice, identifying it as fundamentally pagan and as inevitably failing in its attempt to come to know things and to think well about them. This failure was, they thought, guaranteed by the strange relation between knower and known established by curiosity. That relationship is characterized by two fundamental desires: to own what is known, and to know new things. To own what you know is to establish a relation of dominance over it by making it exclusively yours. In order to do this, you need to cut it out from the herd of other knowables, as it were, rope and tie it, and bring it, now under constraint, into solitary confinement in your mental pen. This sequestration in the direction of ownership attempts, so its Christian critics say, to give those who undertake it a quasi-divine dominance over what they know. The object known, for the curious, lies passive before the gaze of the knower, and is removed from its participatory relation with the Lord who made it. If you try to know things as the curious do, to become curiously learned, you make idols of the creatures you study, things that can be known exhaustively, without remainder, and without reference to the Lord. This attempt must fail, for no creature can be known in this way; what you get when you try it is a simulacrum of knowledge, something like what you get when you substitute for making love with an actual human being making love to a phantasm, an image imagined. The phantasms that the curious attempt to grasp do not satisfy them, which is why the definition of curiosity includes reference to novelty: the curious are driven, desperately, to seek new things to know because they can never be satisfied by the simulacra of knowledge curiosity provides. The fathers root this analysis of curiosity in 1 John 2:16, where there is a division of the love of the world into three kinds: the lust of the flesh, the lust of the eyes, and the pride of life. Curiosity is identified with the second of these three, the *concupiscentia oculorum*. It is an idle, restless, idolatrous attempt to establish intellectual dominance over creatures as if they were not creatures but, instead, mere objects under the complete control of the curious knower. The curious value learning for its own sake, alone, which is the precise Augustinian definition of idolatry: they exchange use for enjoyment.[5]

There is a further and deeper criticism that can be made of curiosity as a species of the catechized appetite for learning. It is that the appetite is ravenous for extinction, for emptying the world of unknown knowables. Augustine writes, in the course of a lengthy and interesting analysis of what it means to want to know some creature as yet unknown, that "even the curious do not love the unknown. It would be more appropriate to say that they hate the unknown because they want to bring it to nothing by coming to know everything" (*sed nec ipse* [sc. the curious] *amat incognita, imo congruentius dicitur odit incognita, quae nulla esse vult dum vult omnia cognita*).[6] To bring the *incognitum,* the unknown, to nothing is to return it

---

5. For more on Augustine's treatment of 1 John 2:16, and the broader patristic understanding of *curiositas,* see my *The Vice of Curiosity: An Essay on Intellectual Appetite* (Winnipeg: CMU Press, 2006).

6. Augustine, from *De Trinitate* x.1.3, ed. P. Agaësse, *La Trinité, livres VIII-XV,* Oeuvres de Saint Augustin, vol. 16 (Paris: Institut d'Études Augustiniennes, 1997), p. 122.

to the nothing from whence it came when the Lord brought it into being *ex nihilo*. This, Augustine thinks, the curious both seek and achieve, because the means they use to attempt knowledge of the unknown guarantee failure to know, and thereby remove the unknown from the possibility of knowledge. When curiosity is extended without limit, as its indissoluble connection with novelty ensures that it will be, then the result is cognitive devastation without limit — devastation, that is, in the strict etymological (Latin: *de* + *vastare*) sense of "laying waste, emptying of goods." It is of course not the case that creatures are removed from being altogether by the curious; they have not that power. But it is the case that they are removed from being as knowable, and in that sense the curious are cognitive killers.[7]

If this critique of curiosity had been the last and only thing that Christians had said about the appetite for learning, then the church would have been a place in which that appetite was not valued, a place in which knowledge and the skills of thought were placed under the ban. But the critique of curiosity is not the last word on the subject. Curiosity is not, as Christians see it, identical with the appetite for learning *simpliciter;* it is just one form of it, the product of one particular kind of catechetical discipline and training. The appetite for learning can be catechized in quite another direction — that of closer cognitive intimacy with creatures understood exactly as creatures, which is to say as gifts from the Lord, knowable and lovable exactly as such. This form of appetite for learning the church has endorsed, and its name is studiousness. It is an appetite for closer reflexive intimacy with the gift. For the moment, this definition will have to remain obscure: it will become slightly less so as we proceed to consider the lineaments of what it means to study and teach as a studious rather than a curious person. But before doing that, it is necessary to say something from a Christian point of view about the relation between learning as such and its particular forms.

Accounting for Learning

In his treatise *De reductione artium ad theologiam [On the Reduction of the Arts to Theology]*, Bonaventure makes the claim that every form of cogni-

---

7. Heidegger saw this aspect of *curiositas* clearly, drawing explicitly upon Augustine. See *Sein und Zeit,* 10th ed. (Tübingen: Niemeyer, 1963), §36.

tion is theology's slave.[8] He includes under the heading of *cognitiones* (forms of cognition or modes of knowing) not only what we might call the disciplines, such things as astronomy and history and literature and mathematics. He also includes the acquisition of particular skills, such as those possessed by the farmer and the shipbuilder and, we might say, though he of course does not, the auto mechanic and the plumber and the computer programmer. He really does mean *all* forms of knowledge and *every* kind of learning, both knowings-how and knowings-that. All are at the service of theology; each is theology's handmaid. Bonaventure does not mean by this that all these particular knowledges are forms of theology, or that theologians, just because they are theologians, know how to make sails or lay bricks or prove theorems in mathematics. Much less does he mean that theologians can prescribe to those who do have such knowledge and skill how they should deploy or extend it. Your friendly neighborhood theologian will have nothing useful to say about how you should fix your car. What Bonaventure does mean is that theology, which is reasoned and reasonable discourse about that God who is the Lord, provides both the frame and the explanation for all these particular forms of learning.

Something of what this means can be seen by observing that there is no Christian mathematics. There is not because mathematics, like all particular knowledges and skills, does not, for the most part, climb sufficiently far up the ladder of generality to give it any particular Christian interest. Mathematics, like all particular sciences, is theology's slave and can be accounted for by theology, and to that extent it is of interest to the church. But only to that extent. Christians, as Christians, have neither special mathematical interest nor special mathematical competence. When we do mathematics — and some of us do, very well — we do it just as the pagans do, and we are and should be judged by the same criteria of mathematical excellence as they. Saying this is quite compatible with saying that Christians do have a special interest in providing an account of what mathematics is. That is because giving an account of what an activity is has not much to do with performing it, a point that can be put only a little differently by saying that it is quite possible to be a virtuoso practitioner of some activity without being interested in or capable of offering an account of what it is that one does as such. Providing a Christian account of the nature of mathematics — as,

---

8. "Omnes cognitiones famulantur theologiae," in *St. Bonaventure's On the Reduction of the Arts to Theology,* edited and translated by Zachary Hayes (St. Bonaventure, N.Y.: Franciscan Institute, 1996), §26, p. 60.

perhaps, the seeking of cognitive intimacy with the eternal order of abstract objects as these subsist in the Lord's nature — has only marginal and indirect effects upon mathematical practice, as is evident from the fact that mathematicians who offer no account of what they do, or one in every particular incompatible with the one just given, can cooperate well with those who offer a Christian account of mathematics.[9]

Practitioners of the particular disciplines taught and learned in our institutions of higher education are typically not much interested in offering an account of the nature of their own activity, and even less in specifying its relation to the practices that belong to other particular forms of learning. Not many biologists, for instance, are interested in discussing what biology is or how best to construe its relation to the study of Renaissance literature; neither are many learned in literature concerned to offer an account of what they do that specifies its relation to biological learning. And when biologists or littérateurs do talk about such exotic questions, they at once cease to practice biology or the study of literature and move to another field. To place particular forms of learning and the catechetical practices that make them possible into an ordered schema by specifying what they share and how they are differentiated one from another is not something that much concerns the contemporary university. But it is something that does, or should, concern Christians. For us, returning again to Bonaventure, theology is the master discipline — or, given her gender, the mistress discipline, the queen of all particular forms of learning, because what theology is explicitly about — the Triune Lord, God of Abraham, Isaac, and Jacob — is that toward which all other forms of learning tend and from which they begin. A complete account of what they are and are for, therefore, is by definition not something they can themselves offer, and when they attempt it, perhaps by specifying their own nature or their relations to other forms of learning, they necessarily transgress their limits.

This may seem controversial. It is certainly not easy to imagine many mathematicians or biologists happily agreeing to the claim that theologians can offer an account of what they do of a precision and scope in

9. It may seem that claiming the compatibility of mathematical activity with rival accounts of what that activity is and is for stands in some tension with my earlier argument that different modes of catechizing the appetite for learning are intimate with different, and often incompatible, modes of attempting to know. But this is not, or not necessarily, so. Offering an account of what one does as a learned or would-be learned person is much less formative of and intimate with the modes of knowing one performs than are the practices into which one is catechized as a neophyte of a particular form of learning.

principle unavailable to themselves, at least so long as they remain mathematicians and biologists. But it should not be controversial. If, as I have claimed, mathematicians and biologists are ordinarily not very interested in these meta-questions, then perhaps they will, more or less happily, give over analysis of them to theologians.[10] Whether or not this is so, two things are certain. The first is that our colleges and universities, whether Christian or not, largely lack interest in or capacity for offering framing accounts of the order and purpose of what they do, and that it is utopian to expect change in this regard — all the forces and powers of the national and transnational scholarly guilds make the offering of such accounts effectively impossible. The second is that Christians, to the extent that we think as Christians about the nature of the life devoted to learning, cannot avoid offering framing accounts of learning's nature and purpose. It is part of the church's calling to do this.

Christian Learning: Preparatory, Ancillary, and Informing Practices

The abiding Christian ambivalence about learning is given conceptual form in the distinction between curiosity and studiousness as catechized forms of the appetite for learning, the former being good because it is compatible with the natures of both knowers and knowables, and the latter being bad because it is incompatible with the same. Christians also have no particular expertise in or concern with the methods and practices proper to particular forms of learning, while we do have a deep and abiding interest in accounting theologically for the kinds of learning there are and their relations one to another. It follows from this that what the Christian archive has to tell us about how learning should be sought will not have to do with the practices proper to particular forms of learning. The archive has nothing to say about how to become a good musician or a good botanist. What it does have something to say about is the practices and attitudes that should inform all particular forms of learning, practices and attitudes that are preparatory for, ancillary to, and informing of what belongs properly to those particular forms. It is to these preparatory, ancil-

10. Or perhaps to philosophers. Certainly some Thomists would say this. I do not take such a view because I do not think that philosophy has either the scope or the autonomy which that view suggests. But it is not necessary further to explore, and much less to resolve, this interesting question for the purposes of this essay.

lary, and informing practices that I now turn, practices that apply to all Christian cultivation of learning, which is to say to the cultivation of learning in all its particular forms. Their absence will damage the cultivation of studiousness, and their presence will nurture it, and in that sense their presence will make those who practice them more properly learned than they would otherwise have been. But, to say it again, while the practices I am about briefly to comment upon are constitutive of a properly Christian approach to learning, they do not contribute directly to the intensification of cognitive intimacy with any particular range or kind of creatures. They are to those particular intimacies rather as the cultivation of a proper understanding of love is to becoming a good lover of a particular human person: that is, necessary but very far from sufficient.

Christian thinking about preparatory, ancillary, and informing practices must begin from thinking about the liturgy. That is because Christian life is lived most intensely and most fully in the liturgy.[11] It is there that the church is most fully herself as *sponsa Christi,* there that she returns most explicitly and intimately the embraces given her by the Lord, and there that she learns most fully what she needs to know in order to be herself. Attending to the liturgically given shape of the Christian life is of great help in seeing what ought to inform a fully Christian pursuit of learning. Liturgy, which finds its most complete form in the liturgy of the Mass but which occurs in one form or another whenever the Christian people gather to worship the Lord, always includes the following elements, though not always in the same form or order.

First, there is a sacrificial gift-exchange, in which the Lord offers himself to his people and the people acknowledge the gift with gratitude, in that way (the only way possible) returning the gift to its giver. The gift exchange occurs in words, as prayer of confession and praise; in the movement of bodies from kneeling to standing to walking; in gestures of self-crossing and raising the hands in prayer; and in the use of material objects (bread, wine, incense, images, books, and so on). In every modality, the Lord initiates by giving the gift, and the people respond by returning it: that is the fundamental liturgical structure.

Second, liturgical work, the work of the people (which is what the word means), is done without interest in or concern for outcome. We do not receive the body and blood or hear the word or sing praises to the Lord

11. I assume here a Catholic understanding of the liturgy, which will be comprehensible by and applicable to other Christians to varying degrees.

because we think that doing these things improves us morally, makes us healthier, provides us material blessings, or conforms us to Christ — even though it may do some or all of these things. We work liturgically because it is the thing to do, because liturgical gratitude is the only way to accept a gift given, especially one of surpassing beauty and value that we do not merit, and because we are in love and are eager to show that love. Inscribing the liturgy's gestures of love into an economy of contract, within which every action carries with it an expectation, even a demand, that something should be given back, would be to corrupt the liturgy. Those gestures belong, instead, to an economy of the gift.

Third, the liturgy is threaded through with lament. Its paradigmatic form is the confession of our incapacity to do what we are in fact doing, a confession that carries with it the implication that it is not we, or not only we, who do it. In the Order of the Mass (for Catholics) there is a confession of sin close to the beginning, in which we make exactly this gesture of renunciation because of unworthiness, a gesture that is repeated in the *non sum dignus* that comes immediately before the reception of the consecrated elements. Confessing unworthiness and lamenting sin does not, as it would in the ordinary contractual economy of exchange, lead to the conclusion that we should forthwith cease what we're doing. It is, instead, a gesture of disowning which is necessary if we are properly to continue our liturgical work. Without such repeated stammering gestures, liturgical work would become ours; with them we enter, performatively, into a condition in which we act with the Lord rather than on our own.[12]

Fourth, the liturgy is repetitive, and in being so it takes — or, better, wastes — much time. This is perhaps most evident if the entire cycle of the liturgy of the hours is prayed: doing that takes something over two hours a day, and if it is combined with the liturgy of the Mass, a substantial proportion of the day is liturgically spent. Wasting time is, in ordinary English, a bad thing: we want, we think, to make the best use possible of it. But in liturgical terms, time, considered as linear time that can be scheduled, divided into minutes and hours, filled up, deployed, and measured by chronometers, is exactly what should be laid waste, and effectively is. Time, considered as it should be, is cyclical rather than linear, and endlessly repetitive in its cycles: there is the cycle of the day, of the week, of the month, and of the year, each grounded, as Christians see it, in the creative work of

---

12. For this use of the trope of the stammer, see Catherine Pickstock, *After Writing: On the Liturgical Consummation of Philosophy* (Oxford: Blackwell, 1998), Part II.

the Lord, each evident, in different ways, in the created order, and each given its liturgical correlate. The liturgy of the hours works on a daily cycle, the Sabbath orders the weekly cycle, and the yearly cycle is given shape by the seasons of the church's year, from the beginning of Advent to the feast of Christ the King. To enter into the repetitive patterns of the liturgy is to lay waste linear time with the radiance of eternity, and in that way to provide a foretaste of heaven.

These aspects of the liturgy, its central grammar, can serve as paradigm for the consideration of what prepares for, structures, informs, and orders the work of learning. It is not that seeking learning is itself liturgical; it is rather that the extent to which seeking learning is well-ordered, aimed at studiousness rather than curiosity, is the extent to which it participates in and reflects, according to its own peculiar nature, the liturgical order. Thought about that order, therefore, illuminates thought about the practices of learning. How, more specifically, might that thinking go?

Prayer as Preparation

One prepares for engagement in the liturgy by settling the soul and turning one's eyes from the world to the Lord. So also for study. There is a long tradition in the Western church of offering prayers before study; and Thomas Aquinas provides, in pithy terms, the rationale for this:

> We reach the knowledge of truth in two ways. First, by those things we receive from another. In this connection, with respect to the things we receive from God, prayer is necessary, as in Wisdom 7:7: "I called and the spirit of wisdom entered me." And with respect to the things we receive from people, hearing is necessary, by means of which we receive from a speaking voice. And second, it is necessary that we apply ourselves by our own study, and for this meditation is necessary.[13]

We pray before study because by so doing we place ourselves in appropriate relation with the Lord as the one who gives wisdom, without which understanding is not possible. Such prayer is essential, and properly liturgical. It serves not only as an invocation of the Lord, but also as a reminder that we do not arrive at understanding by ourselves, or from our own pow-

---

13. I translate from the Latin of Thomas's *Summa Theologiae* 2-2.180.3 ad 4, as given in the third edition of vol. 81 of the Biblioteca de Autores Cristianos (Madrid, 1963), p. 1039.

ers. In that way, preparatory prayer is an instance of the act of disowning so important to all liturgy: whatever learning we have is not solely ours, and not arrived at solely by our own efforts. To forget to pray before we study is to forget to acknowledge what it is that we are doing, and, very likely, thereby to tend toward the curious desire for mastery rather than the studious desire for intimacy.

Thomas mentions not only what we receive from the Lord, but also what we receive from other people, from the *vox loquens* with which the learned speak to us and make a gift of their learning to us. This, too, is important to remind ourselves of in prayer: without the instruction we receive from those who already know what we want to know, and who have the knowledge and skill that make it possible for them to communicate what they know to us, we could not learn. Learning thus involves a double gift: of teaching from the Lord, and of teaching from people who have already received the Lord's gift. Both ought to be acknowledged in prayer. A learner is typically also (and at the same time) a teacher, and so it is also important to pray for students, whenever possible by name. Doing so serves as a reminder that the gifts given by teachers to students are just that — gifts, owned by neither — and that grace is needed to receive them. Praying for students also serves to place teacher and students into the same context, which is the liturgical one of the gift exchange. Such prayer should be undertaken whether or not students know that it is being done.

The place of learning is, by prayers such as these, assimilated to the liturgical, as it should be; and because prayers of these kinds are generic, setting the scene for learning simply as such rather than that for any particular kind of learning, they are practices preparatory to any and every kind of study. But the sense of gift in play here is nuanced, and in one way at least more specific than that evident in the liturgy. There, in the liturgy, the focus is on the prevenient giving of gifts by the Lord to the church and the church's grateful return of them to the Lord. Here, on the site of teaching and learning, this is also true; but there is an added and very important emphasis upon the gifts given by teachers to students and returned by students to teachers. This nexus of giving of course participates in the primary nexus, which is that between the Lord and us; but it is not identical with it.

Augustine, precisely in the course of an analysis of Christian teaching and learning, which he calls *doctrina,* a word that embraces both what is taught and the act of teaching it, says that there are things which do not give out or become exhausted when they are given away by their putative owners, and which possess the additional characteristic that when they are held on to without being given away are possessed in an improper way, a way that guarantees that they cannot be had.[14] Learning is a paradigm case. It is a *res*, a thing: a body of knowledge and the skill to think about it, as has been said. But it is a thing that can be given away without being lost to the one who gives it away, being in this like love and unlike money. And, still more importantly, it is a thing that if not given away, if clasped to the bosom (or kept in the head) of the one who has it, is *non habetur quomodo habenda est*, not had in the way it should be had. If, that is, you are learned and you do not teach in some way, you attempt to extract your learning, and yourself as a learned one, from the nexus of gift exchange in which all Christian life is lived. You attempt, that is, to make your learning a possession, as the curious do; and in attempting that you devastate it, move it from presence toward absence.

These are strong and interesting claims; prayers preparatory to study may incline Christians toward finding them both true and beautiful, which I take them to be. Prayers preparatory to study, of thankfulness for gifts already received (from the Lord and others) and in anticipatory thankfulness for gifts about to be given upon the site of learning, place we who pray them in a properly liturgical place in which we acknowledge, and over time become habituated to, a vision of learning as inseparable from teaching, and of the Lord as the primary teacher. This is what the place of study must be for Christians; and even when a Christian understanding of learning is not shared by all engaged in some particular studies (I have often taught and studied in places where neither my students nor my colleagues are Christians), it remains incumbent upon Christian students and teachers to pray before studies in these ways, discarding, of course, interest in the outcome of such prayers and praying them simply as an act of love for the Lord, for others, and for what is to be studied.

Akribeia: *Attention, Time, Repetition, Inexhaustibility*[15]

Just as the minutest particulars of the liturgy — the movements of the body, the herbs used in the anointing oils, the furniture and decoration of

---

14. I here paraphrase and ornament Augustine's formula, *Omnis enim res quae dando non deficit, dum habetur et non datur, nondum habetur quomodo habenda est*, from *De doctrina christiana* 1.1.1 (Latin quoted from http://www.augustinus.it/latino/dottrina _cristiana/index2.htm, consulted 8 June 2010).

15. I am grateful to Margie Mitchell, who first, long ago in Chicago, brought the importance of this word and its associated ideas to my attention.

the church building — are matters of intense concern to Christians (which goes a good way toward explaining why proposed or actual changes in them prompt such strong reactions), so also are the minutiae of the practices of study, and of whatever creature or ensemble of creatures is studied. And just as the liturgy lays waste to time by taking enormous amounts of it and transforming it, so also does study. The parallels go deep here, as in the other examples canvassed; and bearing the liturgy in mind can help Christians to understand more fully what learning is and how it should be sought.

Akribeia is a useful Greek word for this aspect of learning. It means, roughly, repeated attention to particulars, even of the minutest kind. Luke reports Paul as saying that he has been educated *kata akribeian tou patrōou nomou,* which comes into Latin as *eruditus iuxta veritatem paternae legis,* and into English as "educated according to the strict manner of the law of our fathers" (RSV), or "thoroughly trained in every point of our ancestral law" (NEB), or (rendering *kata akribeian* adverbially) "educated strictly in our ancestral law" (NAB), or "taught according to the perfect manner of the law of the fathers" (KJV). Luke (1:3) uses a cognate term to denote the care with which he has examined the particulars of the Jesus traditions. To attend to something *kata akribeian,* then, is to attend to each and every one of its particulars, and in so doing to regard all of them as important and revealing of what it is.[16] In the case of studying a text, this might mean attending to its rhetoric, lexicon, argument, silences, author, reception, genre, and so indefinitely on. The idea that every creaturely particular is important finds its ground in the thought that whatever is, is good: this applies to every creaturely particular, and it means that nothing is too insignificant to warrant attention.[17]

The most immediate working assumption of trying to learn about a creature or creaturely ensemble with *akribeia* in mind is that the task of learning cannot be completed because what is studied cannot be comprehended. That in turn is because comprehension denotes complete understanding, knowing everything there is to know about what is studied, and since the particularities of every creature are inexhaustible — they include, for example, the very fact that it is a creature, which means in turn that

16. For other scriptural uses of *akribeia* and cognates, see Matthew 2:8; Acts 18:25-26, 23:15, 23:20, 24:22, and 26:5; Ephesians 5:15; and 1 Thessalonians 5:2.

17. On attention, see, particularly, Simone Weil, "Reflections on the Right Use of School Studies with a View to the Love of God," in Simone Weil, *Waiting for God,* trans. Emma Craufurd (New York: Harper & Row, 1973), pp. 105-16.

comprehension of it, were that possible, would include complete understanding of its relation to the Lord — that is in principle not possible. Studious practitioners of *akribeia* know this, and therefore do not attempt mastery of what they study, a mastery that would only be possible if comprehension were possible. They attend, instead, repeatedly to what they study, always under the sign of necessary incompleteness, and with reverence for what is attended to. If every creature is inexhaustible, then none can be mastered: mastery in the sense of dominance is both an impossible task and an improper goal. And yet, the rhetoric of mastery, dominance, and control is everywhere in our academic institutions: we speak as if we can and should master our academic fields and in doing so comprehend the creatures that constitute them.[18] That language, and the attitudes it bespeaks, belongs not to studiousness but to curiosity.

Quietism with Respect to Outcome[19]

Like liturgical work, the work of learning is done without interest in or concern for outcome; and for essentially the same reasons. To attend to the particulars of a creature is a gesture of loving intimacy, and it needs no other justification. We do not seek learning in order to make the world a better place or ourselves better people. Those things may or may not happen; that they do (or do not) is neither the goal nor the motive of learning. The studious do not assess outcomes or undertake their studies with particular expectations. Instead, we attend, lovingly, to what gives itself to us.[20] The curious, by contrast, are driven by goals extrinsic to the act of attentive study, and the extent to which curiosity rather than studiousness

18. Shortly after I had completed my doctoral degree in 1983, the work for which included study and translation of a Buddhist scholastic text in Sanskrit, I recall being asked by a colleague whether I controlled Sanskrit. Even at the time I found this rhetorical flourish in exceedingly bad taste and evidence of deep confusion. No human being can control any natural language, and to speak as if this were possible (as scholars often do: the rhetoric of control and mastery is everywhere in our academies) shows the degree to which the rhetoric and often the reality of *curiositas* rather than *studiositas* is the dominant form of the catechized intellectual appetite in our academies.

19. For a more extended analysis of the idea of a quietism of interest, see my "The Quietus of Political Interest," *Common Knowledge* 15, no. 1 (2009): 7-22.

20. I draw here upon Jean-Luc Marion's formulation of the third reduction: "Autant réduction, autant donation." See, for example, *De surcroît: études sur les phénomènes saturé* (Paris: Presses Universitaires de France, 2002), chapter 1, §4.

dominates our academies is indexed by the prevalence of the idea that seeking learning without interest in (preferably measurable) outcomes is indefensible. This is a matter that Christian teachers and learners who work in colleges and universities should prepare themselves to address prophetically.

Lament and the Stammer

The liturgy is shot through with words and actions that question its possibility. Liturgical agents stammer and lament. So, and for similar reasons, do studious learners. First, we lament our own incapacities: we are, in various ways and to different degrees, stupid, inattentive, lazy, domineering, and blind. Being catechized in the direction of studiousness rather than curiosity does not by itself remedy these defects, but it does bring them to consciousness exactly as defects and permit them to be lamented as incapable of removal by our own efforts. For the curious, by contrast, utopian as they tend to be, even when these defects are visible, they are thought to be removable: all we have to do is work harder and perfect our methods. Then, our defects will be smoothed away, and we will have made ourselves capable of comprehending what we attend to. Lament is not, for the curious, a value, but rather a sign of weakness. For the studious, lament at one's own incapacity for study and one's failures as a student is intrinsic to learning. The extent to which it is forgotten or laid aside is the extent to which the path of studiousness has been abandoned.

For Christian students, lament is prompted not only by awareness of the damaged and inadequate nature of our own cognitive capacities, but also by awareness of the damage to which the world, the ensemble of creatures has been subjected.[21] The world is radiantly translucent, but it is not only that. It is also shot through with darkness. The divine light does not shine everywhere, but the places of shade and shadow exist only as its absence, its lack, its privation. They can be described only by negation, sought only by aversion (the closing of the eyes), and entered only by embracing the loss in which they consist. Such an embrace damages: the eye accustomed to the dark loses, perhaps temporarily and perhaps permanently, its capacity to see; it sustains damage, more or less deep. And the

---

21. For a more detailed analysis of worldly damage, see my *Intellectual Appetite*, chapters 3-4.

places of darkness are also places of chaos and disorder in which the demons of disorder — Leviathan, Behemoth, Diabolos — prowl, making less what was more, expropriating the beauty and order of the place of light and in doing so removing it from its proper glory and turning it into desolation, the place of dissimilarity, anguish, famine, and destitution in which the praise-shout becomes the wail of anguish, trailing gradually off into the peevish murmur of the self-wounding seeker of darkness. The regions of darkness are visible only by courtesy, as rents and tears in the seamless garment of light. They are the places in which knowledge becomes ignorance, vision becomes blindness, beauty becomes ugliness, harmony becomes discord, and, most fundamentally, life becomes death. To seek them is to seek nothing; to live in them is to live nowhere; to offer them is to offer the empty gift; and so to seek to live and to offer is to diminish, to hack at the body of one's being with the sharp sword of a disordered will until the body is limbless, bleeding, incapable of motion, approaching the second death from which there is no rebirth.

The darkness that is damage serves, for Christians, to explain the evil that is good's absence in the world external to ourselves. The corporeal world is out of joint, not as it should be; that is why the ensemble of causal connections that constitutes its activity is so often destructive to beings like us, and to the harmony of the whole. Earthquakes and tsunamis and plagues are, in part at least, the world not working as it should. We tend to call such things "natural disasters," but this is misleading. They are not natural if by that is meant that they belong to the world as it should be, the world as it was brought into being by its creator. Rather, they are anti-natural, instances of the chaos that disorders the world's nature rather than of the order that constitutes its beautiful harmony.

But we need to be careful here. Our intuitions and judgments about what is ordered and what is disordered are not always reliable because we are ourselves disordered and may therefore interpret a painful result of our own disorder as chaotic when it is nothing other than the inevitable pain of self-wounding. If you put your hand into the fire, your flesh will char and you will suffer. But the fact that fire burns your flesh is not itself (probably) an instance of disorder's damage; the disorder lies in your decision to put your hand there. By contrast, the violent death of multitudes brought about by events beyond the control and absent the initiation of human beings, such as the Lisbon earthquake of 1755 or the Indian Ocean tsunami of 2004, it seems more reasonable to think, is an instance of the world's disorder, and not just because such events bring suffering to us.

Any such judgments about what is and what is not evidence of the external world's disorder are disputable, and should always be made with the deep epistemic modesty appropriate to our limited and damaged capacities for knowledge.

Even if we cannot be sure about our ability to discriminate the damaged from the undamaged, the beautiful from the ugly (and our lack of certitude about these things is one more occasion for lament about our own cognitive incapacity), we can be sure that what we study is, at least in the contingent and sensible order,[22] in some respects damaged in such a way that it resists the studious gaze, showing to that look an absence rather than a presence. And this is a matter for lament at least as much as the lacks evident in our own studious capacities. When a Christian student seeks learning about, for example, the violence to which we human beings constantly subject one another, something can be learned. But there will also be a point at which the studious eye notes only chaos and absence, and laments that fact: the city with all its inhabitants is deliberately destroyed in fire; the infant in the womb is intentionally dismembered; the slave is lynched; and so, bloodily and grimly, on. Lament belongs here too, and not just as sadness for pain and death. There is also a properly cognitive lament, a lament that the world is not as beautiful as it should be, and that the efficient causes for its ugliness necessarily remain opaque.

22. This distinction is necessary because intelligibilia (numbers, propositions, and suchlike) are not, in my judgment, subject to damage and occlusion in the same way that sensibilia necessarily *(post lapsum)* are. This, however, is a disputable and speculative suggestion.

From Tourists to Pilgrims:
Christian Practices and the First-Year Experience

Ashley Woodiwiss

Many of us in higher education have had the all-too-familiar experience of first-year students (and their parents or guardians) wondering what practical use this or that major will have for the student once they graduate and enter "the real world." Thus a popular view considers higher education in largely instrumental and self-interested terms. College is a necessary hoop to jump through and a credential to earn in order to maximize one's income-earning potential. I go to college to get a better job than I could if I didn't. And for those of us who teach and administer at intentionally Christian liberal arts colleges, we recognize that such a view exists within our faith-based student and parent population as well.

At the same time, a literary and philosophic genre has developed in the past twenty years that has focused on the phenomenon that John Urry has summed up as "the tourist gaze."[1] In the preface to his volume, Urry sets out nine defining characteristics of the modern social practices that can be lumped under the broader label of tourism. Six of Urry's nine characteristics I find helpful to the topic here at hand:[2]

- For Urry, tourism is a leisure activity "which presupposes its opposite, mainly regulated and organised work." As practice, tourism "has

---

1. See John Urry, *The Tourist Gaze,* 2nd ed. (London: Sage Publications, 2002).
2. The summary that follows is based on and quotes from Urry's *The Tourist Gaze,* pp. 1-3.

I wish to acknowledge with appreciation the assistance provided by my research assistant, Michael Sewall.

come to be organized within particular places and to occur for regularized periods of time."

- Central to the kind of relationships spawned by tourism is movement through space and periods of stay in a new place or places.
- These journeys and stays are themselves outside the normal places of residence and work and are short-term in nature. "There is a clear intention to return 'home' within a relatively short period of time."
- Modern tourism involves "a substantial proportion of the population" and has thus required "new socialized forms of provision" to facilitate the practice.
- The tourist gaze is directed at phenomena in a way that separates them from everyday experience.
- Finally, for Urry, the social practice of tourism in its contemporary form has necessitated the development of "an array of tourist professionals" whose expertise is deployed to sustain and grow the practice.

When this account is relocated to describe the life world of a typical undergraduate student at an American institution of higher education, it becomes possible to imagine that the college experience for many an undergraduate is like that of Urry's tourist: A large percentage of American eighteen- to nineteen-year-olds undertake a temporary spatial relocation to pursue an experience, formed and guided by professional experts, and they are cut off from the everyday experience of family and home community.

Now, of course, one major way that the undergraduate student is not like a tourist lies in the *particular* instrumental manner in which many students think of their college experience. Unlike the tourist, who is after a largely aesthetic experience for personal pleasure, many students explain or interpret their experience of college in coldly rational formulas. College is an externalized experience, one considered necessary for the securing of a well-paying job upon graduation. But setting aside this instrumental dimension to their thought about the *whys* of an education, I still think it quite instructive for us to see the *hows* of the educational experience in the terms set out by Urry's notion of the tourist gaze. The contemporary academic gaze of the everyday undergraduate may come too close to Augustine's "disease of curiosity" (see his *Confessions*), whereby the individual satisfies a baser selfish and consumptive passion rather than ascending to the virtue of wisdom.[3] Thus Urry's tourist and the typical undergraduate

---

3. For a considered account of Augustine and his distinction between *studiositas* and

may be imagined as inhabiting a roughly similar world, where the former instrumentalizes the other for individual aesthetic-consumptive reasons, while the latter instrumentalizes for individual economic-consumptive reasons. Both are detached, disengaged, and disconnected from the object of their gaze. The tourist gazes at (consumes) the ancient structure for a moment of inward pleasure; the student gazes at (consumes) the text for a felt pragmatic necessity.

As a Christian educator, I believe that this tourist gaze, now in its reconfigured undergraduate student form, falls radically short of a fully authentic Christian conception of education. Not only does it fall short substantively of what a Christian account of education calls for;[4] I think it even falls short of the fullness of expectations and hopes for higher education in the hearts and minds of many contemporary first-year students. I believe that while many (if not most) students do possess an instrumental approach to their education, this is not *all* they possess. There is more present. Survey data on first-year students bears this out. Indeed, recent surveys indicate that "questions of spiritual identity remain pertinent" for entering college students."[5] In the forty-third annual report of its survey of more than 240,500 first-year full-time students at 340 of the nation's four-year colleges and universities, UCLA's Cooperative Institutional Research Program (CIRP) solicited responses to a number of questions pertinent to this project. Included in the 40-question survey were items concerning religious and political identity, past religious, intellectual, and social behavior, an evaluation of personal traits, the student's views on current social and political issues, and a sense of what the student considered important to accomplish in life. What do the data reveal? On the one hand, as recent national survey results indicate for Americans in general, so the CIRP sur-

---

curiositas, see two recent works by Paul Griffiths, *The Vice of Curiosity: An Essay on Intellectual Appetite* (Winnipeg: CMU Press, 2006); and, *Intellectual Appetite: A Theological Grammar* (Washington, D.C.: Catholic University of America Press, 2009).

4. The literature on the nature of Christian education, and on higher education in particular, is vast and growing. An excellent start in this field can be found in Nicholas Wolterstorff's collection of essays in his *Educating for Shalom: Essays on Christian Higher Education* (Grand Rapids: Wm. B. Eerdmans, 2004).

5. See David Smith, "Spirituality and Language Pedagogy: A Survey of Recent Developments," in *Spirituality, Social Justice, and Language Learning,* ed. D. I. Smith and T. A. Osborn (Greenwich, Conn.: Information Age, 2004). I am indebted to David Smith, who first cautioned me about under-appreciating the level of residual spiritual interest in the contemporary U.S. college student.

vey of first-year students reveals a significant number who do not affiliate with any religious traditions. While the full adult population who identify themselves as religiously non-affiliated numbers about 16 percent,[6] for 2008 first-year students, CIRP identified 21 percent who identified as such. The 2008 CIRP survey also revealed that only about 32 percent of the first-year students had discussed religion frequently or occasionally, and that, despite the legal drinking age being twenty-one, a full 44 percent of incoming students self-reported having either frequently or occasionally drunk wine or liquor in the previous year. These data seem to point to a 2008 national first-year class of incoming students who could potentially be immune or resistant to a religiously based narrative intended to displace the culturally prevalent self-interested approach to higher education. Yet other findings in this national survey point to a possible alternative conclusion, or at least a more nuanced one. So, for example, while discussion of religious matters might be low for these students, 40 percent believed themselves to be much more spiritual than their peers, while about 76 percent had attended a religious service frequently or occasionally. In terms of their future aspirations, a majority (51 percent) thought it "essential or very important" to develop a meaningful philosophy of life. With these findings, it could certainly be argued that in 2008 "questions of spiritual identity [still] remain[ed] . . . pertinent" for that year's entering college students.[7] It may well be that alongside the instrumental view of education there lies (though possibly dormant) a more aspirational hope among entering students that the college experience will possess some non-utilitarian meaning for them.

So, for those of us who teach at intentionally Christian liberal arts colleges, what resources are available to us to lead our first-year students to "higher ground"? Can we move our students beyond the tourist gaze to something nobler and more consistent with our — and their — Christian identity? In the account that follows, I offer my own attempts to address these questions from within the Christian tradition of particular spiritual practices.

---

6. For survey findings, see the Pew Forum on Religion and Public Life's 2008 survey on the U.S. religious landscape, available at http://religions.pewforum.org/.

7. Smith, "Spirituality and Language Pedagogy," p. 14.

The Project

The Erskine Seminar (ES 101) is a first-semester program for all first-year students enrolled at Erskine College. Erskine is a Christian liberal arts college situated in the Associated Reformed Presbyterian (ARP) denomination and located in a small rural town in what the locals call up-state South Carolina.[8] ES 101 is designed to accomplish a number of purposes related to the transition issues involved in matriculating to a Christian and liberal arts college. The format is relatively straightforward: Each year a text is chosen for all entering first-year students to read before they arrive on-campus. The students then select a particular section of ES 101, joining other first-year students and an instructor. The instructors themselves have great liberty in shaping their particular section of the Erskine Seminar.

For the fall semester 2008 section of ES 101, I chose the ancient spiritual practice of pilgrimage as a way to assist this group of first-year students in reconceiving their academic course of study away from a culturally prevalent "education for employment" perspective to an "education as character formation" view that comports more with both the mission of Erskine College and the tradition of (Christian) liberal arts education.

After a brief account of the institutional context in which this pedagogical experiment was set, I examine the component parts of the course and my observations of each. In my conclusion I suggest that the project was a success, but only in part. There I also examine some of the possible factors involved in this outcome. Perhaps this experiment can help identify some salutary recommendations for those of us who would translate Christian practices into Christian pedagogy as we seek to move our students from tourists to pilgrims.

Erskine College

As a small Christian liberal arts college (570 enrolled students) located in rural South Carolina, Erskine College has possessed a rich academic heri-

---

8. This location is not accidental. The ARP, since its inception in 1782, has been a largely rural and small denomination, with 88 percent of its 286 congregations possessing less than 200 active members. This data comes from the 2006 survey conducted by the ARP General Synod.

tage, with nearly half of its graduates continuing their education in graduate or professional schools (and with a nearly 100 percent acceptance rate into medical and dental programs). But despite this record, in the past few years Erskine has hit some troubled waters: enrollment numbers are down, retention is down, and entering SAT scores for first-year students have declined. Certain demographic characteristics have remained the same, however. Three-quarters of the students who enroll come from in-state South Carolina. At the same time, a current identity crisis has beset the institution, the not unfamiliar story of a Christian liberal arts college struggling to understand the nature of its Christian identity as it pertains to matters of policy, programs, and pedagogy.[9]

The first-year class of 2008, the year of the ES 101 seminar and the subject of this paper, reflected these trends. Of the 147 entering students, 75 percent were from in-state, and entering SAT scores showed a decline for the third year in a row. Perhaps not unimportant for this study, the religious breakdown for that class shows that of the 112 who reported a religious identity, only 8 percent identified with what might be called "traditions of historical liturgical practice" (Catholic and Episcopalian), while 38 percent considered themselves Baptists of one kind or another. This breakdown is consistent with the religious makeup of South Carolina itself.[10]

Erskine College also participates in the annual CIRP survey, so it is interesting to compare Erskine's 2008 results with the national average in respective categories. And once we do, we see why at Erskine my selection of a Christian-based narrative possessed real pedagogical potential. Indeed, the 2008 first-year Erskine class scored significantly higher in those categories related to this project. For example, the percentage of religiously non-affiliated students, while 21 percent nationally, was for those entering Erskine in the fall of 2008 a mere 3 percent. A majority (53 percent) considered themselves spiritually above their average peers. Sixty percent claimed to have spent no hours "partying" in the previous year (as compared to 29 percent in the national average), and only 22 percent reported drinking wine or liquor in the year previous — half that of the national average. A staggering 98.6 percent of entering Erskine students claimed to have attended a religious service frequently or occasionally in the past year, with

---

9. For a particular take on this crisis, see Joe Belz, "Looking for a Miracle," found in *World Magazine*'s 4 July 2009 online edition at http://www.worldmag.com/articles/15536.

10. For information on the religious makeup of South Carolina following the 2000 census, see http://www.thearda.com/mapsReports/reports/state/45_2000.asp.

44 percent reporting discussing religion frequently or occasionally. A final datum is also relevant here: While only 7.5 percent of the national average was attracted by the religious affiliation or orientation of their college, almost 45 percent of 2008 first-year students at Erskine expressed such an attraction to Erskine. The composite picture from Erskine's 2008 CIRP profile is of a seriously religious student body attracted to Erskine in large part due to its explicit Christian identity. Thus, at Erskine, a project that seeks to translate Christian spiritual practices into an intentional Christian pedagogical experience should fall upon quite fertile soil.[11]

These surveys point to how there may be something else than mere economic self-interest to which the educator, and especially the religious educator, can appeal in the hearts and minds of our undergraduate students. There exists a real possibility for the replacement of the narrative of instrumental education with a more noble, and, I would argue, a more personally transformative narrative that fits the tradition of (Christian) liberal arts education and prepares our students for a more soul-satisfying life "in the real world."

The Topic

For ES 101 in the fall of 2008, I sought to develop *the narrative of the pilgrim* as just such a replacement. While there is a growing anthropological and ethnographical literature on pilgrimage,[12] my own recovery of it fell along more traditional understandings. Where the academic literature roams the world over to locate pilgrimages in multitudinous activities both sacred and mundane, I drew from an explicitly Christian tradition and some of the specifics of that tradition with its focus on character, inner discipline, attitude of heart and mind, and, ultimately, pilgrimage as a form of spiritual worship.

If the contemporary academic gaze can be thought of as a species of the "tourist," then, for the Christian pedagogue, can the "pilgrim" be a kind of overcoming? How could such a spiritual practice be translated into

---

11. Other data from the Erskine 2008 CIRP survey will be used to suggest some of the reasons why, given this initial portrait, the project was not more successful.

12. For two examples, see *Contesting the Sacred: The Anthropology of Christian Pilgrimage,* ed. John Eade and Michael J. Sallnow (Champaign: University of Illinois Press, 2000), and *Reframing Pilgrimage: Cultures in Motion,* ed. Simon Coleman (London: Routledge, 2004).

an expression of Christian pedagogy? This question leads to the design of ES 101.

A Journey Begun

"A Journey Begun" picked up on the first-year student's moment of personal transition. It encouraged the fourteen first-year members (ten women and four men) of this section of the Erskine Seminar to envision their college experience in a particular kind of way: as pilgrims, not tourists. I sought to nurture this by the texts chosen, the assignments given, and the way time was spent both in and out of the classroom.

At the outset, both in our initial class meeting and in the syllabus, I followed the "pilgrims, not tourists" theme by stating the following:

> With this in mind, we will adopt some particular (some might say peculiar) *practices* that will, hopefully, shape how we *read,* broaden our *imagination,* and stir our *affections.* In sum, education to be done rightly and well requires, I think, the commitment of body and soul. And in this section of ES 101, we will attempt just such a commitment in order that your collegiate journey, having now commenced, will be one that shapes your person as well as feeds your mind. To accomplish this, we will need to explore theologically and historically the place of the pilgrimage in Christian tradition, to consider certain practices involved in such pilgrimages, and to train ourselves in certain qualities of character necessary to undertake the pilgrimage and to end it well.

I set four course goals. At the end of their ES 101 experience, students should be able (1) to recognize how education, to be personally enriching, requires the presence and practice of certain qualities of character; (2) to understand how the Christian tradition identifies specific qualities associated with Christian higher education; (3) to see in the metaphor of the "pilgrim" how those qualities of character become embodied as practically relevant for the student's educational journey; and (4) to begin to inculcate those practices and qualities of character into their everyday life at Erskine.

Each of the three primary texts was used to focus on a specific aspect of a pilgrimage. So, for example, the designated text for all sections of the 2008 Erskine Seminar was Leif Enger's *Peace Like a River.* This 2001 bestselling novel tells the tale of eleven-year-old Reuben Land, who, along with his sister, Swede, and apparently miracle-working father, Jeremiah, strikes out across the barrenness (wilderness!) of the upper Midwest and Dakotas in search of his fugitive older brother, Davy. For our section of ES 101, we addressed the issue of character, and how this searching journey and quest reveal much to the narrating Reuben, not only about himself, but also about life, love, and the place of sacrifice. So, for example, Reuben reflects upon the difficult economic circumstances the cost of this search placed upon Jeremiah and his two children:

> The good thing about our reduced circumstances, going into Christmas, was that our expectations changed. They lowered themselves to a worthy place.

And as befits many of the chronicles of medieval pilgrimages, the author himself at his story's end reflects upon the limits of language and speech to communicate all that he has seen and heard:

> Is there a single person on whom I can press belief? No sir. All I can do is say, Here's how it went. Here's what I saw. I've been there and am going back. Make of it what you will.[13]

For the second text, Shakespeare's *Merchant of Venice*, we looked at the problem of disordered loves and the need for self-examination.[14] Unlike Enger's straightforward and accessible novel, this text provided a greater pedagogical challenge, since the first-year students possessed very little awareness of sixteenth-century Elizabethan England, or the history of European Christian-Jewish relations. None of the students had read the play before, and many had had no prior encounter with any Shakespearean text. While the reading of Enger's text was a reflective exercise of imagination and appropriation, reading Shakespeare was itself a discipline of self-examination as we struggled with the qualities of character required to simply comprehend the story and then the additional levels of critical appreciation, and to reflect upon why this play has become a central text in the Western imagination. As Barbara Lewalski noted nearly fifty years ago in her article on *Merchant*, "At what would correspond in medieval terminology to the 'moral' level, the play is concerned to explore and define Chris-

---

13. Leif Enger, *Peace Like a River* (New York: Grove Press, 2001), pp. 126, 311.
14. William Shakespeare, *The Merchant of Venice* (New York: W. W. Norton, 2006).

tian love and its antitheses."[15] And so the discussion of the play as we experienced it in ES 101 centered on such topics as friendship, courtship, loyalty, sacrifice, justice, mercy, and forgiveness, but also on pride, avarice, racism, ambition, cold-heartedness, hatred, and the will to violence. Much was made of Shylock's famous declaration: "I am a Jew. Hath not a Jew eyes? . . . If you prick us, do we not bleed? If you tickle us, do we not laugh? If you poison us, do we not die? And if you wrong us, shall we not revenge?" (at III.i). Is this an appeal for an empathetic foundation for some form of benevolent liberal universalism, or, perhaps, a commentary on the ineradicable nature of the human *agon*? What practical consequence for our living as Christians in the world should our confession of love have for us?

Our third text was the autobiographical account of Rory Stewart's walk across Afghanistan in January 2002. With little or no awareness of this part of the world and its histories, the first-year students in ES 101 were thrust into Stewart's account and its seeming inexplicability. The author himself notes in his preface, "I am not good at explaining why I walked across Afghanistan."[16] And coming less than a year after the events of 9/11 and just six weeks after the Taliban's departure from the country, the oddness of the quest becomes even more dramatic. What the students encountered in reading *The Places in Between* was the profound issue of difference and how on life's journey one inevitably encounters ways of life much different than one's own, and even, at times, ways of life inimical or hostile to one's own. How will we negotiate such differences as we journey onward? And how do we handle the mundane quality, the everydayness of most of our life's journey? Stewart's narrative is rich in its careful attention to detail. During the reading of this account, the students considered the place of fear, mistrust, suspicion, and stereotyping in those encounters with others who strike us initially as so alien to our understandings and practices. But they also encountered the need for context, history, and openness to negotiate those encounters empathetically and wisely. Practical concerns (walking sticks, medicines, food, warm clothing, and so on) figured as prominently as more lofty ones (inter-religious dialogue, foreign policy, history, political geography, and so on). There is a certain level of wry irony in the author's writing. It may well be that such a quality is also necessary for one's pilgrimage.

---

15. See Lewalksi, "Biblical Allusion and Allegory in *The Merchant of Venice*," *Shakespeare Quarterly* 13 (1962): 328.

16. Rory Stewart, *The Places in Between* (Orlando, Fla.: Mariner Books, 2006).

The use of such texts is standard pedagogical fare in higher education. At this point, the only substantive difference between my project and a more mainstream approach is at the level of *seeing*. That is, I was simply asking students to read and think about the texts from within the particular Christian context I sought to establish. At this level, the project was working at the level of the *imagination*. One can read these three texts in all manner of ways. I was asking the students of this section of ES 101 to look at them from a pilgrim's perspective. But, clearly, more than just an interpretive frame for reading was required.

The Assignments

Course assignments were developed to attend to different moments in the experience of the course. Each student kept a journal of ten 1-2 page entries for this class. The journal, as a medium for personal reflection, possessed both thematic and chronological qualities. So for the initial entry I asked them to reflect on why they had come to college and what about Erskine in particular had attracted them. Then, for the final entry at the end of the semester, I asked them to return to this topic again. Additionally, each student wrote reflection papers on the course texts. They also had the opportunity to do research based on a topic found in their reading of a selected chapter from John Ure's popular work, *Pilgrimages*.[17] The idea here was twofold: first, to give students an opportunity to read an account of a well-known medieval pilgrim or pilgrimage site; but also, at the same time, to give them an experience in doing research on some aspect of their reading. So, for example, one student, in reading about the pilgrim Canon Casola (in Ure's fourth chapter), encountered the topic of the kinds of Venetian boats used in transporting pilgrims to the Holy Land. This led him to research Venetian boat-building, its rise and decline. These kinds of assignments are also not that unusual in higher education. Rather, we might consider these written assignments as simply *reinforcing* the imaginative work of the students' readings. Again, while necessary, the texts and the written assignments were certainly not sufficient as a thoroughgoing translation of a Christian practice into Christian pedagogy.

17. John Ure, *Pilgrimages: The Great Adventure of the Middle Ages* (New York: Basic Books, 2006).

The Practices

Unlike more routine academic courses, for "A Journey Begun" I also sought to involve students in certain extra-ordinary practices. As I stated in the class syllabus, "All five of our senses will be employed. Hopefully our spiritual sense will also be quickened and deepened." For example, at most class meetings we used the Book of Common Prayer to experience times of corporate prayer and reflection. And we re-created pilgrimages of sorts. I divided the class into three randomly selected groups. To each I gave the assignment to locate a public site in the local area that would constitute the destination for their pilgrimage. For the purposes of the assignment, they were to travel together to observe the place of their destination, and to decide ahead of time the goal or object of their pilgrimage. What did they hope to see? to learn? And what personal importance did their pilgrimage have for them? When they completed their journey, each group shared their insights and lessons with the rest of the class in a fifteen-minute multimedia presentation. These practices involved using the body as well as the mind and spirit. The practices involved shared worship and prayer, shared journeying, and shared reflection.

"A Journey Begun" sought, in thought, word, and deed, to take fourteen first-year students at Erskine College and to refashion their understanding of what their college experience might be all about. Could they cast off an instrumental view of their education and adopt more of a pilgrim's perspective, one about inner discipline, devotion, and faithfulness? How did this pedagogical experiment fare?

The Assessment

An assessment of "A Journey Begun" can be carried out along a number of different lines. How well were the four goals of the course realized? By some conventional measurements and rubrics, ES 101 could be considered a success. Among the fourteen students, there were no failing grades. In both their written work and their verbal work, students demonstrated at least a minimal competency, and, at times, some real excellence. Their writing totaled about thirty pages in a variety of genres (journals, reflection/response papers, group projects, and individual research papers). They participated in class discussion and presented individual and group oral reports of their research.

In some of their assignments, students gave witness to a growing awareness of the world. One student reflected on Stewart's book in an interesting way:

> After our group discussion in class one morning, I began to think more about the "silent character" of *Places in Between*: the women. I did not really notice the fact that women are not present in this book while reading part one and two. . . . Not until we had our group discussion in class did I really begin to wonder why women are not seen as important in countries like Afghanistan. . . . This made me think about how American women, including myself, take so much for granted.

And another student, in reflecting on her group "pilgrimage" assignment, commented, "I think our group projects not only made us understand the world better and different cultures better, but I think [they] also helped us to grow as a class and helped us to open up to one another."

So there is clearly some evidence that some of the goals of ES 101 were at least in part realized. Students began "to recognize how education, to be personally enriching, requires the presence and practice of certain qualities of character" (goal #1). There were some stated efforts "to inculcate those practices and qualities of character into their everyday life at Erskine" (goal #4).

And yet I walk away from "A Journey Begun" somewhat unsatisfied. For by another line of assessment, ES 101 as an experiment in translating Christian practice into pedagogical method seemed to glide along the surface without having a serious substantive impact on the students.[18] Curiously, while the liberal arts goals were partially realized, the more explicitly Christian goals (as captured by goals #2 and #3) fell further short. For example, in their final journal reflection — a return to the question of why they had come to college — only four of the fourteen mentioned growth as a person (and only one as a Christian explicitly), while the rest retained a "tourist"-like instrumental perspective of college as a necessary step for better employment. And the written reports of their group pilgrimages were striking in what they omitted. While all used the word *pilgrimage* in the opening paragraph of their report, none of them set out what that term meant as it related to their project. Nor did they "translate" their

---

18. Admittedly, this observation suffers from lack of data and lack of perspective. Who knows how much influence this course might have on the lives of these students, and when such might be exhibited, if ever?

group project into a pilgrim's way of thinking. Rather, two of the projects were a simple recitation of events with no substantive reflection. Only the third — a visit to a volunteer fire department — included a final paragraph that rose to a minimal level of expectation:

> Our experience put many things into a completely different perspective for the group. Before we visited the department, we thought their job was solely to fight fires when a call arrives. After speaking with Chief Roy, we realized they also handle a variety of situations, including many domestic problems, along with fighting fires. Their training and dedication amazed the entire group.

Thus, in the central experiential moment for this course, one that explicitly provided a pilgrimage-like opportunity, the students in ES 101 just didn't get it. But then again, the assignment *qua* assignment may have in fact not been "thick enough" to adequately capture the pedagogical goal. For don't students in their earlier years have similar kinds of "look-and-see" off-campus experiences known as field trips? And absent explicitly religious sites with "thick" religious meaning and history as the destination for their respective journeys, how else could these students process and reflect upon their experience except through the already formed patterns of personal/instrumental reflections? In this case, a "secular pilgrimage" project faltered because not enough pedagogical formation either preceded or followed upon their experience.

Accordingly, in another version of this course I would undertake some revisions that could thicken the students' experience and perhaps enrich their understanding: (1) the pilgrimage assignment would be to explicitly religious sites; (2) the journal topics would be more directed to address particular qualities of character required for a faithful journey (e.g., "Discuss the place that patience has, or should have, in a pilgrim's journey"); (3) local spiritual adepts would visit the class to discuss their personal experiences; and (4) given the students' first-year status, more effort would go into trust-building, getting-to-know-you activities.

Conclusion

By way of conclusion, let me set out several possible factors that may have contributed to "A Journey Begun" falling short of full project hopes. I do so in hopes of offering some beneficial suggestions for those who would turn Christian practices into Christian pedagogy.

1. Culture is a tough nut to crack.

It might be that the Baptist, anti-intellectual, individualistic culture of South Carolina proved just too tough for a one-off course like this one. Some of the 2008 CIRP survey data tends to confirm this. So, for example, while the national average was at 31 percent for first-year students who reported that they "frequently explore topics on their own," Erskine students scored 10 percent lower. Erskine students also scored significantly lower on the question that asked students to rate their ability to work cooperatively with diverse people. And first-year Erskine students also exceeded the national average pertaining to reading: 28 percent indicated that they do not read for pleasure at all. This data points to the possibility that a partial cultural component factors into this project's shortcomings. One can imagine how in certain Northeastern (Catholic) and Midwestern (Lutheran/Reformed) regions of the United States, a similar project may find greater response due to a more traditional ecclesial and less individualistic religious culture present there. For those who would seek to translate Christian practices into Christian pedagogy, one recommendation is this: *Know your cultural context in order to critically assess the limits of the possible.*

2. Timing is everything.

Given the first point, it may be that the first semester of these students' first year was not the most advantageous time to attempt this project. There is a vast literature containing research into understanding the particular transition issues that confront the first-year college student.[19] A project such as this might work in the first year given the openness characteristic of first-year students. But that first year is also fraught with all sorts of non-academic challenges well documented in the first-year literature. There is an equal probability that my ES 101 simply asked too much of these first-semester, first-year students. A second recommendation is this: *Target your project to an age-appropriate audience.*

---

19. The University of South Carolina has a National Resource Center for the First-Year Experience and Students in Transition that serves as a clearinghouse for this research. See http://www.sc.edu/fye/.

3. Use of time/space is important.

My section of ES 101 met in a too large, too sterile and largely barren class-room in an aging academic building. I should have better used (or abandoned) this classroom space. Historic Christianity has always recognized how space matters for spiritual formation. While the syllabus stated that "there will also be regular individual and group meetings with the course instructor," these in fact were infrequently held. My suspicion now is that given the issues of culture and timing mentioned above, the issue of time and space was even more important for this project to be fully successful. Not surprisingly, given that this was a Christian project, I learned that "going the extra mile" is in fact a pedagogical requirement for a project of this nature. There is in fact a direct personal cost — that of kenotic embodiment — for this kind of pedagogy to flourish. Christian practices are about, in part, self-emptying. Christian pedagogy that seeks to translate Christian practice must itself be characterized by this kenotic posture. So a third recommendation would be this: *Before beginning your project, consider well its personal cost and commit yourself accordingly.*

4. Don't forget to break bread.

Here also less was, unfortunately, less. In the syllabus I had stated, "There will be time for quiet and meditation; there will be time for feasting and play." But in fact there was too little of any of that. Caught up in the greater context of the semester and its load of responsibilities, neither I nor my students caught sight of this possibility in a way that led to a radical un-making of the traditional first-year campus experience. Here, as with the issue of time and space above, a greater intentionality on my part would have contributed more to these students' encountering an educational experience different from the standard individualistic experience found in higher educational practices. So a fourth recommendation would be this: *Consider routine yet extra-ordinary experiences (like shared meals) to further reinforce the extra-ordinary nature of the project that you and the students have undertaken.*

Finally, I point to comments found in the final journal entries from two students. Here we see that perhaps our labors are not completely in vain. While I have considered the experiment of "A Journey Begun" only partially successful, there were moments when I could glimpse the salutary effects of a more successful experiment. One student closed her journal by saying that she "learned that education is more than just learning about science, math, and English. It is also about learning about life." And one male student commented, "Being at college has been a real eye opener. To get anywhere in life, you do not just need to have book smarts, you need to be able to handle real life situations as well." Okay, so it's not Lourdes, Fatima, or Compostela, but maybe it's not too bad for some young, first-year college kids in Due West, South Carolina.

Keeping Time in the Social Sciences:
An Experiment with Fixed-Hour Prayer
and the Liturgical Calendar

James K. A. Smith

Introduction: Orienting Convictions, Pedagogical Hypotheses

This experiment was an exercise in trying to get my practice to catch up with my theory. *Theoretically* I have been convinced that Christian education is not just about the transfer of *in*formation but also about a task of *form*ation — the formation of the kinds of persons that constitute a "peculiar people." In short, Christian education is not just the communication and dissemination of Christian content but the formation of a people who are defined by a certain set of desires or passions which are themselves defined by a certain *telos* — namely, the shape of the coming kingdom.[1]

More specifically, I'm convinced that at the heart of this task is the "conversion of the imagination"[2] enacted through intentional practices that are tactile, bodily, repetitive, and "narratival." We are narrative, liturgical, desiring animals whose actions and orientation to the world are driven much more by pre-cognitive imaginative construals of the world than by cognitive, intellectual perceptions of the world.[3] Our dispositions

---

1. All education, I would suggest, is formative (even modes of education which don't take themselves to be such). The question is, To what *telos* is a given set of educational practices aimed? I'm not suggesting that only Christian education is formation. Rather, what would make a constellation of education practices "Christian" would be the *telos* to which they're aimed (which would, in turn, inform the narratives assumed *by* a Christian education). To think about Christian education as formation is to highlight the *ends* of education.

2. Richard B. Hays, *The Conversion of the Imagination: Paul as Interpreter of Israel's Scripture* (Grand Rapids: Wm. B. Eerdmans, 2005), p. viii.

3. See my discussion of imagination and "social imaginaries" (following Charles Tay-

function as automaticities that are operative, for the most part, without our thinking about them. So a central question for the task of Christian education is this: How can we form those pre-cognitive dispositions — those pre-theoretical, imaginative construals of the world? The shape of a Christian education, then, is not primarily (or not only) figuring out which *content* to disseminate, or from what "perspective" to consider such content, but determining how to enact practices that effect, as much as possible, the conversion of the imagination — the formation and training of an abiding desire for the kingdom.

But when I honestly looked at my own classroom, I realized that I had simply appropriated the *status quo* pedagogies I had absorbed in graduate school. While theoretically I had adopted a philosophical anthropology that emphasized a holistic picture of human persons and human action, I had continued to work with pedagogical strategies that were more appropriate for disseminating ideas and propositions to "brains-on-a-stick." What made my classroom "Christian" (I hoped) was the material being discussed, not the way in which teaching and learning were conducted. In short, my theoretical affirmation of the importance of practice hadn't really touched the practice of my teaching. What would it look like to practice what I theorize?

Concurrent with this realization was a growing intuition that historic Christian practices (including the specific practices of Christian worship) constituted their own pedagogy — that to be immersed in Christian practices was to receive an "education" that was formative and intentional.[4] So might there be ways to extend the pedagogical "genius" of historic Christian practices into the classroom — particularly into the philosophy classroom at a Christian college? These two lines of questioning informed a pedagogical experiment of "keeping time" in a philosophy classroom. In this chapter, I want to outline the course in which this experiment was carried out, introduce and explain the practices that were performed (along with a rationale for why these practices were appropriate

lor) in *Desiring the Kingdom: Worship, Worldview, and Cultural Formation* (Grand Rapids: Baker Academic, 2009), pp. 63-71.

4. I'm not suggesting that Christian practices are the only alternative to "intellectualist" (Taylor) or "brain-on-a-stick" pedagogies. Clearly there could be all sorts of holistic, "practiced" pedagogies. Rather, I'm suggesting that historic Christian practices are inherited practices that are "primed" with an orientation to a *telos* that is directly relevant to the task of a Christian college.

for this course), and then provide a critical evaluation of the experiment: What worked? What didn't? What could I do differently?

Elements of the Experiment

Given that this was a first attempt to appropriate Christian practices in the classroom, I wanted to do so in a course whose themes and content might have a clear resonance with the experiment. I also wanted to experiment with a course that I taught regularly. And, to be honest, I wanted to first try this in an elective course rather than a core course, since I could then at least count on self-selecting interest in the course as a baseline. With that in mind, I settled on a 200-level course, "Philosophy of the Social Sciences," which I teach annually.[5]

The Status Quo Version of PHIL 201: Philosophy of the Social Sciences

In a "normal" rendition of this course — that is, in versions prior to this experiment — the course aims to critically analyze foundational assumptions in the social sciences from a distinctly Christian perspective. As the opening description on the syllabus puts it:

> This course will investigate the foundational assumptions at work in the social sciences, oriented by the conviction that despite being "late comers" on the scene, the social sciences in fact dominate how we inhabit the world. While very few of us will go on to be engaged with social scientific research, *all* of us will be "consumers" of social scientific "knowledge."
>
> Emerging in the wake of modernity and in concert with the rise of positivism, the social sciences have, since the beginning, been concerned with basic philosophical questions when reflecting on "method." What does it mean to have "scientific" knowledge of the "social" world? What counts as "knowledge"? What is "science" in such a context? How has our understanding of "science" changed after the demise of positivism? What are the implications of hermeneutics

---

5. I should also confess that I did not do this in a 300-level course because of "guild expectations" in my department.

for scientific observation and the notion of "objectivity"? But perhaps even more importantly, social scientific analysis assumes particular normative visions of human persons, community, and societal flourishing.

We will engage these questions of method and theory in the social sciences, tackling these issues from a Christian perspective with a Reformed accent. We will be particularly interested in the goals of social scientific theory and research, attentive to the central role of justice in the articulation of a Christian philosophy of the social sciences.

While the course broaches philosophical questions related to methodology in the social sciences (including meta-questions about just what constitutes "scientificity" and the perceived relationship between "objectivity" and secularity), the heart of the course focuses on contesting reductionistic pictures of the human person that are often assumed in the social sciences, along with unveiling, as it were, the implicit norms of human flourishing at work in various paradigms within the social sciences. The "heroes" of the course, in a way, are the two small textbooks used in the middle of the course: Christian Smith's *Moral, Believing Animals* (Oxford, 2003) and Charles Taylor's *Modern Social Imaginaries* (Duke University Press, 2004).

Smith's manifesto-like book challenges some of the reigning reductionisms of the day (such as rational choice theory and an overreaching evolutionary psychology). In particular, Smith emphasizes that the social sciences will never adequately or justly "explain" human behavior unless they honor the fact that humans are "moral animals," that they are "believing animals," and that they are "narrative animals." The action of humans as moral animals is motivated by commitment to values beyond self-interest; in particular, he emphasizes that human cultures are moral orders. And such moral orders are carried and communicated in narratives because humans are also "narrative animals": we make sense of the world *in story.* Even "we moderns," Smith emphasizes, "not only continue to be animals who make stories but also animals who are *made by* our stories."[6] And these stories carry an ultimacy about them because, as *believing* animals, we have to entrust ourselves to an orienting story. "All human persons . . . are, at bottom, *believers,*" Smith says (p. 54). The upshot

---

6. Christian Smith, *Moral, Believing Animals: Human Personhood and Culture* (Oxford: Oxford University Press, 2003), p. 64. Subsequent quotations from this book will be parenthetically cited.

of Smith's methodological manifesto, however, is not to give comfort to religious folk. Rather, the point is that because humans are these kinds of animals, social science will only be able to "explain" human behavior to the extent that its methodological assumptions honor these features of human personhood.

In the context of the course, Taylor's book does dual labor: on the one hand, he provides an archaeology of modernity, which was the matrix for the very emergence of the social sciences; on the other hand, he articulates a philosophical anthropology that is central to the course. Drawing on Heidegger, and criticizing what he describes as "intellectualist"[7] pictures of the human person, Taylor emphasizes that human persons have a kind of "understanding" of the world that is unarticulated (and, in some ways, inarticulable). He describes this "understanding" (Heidegger's *Verstehen*) as a "social imaginary" because it functions more on the affective register of the imagination than the cognitive register of the intellect *(Wissen)*. Thus human action is, for the most part, shaped and driven not by "conscious" decisions but by pre-conscious understanding.[8] This preconscious construal of the world constitutes a "social imaginary" which, Taylor emphasizes, is "carried" in images, stories, and legends, as well as practices. So it is our immersion in narratives and practices which inscribe in us a "social imaginary."

Both Smith and Taylor press the fact that, despite claims to neutrality and objectivity, the social sciences always work with implicit norms of human flourishing and human community, even if they pretend only to be "describing" what they see. Smith in particular is concerned to make explicit what is implicit, to get the social sciences to put their norms on the table. These questions of normativity turn to questions of *justice*. Indeed, while there is a long history of "secularization" in the social sciences, the history of the social sciences also has a strongly "reformist" impulse (particularly from the Marxian tradition) such that what often pretends to be mere description is ineluctably informed by an assumed prescription of "the way things ought to be." Thus the course concludes by trying to explicitly think through the norms of a distinctly "Christian social science" by engaging Nicholas Wolterstorff's *Until Justice and Peace Embrace*.

7. See Charles Taylor, "To Follow a Rule . . . ," in *Bourdieu: Critical Perspectives,* ed. Craig Calhoun, Edward LiPuma, and Moishe Postone (Chicago: University of Chicago Press, 1993), pp. 45-60, esp. pp. 45-49.

8. Recent cognitive science on "automation" substantiates this picture. See Smith, *Desiring the Kingdom*, pp. 59-62.

In past ("normal") renditions of the course, I have tried to press questions about the relationship between Christian faith and social science by having the students read John Milbank's *Theology and Social Theory: Beyond Secular Reason* (Blackwell, 1990) — a difficult, arcane book about which students have protested. My experiment this time around helped me to imagine how I could drop this textbook from the readings while still pursuing the same themes.[9]

A "Practiced" Rendition of PHIL 201: Intuitions and Strategies

Given my theoretical intuitions about pedagogy above, I wanted to experiment with Christian practices to see whether engaging in a specific practice could help frame and contextualize the themes of the course — and ultimately, to determine whether engaging in intentional Christian practices could actually help deepen the understanding of the core themes of the class. In short, my hunch was that, rather than just "adding" something external, performing the practice might actually help us better achieve some of the desired outcomes for the course. My approach was to adopt a couple of Christian "timekeeping" practices: observance of the liturgical calendar and the practice of "fixed-hour" prayer (or "the divine office").

Now, why *this* practice? I have long been committed to prayer as a baseline practice that creates a certain kind of learning space. Echoing Augustine's *Soliloquies,* I have always thought that Reason needs to pray in order to be rightly ordered and attentive.[10] Thus I have always opened all of my classes with prayer. But there were two other reasons that motivated my focus on historic Christian "timekeeping" prayer practices. First, in a way, the practices of fixed-hour prayer and the liturgical calendar explicitly intersected with themes addressed in the books by Smith and Taylor. For instance, in *Moral, Believing Animals,* Christian Smith emphasizes that "human social life is well understood as the 'liturgy' of the moral order."

---

9. I replaced the Milbank text with an anthology, *Readings in the Philosophy of Social Science.* While I'm tempted to say that this change was "unrelated" to the practices project, perhaps unconsciously this was my attempt to give the appearance of "guild-approved" rigor in the course. I'm re-evaluating the use of this book in the course.

10. Something like this intuition is wonderfully explicated by Jewish philosopher Peter Ochs in an important essay that has very much influenced my thinking on these matters: "Morning Prayer as Redemptive Thinking," in *Liturgy, Time, and the Politics of Redemption,* ed. C. C. Pecknold and Randi Rashkover (Grand Rapids: Wm. B. Eerdmans, 2006), pp. 50-90.

Thus he sees cultural practices as analogues of religious liturgies: "Liturgy ritually reenacts a tradition, an experience, a history, a worldview. . . . It is also exactly what human social life more generally does with cultural moral order. All of the social practices, relations, and institutions that comprise human social life generally themselves together dramatize, ritualize, proclaim, and reaffirm the moral order that constitutes social life" (p. 16). And Smith goes on to specifically note *time* as a feature of this meaning-making: "Humans always and everywhere use time to invest time and their lives with meaning through stories. Moral, believing animals recurrently mark time by designating particular dates and seasons that recall what for them is hallowed by invoking and retelling their particular narratives" (p. 78). In a similar way, Charles Taylor homes in on timekeeping as a central aspect of different social imaginaries, contrasting the flattened "one-damn-thing-after-another"-ness of "secularized" time versus the "higher times" of the Christian liturgical year.[11] By observing these practices of Christian timekeeping, students would have a tangible experience of such "world-making" practices, which are likely foreign to them (though the timekeeping and world-making practices of the academic year, or the Hallmark year, are very familiar).

In addition to these explicit thematic intersections, there was also a second reason to pursue these timekeeping practices: I found that considering the adoption of Christian practices in this course actually helped me to hone and revise the learning outcomes for the course. In prior versions of the course, I taught as if I were training a cohort of future social scientists who would be engaged in the generation of social scientific data. In other words, I tended to teach the course as if the students were enrolled in a pre–grad school primer. But the reality is that few, if any, would be going on to become "working" social scientists. However, they would all be inhabiting a culture deeply impacted by social science — a world increasingly fabricated by specific assumptions behind social science (e.g., the role of social scientific research in movie marketing[12]). And, I should admit, I have serious concerns that this "world" and the assumptions behind it are radically different from the kingdom and the "world" for which we hope as Christians. So in the process of thinking about the integration of

---

11. Taylor, *Modern Social Imaginaries* (Durham, N.C.: Duke University Press, 2004), pp. 98-99. I discuss this in more detail in *Desiring the Kingdom*, pp. 155-59.

12. See Tad Friend, "The Cobra: Inside the Movie-Marketing Playbook," *The New Yorker*, 19 January 2009, pp. 40-49.

Christian practices into the repertoire of the course, I also honed its focus: I would teach the course not for social scientific *producers* but rather for social scientific *consumers*. Instead of imagining students as the producers of social scientific data, I imagined them as inevitably influenced by cultural practices that were informed by particular configurations of social sciences — and thus, more importantly, worlds shaped by the implicit assumptions about the human person *behind* these social sciences.

With that in mind, I began to imagine the Christian practices of "keeping time" as practices of *resistance*. Just as I wanted our theoretical analyses to be a kind of apocalyptic "unveiling" of assumptions at work in contemporary culture, so I wanted the received practice of fixed-hour prayer to function as an example of alternative "world-making" — a way of subtly rewiring their imaginations by means of an alternative story repeated over time in the mode of a prayer.[13] The liturgical year is constructed narratively, re-enacting the life of Christ in rhythms of repetition, inviting the people of God into that story such that the story of God in Christ becomes the story of the people of God.[14] As Christian Smith suggested more generally, the liturgical year is a liturgical, narrative dramatization of a moral order; its unique timekeeping is an alternative practice of meaning-making and world-making.

So in the spring semester of 2009, I adopted three related practices as a constellation of "timekeeping" practices informed by the historic Christian tradition. I should also note some of the other factors and variables in this rendition of the course. In this elective course, even within the philosophy major, only about half of the students are philosophy majors (generally sophomores and juniors); the other half are non-majors, often from other social sciences (particularly political science, sociology, and economics). In spring 2009, I had just nine students (plus a visiting scholar from Korea who attended every class): six men and three women; about half were philosophy majors. And generally those who were not did not seem to exhibit much philosophical acumen. There were two seniors, but the majority were

13. For an argument along these lines, see Scott Waalkes, "Celebrating the Church Year as a Constructive Response to Globalization," in *What Comes After Modernity? Secularity, Globalization, and the Re-enchantment of the World,* ed. James K. A. Smith (Waco, Tex.: Baylor University Press, 2008), pp. 219-40; and Scott Waalkes, *The Fullness of Time in a Flat World: Globalization and the Liturgical Year* (Eugene, Ore.: Wipf & Stock, 2010).

14. On the liturgical year as a rhythmic retelling of the life of Christ, see Robert Webber, *Ancient-Future Time: Forming Spirituality through the Christian Year* (Grand Rapids: Baker, 2004).

sophomores. We met twice a week for seventy-five minutes, beginning at 12:05 P.M. on Tuesdays and Thursdays. Because it was such a small class, I moved us from our assigned "standard" classroom to a smaller seminar room with a large conference table. I hope this provides a snapshot of the course in which this experiment was undertaken.

The Liturgical Calendar and Calendar of Saints   The "macro" framing of time was indicated by our observance of the liturgical calendar. Given that this was the spring semester (beginning February 3), it was a particularly rich time in the church year, encompassing Lent, Holy Week, and Easter. Our "location" in time was indicated in several ways. First, I distributed a graphical presentation of the church's calendar, provided an introduction to the very notion of the liturgical calendar, and encouraged students to find ways to observe the calendar outside the classroom. Second, the timekeeping of the liturgical year was imprinted on the syllabus course schedule, including the calendar of saints as "exemplars" to consider.[15] I tried to graphically present this by having the church's "time" overlaid and imposed upon "academic" time in the syllabus design. Third, our midday prayers (more below) were marked by the "season" we were in. For instance, during the Lenten season, the "Alleluia" was omitted from the Gloria. So the prayers themselves "kept time" according to the seasons.

The liturgical calendar is no respecter of persons or days, in a sense. So, for instance, while students are experiencing the anxiety of final-exam prep or the irresponsibility of spring break, the liturgical calendar is indifferent. Spring break, in fact, falls within Lent — what difference might that make? Final exams fall within Eastertide — what's really important here?

Midday Prayer (Divine Hours)   If the liturgical year was the "macro" frame for keeping time, the observation of midday prayer was our "micro" practice of timekeeping. As I mentioned, our course met at 12:05 P.M. each day (high noon, so to speak) — an opportune time to observe the Midday Office. I utilized Phylis Tickle's online version of *The Divine Hours*[16] in order to create a service of prayer for each day. The prayers are prescribed, "given" for each day (as a gift). They are also suffused with the language of

---

15. My appropriation of saints was somewhat eclectic, with a particular interest in honoring women in the church's tradition as well as honoring saints from outside the North Atlantic.

16. See http://www.explorefaith.org/prayer/prayer/fixed/index.php.

the Psalms.[17] They took us into corners of Scripture we might not otherwise encounter. And they often had surprising resonances with themes being discussed in class (particularly regarding justice).

The midday prayer was a mixture of repetition and novelty in a cyclical, rhythmical pattern. On the one hand, it was repetitive in the sense that we opened every class in this way, with this same format. In addition, the final part of the prayer was repeated in every class and became quite a treasured rhythm for the class:

> God of mercy, this midday moment of rest is your welcome gift. Bless the work we have begun, make good its defects, and let us finish it in a way that pleases you. Grant this through Christ our Lord. Amen.

One could sense our shoulders relaxing in reception; some days the prayer was like a collective sigh. (One day, when we were watching a film, I neglected to prepare a prayer, and several students expressed disappointment, and basically scolded me for shirking my duties, particularly because they missed this final element of the prayer!) Every day we prayed the Gloria and the Our Father.

And yet it was repetition with a difference. During Lent, the absence of the "Alleluia" from the Gloria got to be quite noticeable, almost grating, and seemed to add to our hunger for Easter (despite being just one word!). The Prayers for the Appointed Week would be repeated just a couple of times, but then might come back to be prayed again. Over the course of the semester we were taken through long portions of Psalm 119, and read from most passages only once. And the collects for saints and martyrs would always be different as we met new heroes of the faith.

Student Journals Students were also required to keep a "time journal" as a third element of timekeeping, meant to tie together the first two through reflection. In this practice, the students were invited to reflect on any aspect of how they inhabited time — how they organized their time, how their rhythms were shaped, what happened when they "ran out of time," and much more. The journals did not have to reflect on the course discussions or timekeeping practices, but students often made connections between course content, course practices, and their "extra"-curricular expe-

---

17. Following Thomas Long, John Witvliet has described the Psalms as "God's language school" in *The Biblical Psalms in Christian Worship* (Grand Rapids: Wm. B. Eerdmans, 2007), p. 12.

rience of time. I gathered these journals several times throughout the semester and evaluated them simply on the basis of effort.

An Evaluation of the Experiment

My pedagogical goal in introducing Christian practices into the philosophy classroom was to enhance learning. More specifically, my goal was to see whether the practices would help students absorb an "understanding" of the core issues in philosophy of social science as contextualized within a Christian education. One might say that this was an alternative paradigm to common parlance about the "integration" of faith and learning. Rather than simply integrating concepts or content, I was aiming to enact practices of formation that would inscribe an "understanding" of the course themes *and* deepen theoretical "knowledge" of course content. So the evaluative question to ask is *not* only, or even primarily, "Did this make the students interested in fixed-hour prayer or the liturgical calendar?"[18] but rather, "Did this give them insight into the argument of the course and texts? Did the Christian practices of 'keeping time' contribute to their understanding of the critical project of the course?" In my evaluation of the course — based on observation and student feedback — I'd like to summarize roughly what worked, what didn't, and what I see as possibilities for the next rendition.

What Worked: Positive Outcomes

Overall, I think the inclusion of the practices made a positive contribution to the course. At a baseline level, students simply expressed their appreciation for midday prayer as a contemplative respite in the middle of their day. It became clear that this was a bit of a decompression time for them. Some students, who perhaps struggled with a kind of piety that required "spontaneous" prayer, found written, fixed-hour prayers to be a gift that helped them pray. While this is not directly related to the learning out-

---

18. Not that I'm opposed to that! Given that I think a Christian education should be conducive to deepened discipleship, and given that I think these practices are conducive to such, I'm actually quite happy if this is a cognate outcome. But such an outcome would be insufficient, I think; or at least, this would not be enough to confirm my hypotheses.

comes of the course, it seemed appropriate to me that students might find such a gift in a Christian college classroom.[19] Even if this were the only outcome, I'd do it again just for this reason.

But I'm also confident that the practices did contribute to the learning objectives of the course. For instance, at the conclusion of the final exam, in a non-graded reflection question, I asked the students to reflect on the midday prayer rhythm, whether it connected in any way with themes in the course, and if so, how. (If anything, during the course I tended to err on the side of *not* trying to make the connections too explicit.) One student responded: "The midday prayer was most significant for me as an embodiment of the sort of understanding through practices emphasized in Smith and Taylor. . . . As a part of class I thought it was a great way to focus or orient what we were doing (in sacred time?) so I think it was definitely valuable." For this student, then, the practice connected with the core theses of Smith and Taylor. But it also worked as a means of "framing" or contextualizing our class as a time and space to explore these themes in a certain way, with a certain vested interest, within a certain story.

Another student teased out the connection between the practice and the themes of justice we discussed with Wolterstorff:

This prayer was a good way of understanding the theory that *action* comes before belief. It is by "doing" prayer and doing it together that we live our Christian commitment. Obviously there is more to follow. . . . We cannot stop here. What we say in prayer is meant to not only influence and shape our contemplation of God, but also our commitment to world-formative action.

In the students' journals (unfortunately, only a few students seemed to take this requirement seriously as a mode of reflection), it was interesting to see how students found intersections with other courses (including several concurrently enrolled in a linguistics course) and their daily rituals and routines. Sometimes even playful entries were getting at something significant, as when a student talked about her experiment with a windowsill garden:

---

19. In *Desiring the Kingdom,* chapter 6, I suggest that the unique (some might say "strange") configuration that is a Christian college presents a kind of "monastic" opportunity to observe routines of daily worship and prayer.

Now we've talked in my soc/comm. class about the Western perception of time as a commodity. "That's a waste of time." "I don't have enough time." "Time is money." "How will you spend your time?" With this perception of time, how are our liturgical practices affected? Our prayer time — the midday moment of rest — is a welcome *gift*. We choose whether or not we will give it. It is, we think, something to give. But is it?

I'm growing plants on my windowsill. One of the pots has "thyme" seeds. (I don't even know what thyme is used for, but I thought I'd plant it anyway.) This has been the subject of some lousy jokes: "Look! My thyme is growing!" As though one could grow "time." Again, it's only funny b/c we can understand an idea of time as a commodity.

[The garden externalizes time in a way similar to the syllabus or prayer ritual. Thus she goes on to note:] The actual plants are causing me to think differently about time as we mark it in seasons. At least in Michigan we notice the cycles of life. Death and hibernation in fall and winter, then this wonderful season when the world comes back to life. . . . I notice it more when it's right on my windowsill in pots.

Another student noted, in depth, some of the tensions between "natural" time and "cultural" time, making these observations:

The way in which time is spoken of, ordered, and orders our world seems self-evident: there are sixty seconds in a minute, sixty minutes in an hour, and twenty-four hours in a day. That makes sense, and I am not sure if I can really conceive of time passing any other way. However, what I have noticed is that although our modern world recognizes roughly thirty days per month and twelve months per year, and although that may indeed be based on astrological and agricultural markings, my conception of time seems almost entirely separate from nature. Nature does not govern, order, or create my life; I do. Or, at least that seems to be the case.

In thinking about time, I noticed how the sun rises and still I sleep, the sun sets and still I wake, how I travel distances in extremely short amounts of time, and how the seasons pass and I am generally unaffected (except of course in the bleak oppression of the Michigan winter, but I'll come back to that). Coats, heating, hearty food, vitamins, vaccination shots — countless precautions are taken in my daily life against the dangers of our world and, yet, I don't seem to notice. Does this distance me from nature, from His creation? Theoretically, of course, I can live entirely separated from the natural world.

But the student went on to note how much culturally constructed time can trump the rhythms of nature, building connections to Taylor:

> Yet, more mundanely, my days are not oriented around the natural world, which may be to say that my days are not ordered around His creation. One of my hopes with the daily prayers, as seems fairly obvious, is that my life would be *re*-ordered, given a new and more spiritually disciplined rhythm. But for it to be *re*-ordered, does that not mean that it was and is *dis*ordered? If so, then what has disrupted this order? Setting aside the inevitable and pervasive disorder of sin in my life and taking a more socio-political perspective, I would venture to guess that this is a conflict of the type that we have been discussing, particularly in relation to Calvin College.
>
> As Charles Taylor noted, social imaginaries almost always overlap and interplay throughout society. Thus, I would guess that there are conflicting social imaginaries internalized in me, specifically seen in my discomfort with how my life is ordered. Of course, discerning all the clear-cut social imaginaries in my life would be a formidable task; however, I think it is safe to highlight two probably simplified imaginaries that are in specific conflict about how to view time.
>
> This insight has already been made in our course; however, recognizing that the daily prayers are meant to be much more than spiritual commodities has brought me to the conclusion that fairly drastic measures must be implemented in my life if I wish to live according to His time. That is, it is not enough to simply read words off a page three times a day. Or rather, that reading them like anything else will not achieve the desired affect. At a recent Sunday church service, one of the leaders invited the congregation to join in an altar call. As this church did not regularly perform this ritual, he took a short time to explain what it meant for him and the tradition of this church, and I really appreciated what he had to say.

And while I was hoping that engaging in the Christian practices would illuminate Taylor and the course materials, this student's journal indicated that the illumination went the other way as well:

> In short, he summed up my current intuitions about prayer-life, worship, and Western Protestant Christianity at large (or maybe not that broad, but what I've experienced as of late). In my view and as we've discussed in class, Christianity as right-belief has become too heady

153

and not embodied enough. Sharing this critique, the leader discussed how altar calls, specifically in his memory of revival services, are much more embodied than in-pew prayers. The reasons he gave were bodily: there is the motion of coming to the altar, bowing or even prostrating oneself, the pain of kneeling for extended times, and even the smell of the carpet. In this way, he said, such prayers become much more memorable — they last, which is to say that they are meaningful and perhaps transformative.

That type of liturgy is the type that I want and that desire leads me to think that spiritual, Christian *practices* must be structured into my daily life in order for my life to be ordered by His ways. It would be wrong to say that the places I have seen this dis-embodied Christianity do not do things, because they do. However, the activities my previous church and other Christian communities engage in do not seem to be the same kind of practices I have in mind. Rather, they seem to be easier solutions to the nagging guilt of personal transformation, social activism, or the call towards righteousness. I am coming to see what it means to be a follower of Christ, what it means to commit myself to His righteousness and Kingdom. And that is that I cannot sporadically charge myself with "spiritual" activities. Rather, the mundane, dirty, and difficult task of working towards a more just society is the nature of discipleship. For example, it would never be enough to simply pump money into the Third World, expecting a modern, developed, and fed society to arise. Instead, serious investments of all resources — time, money, persons, and even institutional restructuring in certain societies — are needed to bring about actual and meaningful change.

Likewise, my own life requires that serious investment if I want to be changed, ordered more in His image. And for that to happen I think I need to deconstruct and probably do away with the beliefs about the world that certain imaginaries hold. I also do not think that it is merely the reward of being more "in touch" with nature that this kind of reordering would yield. My hunch is that living less according to the regnant understandings of time and more towards a Christian understanding is a deeply transformative spiritual discipline precisely because living as such means that I give up my time, my daily life, to the Lord.

This was exactly the kind of critical evaluation of cultural practices that the course had always tried to achieve. And here it seems the engagement in intentionally formative practices helped crystallize this insight. Thus the practices of fixed-hour prayer and the liturgical calendar, rather than being a distraction from or addition to the course, functioned to deepen the course. The way the practice worked — through repetition, communal participation, submission to a tradition, and so on — was a kind of *performance* of themes addressed in the course. While course readings from Christian Smith and Charles Taylor were reflectively inviting students to see how, and to what extent, their world is constructed by practices, students also began to see how the practice of fixed-hour prayer was constructing the world differently.

What Didn't Work (Or, What I'll Do Differently Next Time)

After trying the experiment for one semester, I was convinced of its viability and value, but also immediately learned some lessons about its limits and problems:

- Only meeting twice a week makes it difficult to maintain a real rhythm of "alternative" time. Indeed, the full effect of Christian timekeeping practices would require that they be integrated into a larger, extra-classroom, co-curricular pattern. Some of the students did this (e.g., in observation of Lent, through chapel participation), but just observing midday prayer twice a week is almost entirely insufficient. A course that met three or four times a week would feel this rhythm more strongly.
- Because of some of my own theories about the irreducibility and sufficiency of the practice *as* its own "understanding," I was reticent to really push the connections between the *content* of midday prayer and what we were discussing in the course. I wanted to have the practice "do this work" without having to be supported by constant commentary and meta-reflection (just as I think Christian practice is formative in and of itself and doesn't require that we understand or constantly *explain* what we're doing in the practice). In addition, my theoretical assumptions about practices tended to emphasize form rather than content. However, I now think my reticence in this regard still harbored a kind of dichotomous construal of the relationship between practice and reflection *on* the practice.[20] I could have

20. For a relevant discussion of this point, see Rebecca DeYoung's chapter in this volume.

commented more specifically on *what* we prayed and made time for student reflection on the prayers within class time, making reflection on the content of the prayers part of the practice.

- The actual "textual" connections to "time" came quite late in the course, so any "aha" experience was significantly delayed. Perhaps there are ways that I could flag this ahead of time.

- In general, I feel like I simply didn't have time (or didn't *make* time) to fully utilize the resources of the practice (it was enough to just keep generating the prayers for each class, doing a bit of research on the saints and martyrs, etc.). For example, I underutilized the calendar of saints, and it might have been a good occasion to raise issues of justice by focusing on exemplars. Indeed, even explaining the cult of the saints would be a rich way to get at a very different social imaginary. Later renditions of the course will be able to build on this.

- Given my persistent critique of "intellectualist," content-centric paradigms in Christian education, the Midday Office is still quite a "heady" practice. I'm left with two trajectories of thought about this: (1) Perhaps I need to re-evaluate what counts as a "practice" and honor the fact that even "heady" routines can count as practices or repertoires. In this respect, I think these practices are still unique because they are communal, and because they are repeated.[21] (2) Ideally I would like to find bodily rituals and movements to accompany this. (I encouraged students to pursue these practices in ecclesial contexts — e.g., Tenebrae.) This might include aspects of posture in prayer (which seems risky to me, only because of an awkwardness that might accompany asking students to kneel[22]), but could also include observing time by "feasting" on some saints' feast days. Perhaps there would be a way to have students select a saint and have students host a "feast" on that day.

In sum, I was encouraged by the fruits of this investment and hope the experiment might be a catalyst for others to imagine how a range of Christian practices could be employed in the service of intentional pedagogy.

21. I will explore these elements of liturgical practices in more detail in *How Worship Works: Imagining Liturgy as Literature*, Cultural Liturgies, vol. 2 (Grand Rapids: Baker Academic, forthcoming).

22. However, if David Smith can ask his students to sit on the floor in the dark (see his chapter in this volume), perhaps I shouldn't be so nervous about asking my students to kneel for prayer.

How Christian Practices Help to Engage Students Morally and Spiritually: Testimony from a Western Civilization Course

Glenn E. Sanders

I want to give testimony about the ways that Christian practices have changed my teaching.[1]

Specifically, over the past six or seven years I have puzzled often about how I might "step up" my moral and spiritual engagement with students. The ambiguous wording is deliberate. The accurate alternative involves some ugly repetition: I want to be a moral and spiritual person teaching moral and spiritual beings in moral and spiritual ways. I teach history, however, not ethics or religion. Moral and spiritual principles are important, but I am mainly interested in the ways those principles "play out" (or not) in the complexities of real life. Some understanding of those processes as experienced in the past should help my twenty-something students as they enter adulthood.

An appeal to Christian practices has helped me start accomplishing this goal. Practices have provided me new reasons and ways to encourage intellectual and emotional hospitality in the temporary classroom community. They represent specific elements of Christian spirituality that help

---

1. Thomas Hoyt Jr. defines *testimony* as the Christian practice in which "people speak truthfully about what they have experienced and seen, offering it to the community for the edification of all." It "tells the truth. It also ties individuals to communities. . . . It guards the integrity of personal and communal life, as much on the grand stage of history as in the small exchanges of home." (See his "Testimony," in *Practicing Our Faith: A Way of Life for a Searching People,* ed. Dorothy C. Bass [San Francisco: Jossey-Bass, 1997], pp. 92, 94, 103.) I have cast my report and analysis as testimony to suggest the permeating effect of Christian practices. Hoyt writes, "Christian testimony has two dimensions. One is testimony to the church and the world, where witnesses tell others about the action of God. The other is testimony to God, where witnesses tell God the truth about themselves and others" (p. 102).

mediate my students' encounters with dominant past cultures. Together we grow spiritually as we negotiate the complexities and discontinuities of the past, of culture, and of "real life." Indeed, we get regular reinforcement — even catechesis — in the imperatives of faith as lived in particular historical, cultural, and aesthetic contexts. This common work gives us the emotional resources of friendship and challenges us to build deeper understanding and — if all goes well — meaningful application.

The Underlying Concerns

I side with the teachers, scholars, and moralists who hold that the college classroom should help students live as "moral, believing animals," even "desiring, imaginative" ones.[2]

A recent assessment from William Chace, former president of two nationally renowned institutions, Wesleyan and Emory, presents the opposite view:

> Some critics will complain that the university is not fulfilling its role as a moral academy devoted to the inculcation of specific values. Given its lamentable record in only fitfully honoring that responsibility, I conclude, with mixed regret and relief, that it should no longer try to do so. The morality it teaches, which must be seen as the best it can do, will come by indirection and example: teachers devoted to exactitude of thought and honesty of finding, libraries retentive of all learning and belief, and researchers determined to test, again and again, what is "obvious and settled" knowledge.[3]

According to Chace, even with such concentrated brainpower, wealth, and social capital, the university as an institution can only *indirectly* address common morality. At best it can teach its students only devotion, exactness, integrity in drawing conclusions, respect for all, and

---

2. The first phrase is from Christian Smith's *Moral, Believing Animals: Human Personhood and Culture* (New York: Oxford University Press, 2003); the second is from James K. A. Smith's *Desiring the Kingdom: Worship, Worldview, and Cultural Formation* (Grand Rapids: Baker Academic, 2009).

3. William M. Chace, *100 Semesters: My Adventures as Student, Professor, and University President, and What I Learned along the Way* (Princeton: Princeton University Press, 2006), p. 330.

critical rigor, and these only through example. Both the thinness of the list and the relinquishment of responsibility are striking. Both deficiencies suggest serious failings within the brick and mortar of the university, including loss of nerve, ill will, broken communication, confusion of life priorities, sloth, distraction, ignorance, and postmodern hangover.

The response of some has been a critical re-affirmation of the humanistic tradition as a resource for addressing modern excesses.[4] But a group of Christian scholars has recently offered significant critiques of both this re-affirmation and its underlying assumptions, promoting instead a wholesale refashioning of curricula, institutional identities, and pedagogies based on Christian ideals of human flourishing.[5] For example, James K. A. Smith has emphasized the importance of worship for reforming the desires of students. Humans are "desiring, imaginative animals" whose identities depend on the habits and "social imaginaries" that arise from the "liturgies" in which they participate — the collection of spaces, calendars, icons, and practices that communicate particular patterns of thought and living. Teachers should draw on elements of Christian liturgy to direct the imaginations and desires of students toward Christian ideals of flourishing.[6] Perry Glanzer has recently followed up on Smith's approach by arguing for general education curricula based on six "great creational identities" that allow focus on "the purposes, virtues, and wisdom" needed for each identity context. These identities are universal, social, complex, and interrelated in ways that require serious, critical thought to determine "present and future identity commitments more deeply and in more complex ways."[7]

---

4. See, for example, Anthony T. Kronman, *Education's End: Why Our Colleges and Universities Have Given Up on the Meaning of Life* (New Haven: Yale University Press, 2007).

5. A very good summary of both the critiques and the recommendations is Perry L. Glanzer and Todd C. Ream, *Christianity and Moral Identity in Higher Education* (New York: Palgrave Macmillan, 2009).

6. Smith, *Desiring the Kingdom*, pp. 37-73, 155-214.

7. These six identities are student, friend/neighbor/enemy, marriage/family, citizenship, race/class/gender, and "steward of creation" (Perry L. Glanzer, "Moving Beyond Value- or Virtue-Added: Transforming Colleges and Universities for Redemptive Moral Development," *Christian Scholar's Review* 34 [Summer 2010]: 379-99). This emphasis on student identity is the latest refinement in a contemporary emphasis on education-as-virtue-formation that has roots in the writings of Alasdair MacIntyre and Mark Schwehn. The strength of Glanzer's version is its attention to recent emphases in adult formation, concepts of individual vocation, and the role of co-curricular practices as important for holistic student formation.

But while these recommendations address broad frameworks for educating students, they require something more — a revising of concrete pedagogical approaches to match their high ideals. The kind of student formation described by Smith, Glanzer, and others calls for a level of emotional and spiritual engagement far beyond that which is normal in the modern college classroom.[8] Attention in a course to particular overarching virtues is potentially beneficial, to emphasize either virtues that govern learning and action (intellectual and moral virtues) or virtues that provide frameworks for interpreting particular subjects.[9] Both emphases might call forth imaginative moral and spiritual responses from students — perhaps new ways to relate to an academic discipline or new ways to apply learning. The complementary study of vices offers help on what to avoid.[10] Smith and Glanzer also point to the inspiration of Christian liturgies and to the role of co-curricular programs.

An emphasis on Christian practices gained my attention because their application promised to provide a rich moral and spiritual engagement with students. Practices can potentially address the type of student formation that Smith emphasizes — the development of new "social imaginaries" and habits. They can also allow regular attention to the virtues particular to each practice (for example, patience in relation to community-building). They represent concrete ways of Christian "being-

8. For example, the specifically Christian ideal of formation privileges what Robert C. Roberts calls "emotion-virtues" as "an essential medium in which Christian teachings get incorporated into the life of the individual believer" (*Spiritual Emotions: A Psychology of Christian Virtues* [Grand Rapids: Wm. B. Eerdmans, 2007], p. 5). "Emotion-virtues" include contrition, joy, gratitude, hope, peace, and compassion. Humility is the *sine qua non* required to cultivate these (pp. 78-93). On the place of virtues in Christian formation, see also the recent volume by N. T. Wright: *After You Believe: Why Christian Character Matters* (New York: HarperOne, 2010), p. 234.

9. For the first approach, see Paul J. Griffiths, *Intellectual Appetite: A Theological Grammar* (Washington, D.C.: Catholic University of America Press, 2009). For the second, see Daniel G. Groody, *Globalization, Spirituality, and Justice: Navigating the Path to Peace* (Maryknoll, N.Y.: Orbis Books, 2007); see also *Spirituality, Justice, and Pedagogy,* ed. David I. Smith, John Shortt, and John Sullivan, special issue of the *Journal of Education and Christian Belief* 10 (Autumn 2006), and my essay, "Exposing Students to Intractable Problems: Christian Faith and Justice in a Course on the Middle East" in the latter volume (pp. 39-62).

10. Cf. Paul J. Waddell and Darin H. Davis, "Tracking the Toxins of *Acedia*: Reenvisioning Moral Education," in *The Schooled Heart: Moral Formation in American Higher Education,* ed. Douglas V. Henry and Michael D. Beaty (Waco, Tex.: Baylor University Press, 2007), pp. 133-53.

in-the-world," ways deeply embedded both in the spiritual tradition and in the working of the Holy Spirit. Craig Dykstra's definitions are particularly helpful:

> Engagement in the church's practices puts us in a position where we may recognize and participate in the work of God's grace in the world.
>
> [Practices] become arenas in which something is done to us, in us, and through us that we could not of ourselves do, that is beyond what we do.
>
> The practices of Christian faith turn out in the end not primarily to be practices, efforts. They turn out to be places in the contours of our personal and communal lives where a habitation of the Spirit is able to occur. And it is this that is the source of their power and meaning.[11]

Trying to make a course into an experience "where a habitation of the Spirit" might occur was a heady goal. But the attempt matched my interests, convictions, and commitments regarding student moral and spiritual development.

Year One: Discovering Three Ways to Engage Students Morally and Spiritually

I selected my Western civilization sequence in 2008-9 for my trial efforts at applying Christian practices. "Civ." is intensively team-taught and central to the core curriculum; pairs of tenured English and history professors work daily with sections of fifty to sixty students (primarily sophomores), commenting during one another's presentations and grading all the essay exams and sometimes papers. The course has a tradition of forty years behind it, yet a strong sense of collegial responsibility within the "Civ." staff of ten teachers keeps the course fresh. Current students collectively see the course as a rite of passage, and alumni regularly identify the course as intellectually and spiritually transformative.

The course's up-front advantages for the application of spiritual practices are noteworthy. A long-standing emphasis on "big questions"

---

11. Craig Dykstra, *Growing in the Life of Faith: Education and Christian Practices*, 2nd ed. (Louisville: Westminster John Knox Press, 2005), pp. 41, 56, 64.

and real-life Christian responses provides a congenial environment, as does an emphasis on synthesis and interpretation central to the course's goals and reinforced by the combination of disciplines. The course encourages intense discussions and regular writing, with an emphasis on thesis-based argument and analysis. Affective bonds help mold this environment; daily contact means that teachers and students become close over the two semesters of the sequence. Years of collective work on the "Civ." staff have encouraged deep friendships between English and history teachers, as well as the sharing of disciplinary insights and pedagogical techniques.

Working from Dykstra's definitions, I set some initial goals for my application of practices:

- To form the teacher spiritually (practices as ideals, reminders, goads, means, etc.);
- To challenge default teaching styles and approaches with new ones;
- To help students "live into" Christian practices and thus grow spiritually as well as intellectually.

I decided to pursue the first goal by keeping a journal of ongoing reflections about my own efforts to follow spiritual practices; the exercise of writing proved invaluable. As for the second goal, I did not initially realize that my desire to change my default teaching style would count, in Etienne Wenger's term, as largely a revision of repertoire.[12] I merely sought some new approaches. The third goal, I came to realize, ignored the need in my particular institutional context to teach students *about* Christian spiritual practices in the first place.

I initially hesitated to choose a single practice as a guide for reframing the course, perhaps because the various practices are interrelated, or because this particular course had many, varied goals, or because I had to design the course with someone else, or because my own goals were still unclear. I finally developed a working list of priorities that seemed appropriate (see the table on p. 163).

These in turn guided my course revisions for the fall 2008 semester. I began each unit with a class covenant that I had prepared. I revised my presentations to emphasize the goals of each lesson, the specific narratives

12. Etienne Wenger, *Communities of Practice: Learning, Meaning, and Identity* (Cambridge: Cambridge University Press, 1999).

	Core Christian practice	Personal disciplines, exercises	Related classroom exercises
Primary	Shaping communities through hospitality	Listening, prayer	Greeting, office sessions, afternoon sessions (see below)
	Discernment	Study	Close reading, discussions
Recurring	Honoring the body	Exercise	Historic appeals to body symbolism (e.g., the "body politic")
Secondary	Keeping Sabbath (rhythms)	Sabbath-keeping	Observances that emphasize temporal rhythms: use of the "Peace" as a classroom greeting; Advent celebration (linked with Thanksgiving break)
	Testimony (historical faith framing)	Self-reflection	Afternoon sessions (see below)

that framed the lesson, and the regular discussion of texts in small groups of two to four students. The most significant revision, however, was the establishment of one-hour afternoon sessions once a week for those students who could attend. I made other arrangements for those who could not.

The revisions were mainly intended to de-center my part of the course — that is, to counterbalance my predilection for straight lecture with exercises designed to shape community through hospitality. The periodic recitation of a class covenant would set the tone; classroom use of student-generated framing narratives (brief summaries of historical events drawn from the day's textbook assignment) and small-group readings of texts would carry the class through the various lessons; and special afternoon sessions would provide space for considering the select spiritual practices.

In hindsight, my sense of how to apply specific practices remained vague. Also, despite the high place of "shaping community through hospitality" on my list of priorities, I was still depending on individual initiative, both my own and that of the students. I put together these changes for the history part of the course alone, without consulting my literature partner. The preparation of framing narratives remained the responsibility of individual students. I seldom allowed adequate time in the heat of the class period for the text-reading exercises to build adequate interchange between students. I tried during the afternoon sessions to find ways to relate the practices on my list to specific class material, but within a few weeks of the semester's start, I had become frustrated with what were little more than review sessions. My journal records,

> The problem is a familiar one — the grading for two sections grabs priority one, then I fill in daily with student and colleague meetings, then formal committee meetings, ongoing projects for committee, . . . then *always* some add-on. . . . I've managed to keep the afternoon sessions going [four per week], but they've become mainly review sessions. I like the new presentation format, but I'm still not into texts adequately, and the "decentering" isn't working too well.

While it is too much to say that this first attempt to apply spiritual practices worked against my initial goals, to say that my efforts remained abstract, overly complex, and even inchoate is accurate. The idea of application appealed to me, but I did not significantly modify my repertoire of classroom activities or assignments. As my frustrations indicated, the process itself was sidetracking my own spiritual/moral engagement with the students. Their own engagement had no clear or directed opportunities.

Regular review of course material was certainly a goal when I established the afternoon sessions. But I started them mainly to gain additional time for conversations with students — usually a half-dozen to thirty, scattered around the horseshoe-shaped classroom that we had used in the morning. There was never additional reading for the week's single hour, and seldom any during the session. At least for the first month or so of the semester, I would come to the session, teacup in hand, and informally shoot from the hip. We would discuss life experiences for a while, then gradually move to course material. At first I hid my efforts to draw on spiritual practices, only allowing them to guide my framing of questions for review. The afternoon sessions were still very far from what they would ultimately become: concentrated moments when our developing spiritual friendships would allow me to teach about practices, suggest how practices can provide ideas for critically assessing historical events and literary works, explore the "lived theologies" behind practices, and ultimately provide opportunity to employ the spiritual practice of community-building.

Given my initial problems, the transitional phase that followed is significant, for it illustrates how, in trying to apply spiritual practices to teaching, the teacher's own attempt to follow the practices can provide imaginative insights for negotiating the course. The busyness of mid-semester and the approach of Advent led me to explore whether greater attention to one of my secondary practices, Sabbath-keeping, might overcome my impasse. The journal entry for 20 October 2008 reads:

> My paper [for an upcoming conference on the application of practices] is leaning more toward "Identifying Spiritual Problems in Teaching," with an emphasis on what to do in the midst of a busy semester. One possibility: the *rhythms of crystallization* [e.g., imaginative response], the day-to-day, week-to-week rhythms in which you sense the needs of others and yourself and find a response (or not) within.

I had recognized all along that my own spiritual condition would affect the application of practices. Elsewhere in the journal on the same day, I had written this:

> It all seems *fancy-stepping* — either a *dance* (Shaker play this semester) or a *labyrinth turn* or a *garden pruning* (which branch?) — to know what to do next, both to get going short-term and to keep going long-term, with *minimal stumbling* or *miscues*. One key: *realizing* sin-as-inner-object and *living in* repentance and grace.

Such realizations proved essential for moving my efforts from a relatively superficial structural approach to a clearer, more deliberate application that intermingled course material, personal experiences, and traditional spiritual practices. The focus on "Christian time" suggested the need for a concrete topic that would appeal to the various needs of students while respecting the integrity of the course material and the freedom to seek spiritual as well as cognitive insights. A November progress report for the project listed my initial title for the paper as "Healing the 'Busy Semester Syndrome': Christian Practices as Reminders to Teach Important Things."

A third phase began with an afternoon session experiment during a week's lesson on Shakespeare's *Hamlet*. By November I had decided that the sessions would benefit from more direct references to particular spiritual practices. I worked with about a dozen students to identify what *dis-*

cernment meant. Then I shared with them some basic ideas about the subject from the Christian tradition — in particular, Jesuit ideas about individual discernment and Quaker practices of collective discernment. Then I asked a direct, simple question: "Was Hamlet discerning?" Student response was marked: No, he wasn't. He had not been systematically self-reflective. He had not sought adequate counsel nor listened well to advice.

I left the session feeling that something new and important had happened. I had reviewed the features of a particular Christian spiritual practice, identified a problem of interpretation that seemed related, and then brought the two together to see whether the elements of practice might help address the problem. Because the inquiry remained open-ended — the spiritual practice might not shed any light at all — I was able to respect the integrity of both the practice and the subject matter. And ultimately, because students could relate directly and intimately with the spiritual practice, they had a new tool for both appreciating the subject matter and reflecting on personal identity. Indeed, we were starting to *exercise the practices* together that we had discussed — discernment or testimony, for example — as we examined the previous week's subject matter alongside spiritual/moral concerns.

At this stage I began to notice that the pairing of a spiritual practice with a concrete historical event or literary work allowed useful contrasts. Interpreting texts with practices in mind added fresh examples, story lines, contexts, analytical categories, and distinct general angles or worldviews to our reading. For example, to explore Christian ideals of community in the early church, then to contrast these ideals with the imperial ideology of the *Pax Romana* as suggested in Virgil's *Aeneid* is an acceptable way to emphasize observable differences. To appeal to the spiritual practice of community-building provides categories and counter-categories for thinking about Roman life. More importantly, it poses a range of questions about the character of community as young American Christians experience it today, sometimes providing stark contrasts with past Christian and non-Christian experiences.

Focused appeal to particular practices and their use with concrete historical examples and literary works represented a new way of addressing the course's Christian ideals. I was introducing students from evangelical and non-liturgical backgrounds to traditional ways of Christian living. Given the backgrounds of most of my students, this effort to teach the practices increasingly seemed necessary. Students often had rudimentary understandings and appreciations, but for most the concrete practices represented a new way to "package" spiritual teachings and applications in ways that respected the work of the college classroom. The comparative approach meant that the subject matter and the practices remained separate and could interrogate one another. The level of analysis in the afternoon sessions fit well with the curriculum's goal of building critical thinking abilities during the sophomore year.

My application of spiritual practices seemed to be succeeding.

I would only later realize that I was not fully applying spiritual practices in my classroom, at least not in the sense that the course had students following a particular practice as they learned course material. There was no reinforcement of specifically Christian practice within the learning process. I was now abstracting key general principles from Christian spiritual practices and using them at the level of ideas to broaden the range of interpretation — not a negligible usage. But was a broader range enough? Could this approach exercise the moral and spiritual imaginations of students to the point that their emotions and attitudes changed in line with a particular practice?

Before the spring 2009 semester, I met informally with current and past teaching partners to gather their impressions. Beforehand I prepared a guide for our conversations. It provided a useful summary of what became a systematic application of the new approach:

> I think it useful to conceptualize the regular class sessions as "basic ideas, facts, and relationships" and the afternoon sessions as "Christian sensitivity training" to both academic and spiritual practices. So far I've addressed discernment, vocation (and "life rhythms" related to the Christian year), and community-building. Each time I have linked the practice to a particular literary work or set of events: discernment and *Hamlet*, vocation and *Paradise Lost*, and community-building and revolutionary national identity.

The chart on page 168 suggests the approach that I pursued throughout the spring semester. I kept the chart in my journal.

I had come upon a way to regularly apply principles drawn from spiritual practices. A lesson in late April on World War II pointed to an unexpected benefit. The subject was Nazism. I decided to draw on the spiritual practice of testimony to look at Dietrich Bonhoeffer's martyrdom as an illustration of Christian response to modernist secular nationalism. I showed students videotaped interviews of Bonhoeffer's friends and rela-

Week	Class topics	Practice(s)	Rationale, method
1	American and French Revolutions	Community-building	National communities: asked "How are communities created, maintained?"; discussed the *ties* that made *their* communities; closed with Isa. 49
2	Revolutions, *Faust*	Community-building 2	Romantic community, problems of ideological ties
3	Ideologies, Industrial Rev., 1848, early American republic, Jackson, Tocqueville	Testimony? Housekeeping (stewardship)?	Community to democracy, nature of local and national democracies, influence of economic changes, test review
4/5	National unification, American westward expansion, slavery, "Ivan Ilych," Marx	Discernment — of social and political conditions	Turn to *realism* — as a spiritual problem

tives. The interviews made clear the interrelations between Bonhoeffer's character, his theology, and his responses to Nazism. In words and deeds he testified about the regime's injustices and evils.[13] Conversations with students made clear, however, that in addition to providing principles for interpreting an event, the appeal to testimony revealed how a particular practice grew out of a particular theology — Bonhoeffer's own intensely reasoned reflections. Bonhoeffer's example showed students how Christians might live their faith deeply in response to and engagement with the dominant culture. It showed how a culturally embedded theology played out in concrete events and relationships through a particular, related practice. This approach fit with the course's established goal of addressing Christian ideals in historical context.

At the end of a year, my application of spiritual practices had led to some restructuring of the course. The afternoon session in particular now included overt references to particular practices as means for explicating the subject of the week. Because I had to use part of each session to teach the practice of the day, the session also provided students a chance to ex-

---

13. *Dietrich Bonhoeffer: Memories and Perspectives*, directed by Bain Boehlke (Minneapolis: Trinity Films, ca. 1983), VHS.

plore the character and significance of, for example, community-building and discernment. Along the way I had discovered that certain practices like testimony allowed insights into particular historical theologies and their cultural contexts. It was thus with some confidence that I began consultations with colleagues about their own applications of spiritual practices.

I soon recognized that I had been more or less simply *talking about* practices. My students did not yet have a specific practice that they could learn course material *through*. Perhaps my enthusiasm during the latest phase of the project had blinded me to the omission. Despite good student responses regarding the afternoon sessions (below), my failure to select a single practice by which I might imaginatively structure assignments or set the trajectory of the course had limited my engagement with students about moral and spiritual concerns.

Year Two: Making the Practice of Community-Building Central

After this realization, I felt a need to find a practice to fill the omission. But such an after-the-fact attempt seemed an artificial add-on. To some extent I had felt this way at times about the entire attempt to draw on spiritual practices. I imagined that the application of practices to core courses like Western Civilization would often seem artificial because such courses have a received quality about them. They seem delimited by disciplinary perspectives, a narrow repertoire of classroom approaches, the core curriculum, or other factors to such an extent that any appeals to practices or to moral/spiritual formation would always seem separate endeavors.

One of the chief arguments for overt considerations of moral and spiritual matters in college classrooms, however, is the fact that all aspects of campus life necessarily point toward *some* assumptions — perhaps inchoate or conventional — about human identity, ideals of human flourishing, and models of beneficial social relations, even when these assumptions remain unstated or unacknowledged. The received quality of any course is natural and a matter of degree. The application of spiritual practices may always seem somewhat after-the-fact, but that reality points to the effort needed to match practices to the moral/spiritual order already present in the course, not the impossibility of such a match. The first step must therefore be to determine the best fit between the course's features and goals and a range of spiritual practices. What practices are already within the course *in embryo*?

169

Because "Civ." already had a long-standing, strong emphasis on *community*, I began to explore how a focus on the practice of *community-building* might affect the course. Larry Rasmussen writes,

> The shaping of communities is the [Christian] practice by which we agree to be reliable personally and organizationally. This practice takes on life through roles and rituals, laws and agreements — indeed, through the whole assortment of shared commitments and institutional arrangements that order common life. In one sense, then, shaping communities is not just a single practice of its own. It is the practice that provides the choreography for all the other practices of a community or society.[14]

Rasmussen also lists eight qualities common to the church community when it properly lives out the radical character of the gospel:

- A sense of divine power as the power for peoplehood
- A basic equality that dignifies the varied gifts of varied members
- Forms of address that tend more toward "brother" and "sister" than titles
- A sharing of resources with a view to need
- An effort to cross social boundaries for a more inclusive community
- An uneasy relationship to every dominant order, every "Caesar" .
- An empowerment of all members, either as laity or within a new religious order
- A conviction that somehow all this is good news and a vanguard example for the wider world[15]

Given the character of the classroom as a temporary collection of learners with different needs and abilities, not all of these features would

---

14. Larry Rasmussen, "Shaping Communities," in *Practicing Our Faith: A Way of Life for a Searching People,* ed. Dorothy C. Bass (San Francisco: Jossey-Bass, 1997), p. 120. The literature on community, Christian and otherwise, is voluminous, as is that on the role of community in spiritual formation. For the modern era, the classic starting place is Dietrich Bonhoeffer, *Life Together and Prayerbook of the Bible,* ed. Geffrey B. Kelly and trans. Daniel W. Bloesch, vol. 5, *Dietrich Bonhoeffer Works* (Minneapolis: Fortress Press, 2004). Another treatment of the subject as Christian practice is Jonathan Wilson-Hartgrove, "Living as Community," in *On Our Way: Christian Practices for Living a Whole Life,* ed. Dorothy C. Bass and Susan R. Briehl (Nashville: Upper Room Books, 2010), pp. 53-70. Wilson-Hartgrove's chapter represents community from the perspective of the "new monasticism."

15. Rasmussen, "Shaping Communities," p. 128.

be appropriate to emphasize. But the classroom definitely involves "shared commitments and institutional arrangements that order common life." Both within individual sections and across them, "Civ." already promotes a sense of community based on the valuing of gifts and the empowering of students. And the attempt to draw on multiple practices fits with an emphasis on community as "choreographer."

In the summer of 2009 I approached my fall teaching partner and explained my project. We were going to try systematically to build student learning communities in light of this spiritual practice. The effort was largely a modification of previous approaches. This time the students would generate their own covenant in a beginning-of-school activity designed to demonstrate an emphasis on group work. In place of the framing narratives and in-class text readings, out-of-class group assignments would use questions to highlight an important general theme for each unit — for example, the recurring significance of humanism from the Renaissance to Milton's *Paradise Lost*. With limited success I had tried an online assignment during the spring semester for those students who could not attend afternoon sessions. My colleague and I decided to enhance the online activity. We would split responsibilities: I would use the afternoon sessions to focus on spiritual practices, and she would manage a class blog revised to parallel the session work.

In addition to the daily routine of meeting, the out-of-class group assignments and the afternoon sessions were the chief contributors toward a sense of community. In the fall of 2009 we allowed the out-of-class groups of four or five to self-select. This approach hurt performance, since groups tended to contain students of like ability, and some groups became dysfunctional (there were late or incomplete assignments, tensions among members). In the spring of 2010 we dictated groups based upon current GPA, including students of high, average, and low ability in each group. This change proved successful (see below). We realized early on during the fall that group discussions benefited from our distributing very specific questions. In the spring semester we made a special effort to create a set of questions that built week to week on themes emphasized throughout the unit. I developed afternoon session topics to cohere with unit themes as well. Before the spring 2010 course I was able to prepare a chart outlining themes, group topics, and emphases for each afternoon session.

The afternoon sessions in 2009-10 ran much more smoothly than in the previous year. The sessions were mainly times for discussion, with some brief group exercises or film viewings. Often I would introduce a spiritual practice in its "secular" form (e.g., "What is community in general?") and then ask about specifically Christian aspects of the practice (e.g., "What does the Bible say about 'community'?"). Once we had identified these, I would direct our discussions toward some topic of the week (e.g., early nineteenth-century nationalism), then explore any insights that the Christian aspects of the practice might suggest for the topic (e.g., "Did early nationalism have any of the characteristics of Christian community that we saw in the Bible?"). The sessions resorted less and less to simple review.

With this improved use of principles drawn from spiritual practices to analyze subject matter, I began to feel relief that all along the afternoon sessions had actually provided a means for building community and for embodying other practices. The regular directness of exchanges built a high level of trust that in turn supported intense reflection, with a level of self-revelation unusual for a classroom.[16] The discussions often became a chance to think about spiritual life and individual identity in relation to spiritual practice, the virtues that the practice encouraged, and historical and aesthetic contexts. The sessions strengthened the existing sense of community. We talked about discernment, then tried to practice it. We saw how Bonhoeffer's testimony fit in its historical and theological contexts, then practiced with our own testimonies. As Rasmussen suggests, an emphasis on community-building — even in the temporary community of the classroom — can choreograph and provide a context for the exploration of the other practices.

I have continued after the 2009-10 academic year to depend upon the afternoon sessions, but with refinements. In particular, I have tried to reinforce the idea of community as a framework for considering the other practices. Inspired by ancient Egyptian monastic usage, I now call the afternoon gatherings "afternoon conference."[17] A seminar on the Christian tradition of the seven capital vices ("deadly sins") introduced me to spiritual conference among the monks, and the similar goal of personal formation led me to co-opt the name. That seminar also suggested the need to

---

16. In a session drawing on the spiritual practice of forgiveness to discuss decolonization and the American civil rights movement, one student revealed her struggles with sexual abuse, another with an eating disorder. While I allow such disclosures as a way of clarifying an idea ("What is forgiveness?"), I do not promote them. The goals of the session require the discussion to move on and relate such personal experiences to external concerns (e.g., "What kinds of forgiveness might better race relations?").

17. Cf. John Cassian, *Conferences*, Ancient Christian Writers Series 57 (Mahwah, N.J.: Paulist Press, 1997).

augment my consideration of specific virtues and vices associated with particular practices. In addition to regular emphasis during the hour, I hope to encourage students to synthesize Christian practice, consideration of virtues and vices, and specific subject material with group exercises, such as one asking students to compare and contrast Aquinas's understanding of the vice of discord with Tocqueville's account of individualism, and also the kinds of well-functioning social relations that the two men suggest. Finally, I have begun to enrich and expedite discussions about spiritual practices by using slide presentations in afternoon conference. An introductory presentation introduces definitions of practices and a list of almost twenty, with particular emphasis on hospitality, testimony, discernment, community-building, healing, study, and friendship — the seven that I think students might be able actually to exercise during the hour-long conference. They are certainly seven practices essential in a classroom successfully engaged with moral and spiritual concerns.

What Was Gained?

An assessment of these efforts needs to address three questions:

- Did the three emphases in the afternoon sessions — instruction in practices, practices as interpretative tools, and the "lived theologies" behind practices — contribute to both the learning of subject matter and the exploration of moral and spiritual concerns?
- Did the attempts to privilege the practice of community-building benefit student learning and help engagement with moral and spiritual concerns?
- Did an emphasis on spiritual practices lead in general to "a moral and spiritual person teaching moral and spiritual beings in moral and spiritual ways"?

Regarding question one, two surveys showed nearly unanimous affirmation of the afternoon sessions:

	Benefited from afternoon sessions?	Benefited from online forums?
Spring 2009	y = 19, n = 0	y = 8, n = 4
Fall 2009	y = 34, n = 3	y = 11, n = 13

Comments suggest that students especially valued the extra time and safe space that the sessions provided for exploring the relationships of subject matter to personal spiritual life:

> Yes! I actually enjoyed [the afternoon sessions] more than the class itself! It was easy to state your opinion because in class I often felt confused and I didn't always understand, but I enjoyed the afternoon sessions because I could give my opinion and talk about things that related to what I knew or how I felt about a certain topic! I really liked involving my spirituality in the topics as well!

> I feel as though I have learned so much about principles and values that I will carry with me through the afternoon sessions. Yes, they were absolutely beneficial. I enjoyed the ideas behind the literature that we discussed. I feel like I had a better understanding of the overall experience of people during different time periods. . . .

Some students also seemed to understand and appreciate the appeal to spiritual practices as means of interpretation, in particular as a bridge between study and real-life application of the humanities. When asked one semester whether they recognized themes or approaches in the afternoon sessions, fifteen students out of seventeen acknowledged that they did. Two students commented:

> Real life application! You encouraged us to think about how the history and literature related to our lives. You challenged us with questions that forced me to think and reevaluate myself. It was neat to see how the topics discussed in the afternoon session seemed to encourage everyone in the group to share their perspective.

> Yes — they're not so much a recollection of knowledge or a test of any sort, just a way to apply the history we've learned practically and grab the themes from it rather than monotonously recalling facts and information.

These responses suggest that the treatment of "lived theologies" behind practices had less effect than the other two emphases, perhaps because the Bonhoeffer example is still the only one adequately developed. The responses also point to some success for the emphasis on community-building (question two). Similarly, students by far preferred weekly out-of-class group meetings over regular quizzes:

	Benefited from weekly group meetings and reports?	Would prefer regular quizzes to group reports?
Fall 2009	y = 42, n = 7	y = 4, n = 45
Spring 2010	y = 24, n = 4	N/A

One student's comments from spring 2010 suggest some of the sentiments behind these numbers:

> I have found [out-of-class group work] very beneficial. I have built relationships with people that I guarantee I would have never tried to cultivate without the group work outside of class. The groups give a sense of community to the class.

As for question three, "Did an emphasis on spiritual practices lead in general to 'a moral and spiritual person teaching moral and spiritual beings in moral and spiritual ways'?" I would answer yes. Certainly I have benefited from the regular, consistent emphasis on practices, their accompanying virtues, and the constant need to re-educate my desires. The survey data suggest that the students felt themselves moral and spiritual beings throughout the course, and that they often learned the subject matter with moral and spiritual ways in mind.

Christian Smith's recent empirical study of spirituality among young adults resonates with these conclusions. Smith identifies several "theoretical mechanisms" that contribute to a high level of religiosity: socialization through both "formal teaching and informal modeling," the maintenance of relationships, the reinforcement of beliefs about what is good and true, habituation, the maintenance of a sense of identity, and a strong commitment to a belief system.[18] This list closely matches the classroom application of spiritual practices described above. The emphasis on community in both the group activities and the afternoon sessions promotes socialization and relationships. The use of practice-inspired principles to analyze subject matter allows exploration of beliefs and identities in ways tied directly to the Christian tradition, at the same time promoting virtuous habits associated with particular practices. Smith's study also cites various measures to conclude that religiously devoted young people live noticeably healthier and more productive lives than the less devoted.[19] Such results do

---

18. Christian Smith, *Souls in Transition: The Religious and Spiritual Lives of Emerging Adults* (New York: Oxford University Press, 2009), p. 241.

19. Smith, *Souls in Transition*, pp. 257-78. Measures include quality of parental rela-

not count as God's full shalom, but they point in that direction and suggest the goal behind the application of spiritual practices to teaching: the reinforcement of interrelated cognitive, emotional, and spiritual qualities in young adults as a means to personal and communal formation to the fullest — in other words, the reordering of students' loves so that they truly desire God's kingdom.[20]

---

tions, giving and volunteering behaviors, moral orientation, risk behaviors, mental health, attitudes regarding consumption, and character of sexual relations.

20. Cf. Smith, *Desiring the Kingdom*, pp. 215-30.

Thrill Rides and Labyrinths:
The Pedagogical Logic of Freedom and Constraint

Matthew Walhout

The broad aim of this book is to link the logic of Christian practices with the logic of classroom teaching. In this chapter I will examine some connections that might be made even in the science classroom, particularly in science courses that serve as cognates within pre-professional programs. I'll do so in three parts. First, to start with a vivid example of "logic-linking," I will describe a teaching strategy popular among teachers of introductory physics. The strategy is to situate physics within the broader context of an amusement park and to motivate students by way of their extra-scientific interest in thrill rides. I will point out analogies between the physical constraints and freedoms that make a ride thrilling (as opposed to terrifying) and the contextual constraints that this teaching strategy employs. In the second section, I will build on the contextual discussion of constraints and freedoms and state explicitly what I find to be the most salient differences between Christian and secularized, public education. Third, I will describe my own attempt to situate two physics courses within a framework of Christian goals and aspirations, specifically those of aspiring pre-service teachers and health-science majors. I have used the guiding metaphor of a prayer labyrinth to re-narrate the traditional aims of these courses and to invite students to reflect contemplatively on their work and learning.

Dynamics of a Thrill Ride

Students in introductory physics courses have started to take the tools of learning into their own hands. Their teachers send them off into the world with handheld microprocessor devices that can record and display data from built-in accelerometers, barometers, and other instruments. One of the most popular destinations is the amusement park, where students can experience the physical and psychological thrills offered by rides that rotate, spin, fall, turn, bounce, and undulate, while the instruments they carry keep track of the numbers and graphs that represent these motions.[1] In this way, students feel the world's effects on them before they take account of their experiences retrospectively in a mathematically analytical mode.

A physics teacher in this situation aims to have students understand the concepts of velocity, force, and acceleration, as well as Newton's principles of motion, which formalize the relationships between these concepts. For the purposes of this chapter, I will skip the formal details and focus on ideas that, while fitting into the Newtonian framework, also provide a vocabulary that can be extended beyond the strictly mechanical arena through the use of analogy. My intention here is to examine the physical constraints that make a ride such as a roller coaster possible. What goes into the ride's construction and operation that allows the rider to get a taste of danger while maintaining an ultimate sense of security? How does one design a "thrill" or induce that satisfying kind of fear that is never quite raised to the level of mortal dread? I will suggest that an important part of the design is to be found in the set of physical constraints that is employed.

Roller-coaster enthusiasts know the fun challenge of making it through an entire trip with both hands raised above the head. The possibility of a hands-free trip — in which one can overcome the felt need to hang on for dear life — is one consideration in the design of an enjoyable ride. The designer has to set up a fine balance between forces that will surprise and unsettle a rider and constraints that will ensure safety. The unsettling forces usually come from carefully shaped tracks as well as springs and pivots that allow the rider's car to jostle or spin in unpredictable ways. These same elements are also responsible for providing safety. The wheels on a car are designed so they cannot let go of the track; the chassis springs and pivots are designed to prevent damage to the car or the rider. But of course, the most obvious protective constraint is the restraining bar or seatbelt. This harness system is fully dedicated to security; it should generate no surprises! By securing the rider snugly inside the car, the safety restraint provides the most direct source of emotional reassurance. It does the hanging-on work, so the rider doesn't have to.

---

1. Science educators can find curricular ideas in books such as Nathan Unterman, *Amusement Park Physics: A Teacher's Guide* (Portland, Me.: J. Weston Walch, Publisher, 2001).

We can think of the seatbelt as an "internal constraint," since it is inside the car and within the rider's immediate field of awareness. By constrast, the tracks, wheels, and chassis mechanisms can be thought of as "external constraints." The rider cannot see, touch, or control them and does not normally give them much conscious thought. Although both kinds of constraint provide safety, the internal ones add assurance while the external ones create the possibility that a rider will encounter jarring surprises and thrills. Putting it this way suggests that designers can configure constraints in particular ways in order to accomplish a tradeoff between different types of freedoms. Without a seatbelt, a rider would have the freedom of unconstrained motion inside the car — a kind of rattling motion that might lead to injury and ejection. But with a seatbelt, the rider is freed from feelings of mortal dread and free to enjoy the excitement that comes with new and unexpected encounters.

All of this exemplifies the way in which freedom rests upon constraint. Ironic as it may seem, real freedoms are always limited freedoms selected from specific, often mutually exclusive, types. It takes a framework of external constraints (tracks, gravity, wheels, springs) to define the types of freedom that are possible, and the preference for one freedom over another within that framework is met through additional, internal constraints (safety harnesses or seatbelts). The important point is that establishing a particular kind of freedom requires setting up certain internal constraints within a broader context of external constraints.

Once we recognize that different forms of freedom emerge within different configurations of constraints, we might be led to ask which forms of freedom we want. This is a question about motivation, and it gets at the character and the ultimate concern of the people entering into the framework. In the case of fun-loving teenagers at an amusement park, the motivation seems clear: they want to have as much fun with their friends as possible! For these students, the demand for fun might function as an external constraint on what a physics course can accomplish — fun may be the *sine qua non* of their emotional and intellectual investment. The physics teacher can acknowledge and build upon this motivation in order to accomplish other goods of science education. She hopes that the students have their fun *and* learn something about physics through the experience. Moreover, these wishes are nested within the teacher's overarching desire to help the students develop into good, healthy people who can contribute to societal well-being. The contextual motivation that she brings to the amusement park is broader than the typical student motivation. The fun that students might regard as an external constraint is, for the teacher, a potential internal constraint of the course. She can use it pragmatically as she designs the kind of learning experience that the students settle into — an experience that might be made more thrilling or more dreadful by the choices that she makes.

Once the teacher adopts a pragmatic strategy that engages students' extra-curricular interests, she is faced with the moral question of (to put it starkly) where to lead students once they have taken the bait. What was the point of getting them hooked in the first place? This ultimately bears on the question of what it means to teach, or what teaching *is* and what teachers *are for.* Any attempt to answer such questions will reveal ways in which the teacher's specific classroom strategy is itself nested within a complicated framework of priorities and concerns, such as the standards of public education, the shared values of a local school system, the division of labor within a specific school, and the diverse personal commitments of teacher and students. Whatever the teacher does, it seems she must choose a path that allows her to negotiate the entangled network of expectations. Somehow she must find her way from the complex external world into the internal world of the classroom, and somehow the external world must allow her to make sense of the internal one. Moreover, her way of moving between the two worlds will define the path by which students will follow her lead. Her students will learn her way of operating, her way of prioritizing, her way of valuing. They will find themselves in her framework and will have to contend with its particular structure of internal and external constraints — not physical constraints like springs or walls, but axiological constraints that define their classroom experience and shape their conception of its aims.

I have introduced the term *pragmatic* to describe pedagogical decisions and actions that are taken in order to help students flourish. The pragmatic teacher elects to use certain tools and methodologies because they can be put in service of her vision for students. And here I mean a long-term vision that guides the teacher's understanding of what kinds of people her students can (and perhaps should) be, a vision that is deeply connected with her conceptions of human purpose and human nature. The pragmatist is purpose-driven, defining the end goal or *telos* of her work not simply in terms of testing rubrics, institutional standards, and disciplinary content, but in terms of the possible human outcomes that rubrics, standards, and content might serve.

This way of putting things may provide some justification for pragmatic teaching strategies, but it also points to a teacher's responsibility to do more than lure students into a particular area of study or to "make learning fun." No doubt, the thrill of roller coasters may be a legitimate way of leading students into the world of the physics classroom, but what happens when the thrill wears off and the hard work of analysis begins? At this point the teacher must appeal to additional motivations that can sustain interest in the course. If she fails to do so, the students may sense that they have fallen prey to a bait-and-switch pedagogy. They may think they have been taken for a ride. Perhaps most importantly, they are likely to lose faith in the person they perceive as having led them along a bread-crumb trail of immediate thrills into a thick and threatening forest. If this risk of losing faith is a serious concern for the teacher, then her interest in students' axiological frameworks will motivate her to do more than dress up the course to make it attractive when seen from the outside. She will be as concerned with leading students through (and out of) the course as she is with leading them into it.

Models of Pedagogical Interaction

I am portraying the classroom as an axiological nexus, where the teacher's broadest conceptions of human flourishing mingle with and give shape to those of her students. But, one might object, won't this characterization put the teacher in a difficult moral bind? Haven't I painted her into a corner? How can she bring her own axiological structures to bear on students without running afoul of rules forbidding coercion, entrapment, or indoctrination? This gets at a legitimate concern, and my response is twofold. First, people risk breaking these rules whenever they interact with each other; such are the dynamics of power in any social context. Teachers do indeed take on moral responsibilities in their jobs. As I see them, these responsibilities are neither avoidable nor impossible to fulfill. Second, I suspect that at the secondary and post-secondary levels, teachers can take preventive measures against charges of indoctrination by engaging students' capacities to think critically about frameworks. A teacher can openly admit that she has a certain way of seeing the world and that it affects the method and content of her teaching. She may even make a habit of pointing out how and when her personal perspective is playing an active role in the course. As she does this, she can also state explicitly that she intends only to invite students to understand her perspective and not to indoctrinate them into it. The goal is not to have students accept her axiological framework as normative but to make them aware of what her framework is and how it shapes her teaching practices. By having this element of open "pedagogical confession" in her repertoire, a teacher can exercise full and open disclosure and thereby build a degree of trust that would not exist if the pedagogical framework were not made explicit.

Of course, even if teachers accept this last suggestion, there is still the question of which freedoms, constraints, and classroom practices they will choose based on their axiological frameworks. This question can be answered in many different ways, and to suggest the range of possibilities, I want to examine three pedagogical models that represent alternative approaches to the issue of axiology. I will call them the Secular-Divisionist model, the Hermeneutic-Mediator model, and the Christian-Pragmatist model. This list is meant to be illustrative, not exhaustive, of the models that might be identified.

The Secular-Divisionist framework regards students as rugged individualists who tote their axiological baggage in and out of class without unpacking it. Integrating course content with an individual's system of values is left as a take-home exercise. This *laissez-faire* approach seems to dominate public education today and is consistent with a broader individualism in modern culture. As philosopher Charles Taylor has described it, the trend is to imagine each human being as an "atomistic self" with its own private interests and motivations, which are meant to be served by social and political structures.[2] Supported by a consumer-based economy that can serve self-interest very efficiently, this mind-set has come to regard a great number of human interactions — even education — as cash-and-carry propositions. Teachers have become vendors of a commodity; those vendors who ask questions or offer guidance during the transaction run the risk of crossing into axiological territory where they are thought not to belong.

I take Stanley Fish's recent book, *Save the World on Your Own Time,*[3] to be an example of Secular Divisionism. The book is a meandering tirade against faculty who think that the right to free speech entitles them to advocate in the classroom for political causes. While there is a legitimate ba-

---

2. Charles Taylor, *Sources of the Self: The Making of the Modern Identity* (Cambridge: Harvard University Press, 1989); Charles Taylor, *A Secular Age* (Cambridge: Harvard University Press, 2007).

3. Stanley Fish, *Save the World on Your Own Time* (New York: Oxford University Press, 2008).

sis for critique here, Fish overreaches when he suggests that teachers are hired *only* to convey the knowledge and analytic skills of their disciplines and *not* to engage any external motivations that technical competencies might serve. In maintaining a strongly secularized conception of the university, Fish makes "character formation" an extra-curricular activity that should not be a topic of classroom discussion under any circumstances. The kind of pedagogical confession that I have recommended is ruled out of bounds. So, by adopting the Secular-Divisionist framework, Fish excludes a strategy that could help to guard against the kind of indoctrination he opposes.[4]

One alternative to Fish's framework can be identified in writings of the late Martin Eger, a scientist-turned-philosopher who was concerned with the roles and perceptions of science within a broad cultural context, particularly within education. Eger's essays, published recently in a book titled *Science, Understanding, and Justice*,[5] seem to fit what I am calling the Hermeneutic-Mediator framework. The ultimate concern of education for the Hermeneutic Mediator is this: that mutual acknowledgment and reasoning become possible between people who have different self-understandings, or who, in other words, recognize different configurations of interests and constraints in their lives. An important part of the Hermeneutic Mediator's teaching repertoire involves open discussion of the various motivations and perspectives that teachers and students bring into the classroom. Eger encouraged science educators to adopt this approach, so that students learn to appreciate the interpretive, philosophical, or hermeneutical side of science as well as the applied, technological, or instrumental side.[6] This balanced appreciation can be threatened, he thought, when standard curricula are adopted solely on the basis of scientific educational research. Such research tends to focus on technological skills and to produce prescriptions for character-formation curricula that are unconnected to the axiological structures of many students and their communities. Eger suggests that unreflective adoption of research-based curricula might tend to turn teachers into technicians and schools into factories of externally defined societal goods.

---

4. If he were to teach a course based on his own book, and if he were to approach the indoctrination issue as I have suggested, he would have to acknowledge the ways in which his teaching reflects his own axiological views.

5. Martin Eger, *Science, Understanding, and Justice: The Philosophical Essays of Martin Eger*, ed. Abner Shimony (Chicago: Open Court, 2006).

6. For a historical overview of the two-sided conception of science, see Peter Dear, *The Intelligibility of Nature* (Chicago: University of Chicago Press, 2006).

Education itself might become an instrumental science, running roughshod over the concerns of traditions, families, and communities. In Eger's own words, "Science in a high school or college classroom is *science outside its own institutional boundaries:* It is not at all clear in this situation whether the interest and inner logic of a particular science, or the interest of education (or some condominium of the two) should dominate."[7]

Eger attempted to balance the two sides of science (the technological and the philosophical) by requiring that educators become sensitive to the historical and hermeneutical concerns that standardized curricula have tended to ignore. Science teachers should be concerned with engaging a full range of human interests and values and should take contextualization seriously. This does not mean simply that real-world engineering problems and social controversies should get "covered" in class, in the sense of their being touched upon, mentioned, or described by a teacher delivering some expertly packaged content. Rather, Eger urged that a pluralism of human concerns be brought to bear in the recognition and definition of such problems *as* problems.[8] Axiological matters have to be put on the table and discussed with openness and charity, even in the science classroom. Eger therefore saw promise in what he called "a new ecology of education" and proposed that the focus of teacher education should be shifted

> from the teacher as a means of transmitting prepackaged curricula, as a trainer of puzzle solvers for the science-system, to the teacher as carrying out primarily the hermeneutic-communicative action of science. In so doing, [the teacher] does not neglect the other interests, but puts them in perspective. Above all, the teacher must *embody* that perspective.[9]

This brings me to my third and final pedagogical model, befitting someone I will call a Christian Pragmatist. It is the model with which I have experimented, as will be described below. The Christian Pragmatist has a lot in common with the Hermeneutic Mediator. Like him, she rejects the anti-historical, anti-hermeneutical individualism behind *laissez-faire* peda-

---

7. Eger, "Rationality of Science and Social Controversy," Chapter 22 in *Science, Understanding, and Justice,* p. 313.

8. Eger, "The New Epic of Science and the Problem of Communication," Chapter 20 in *Science, Understanding, and Justice,* pp. 281-94.

9. Eger, "The 'Interests' of Science and the Problems of Education," Chapter 16 in *Science, Understanding, and Justice,* p. 230.

gogy. However, she does not face the mediator's daunting task of attending to an irreducible plurality of external student interests. Instead, she aims to make the internal-external connections only within the single, overarching narrative of the Christian gospel. For the most part, she can assume that her students share her basic understanding of this narrative and that they see themselves as having a role to play in it. Their common story provides the *lingua franca* of the classroom, a way of speaking about the gift of grace and God's call to share the love revealed in Christ. It allows them to put disciplinary academic studies into a single context of ultimate concern. Commitment to a Christian *telos* inspires open reflection on the setting of priorities and the refining of personal motivations. Such reflection, or axiological ordering, is a pragmatic exercise; it is undertaken as a means toward an end, the end of Christian faithfulness. This agenda fits best within Christian schools, which are institutions constructed in order to further it. I would even suggest that a teacher should act as a Christian Pragmatist if and only if she is employed at such a school. For here and only here have the appropriate freedoms and constraints been put into place.

When students and teachers reflect together upon a shared interest in Christian axiological ordering, they can hope to find links between internal course material and the broader concerns of faithful living. This activity may function as do other reflective practices that are long-standing traditions in the church, such as confession and *examen* prayer. It may also build mutual trust between the participants and thereby establish an important set of freedoms and constraints internal to the course — just as the seatbelt on a roller coaster establishes the possibility of an enjoyable, hands-free ride. In terms used by Etienne Wenger, attentiveness to axiological ordering qualifies as part of the repertoire of a community of practice: "The repertoire of a community of practice . . . includes the discourse by which members create meaningful statements about the world, as well as the styles by which they express their forms of membership and their identities as members."[10] The repertoire in this case belongs to a learning community, and it is a critical resource for what Wenger calls the educational imagination, through which the community orients itself in the world, forms an identity, reflects on its situation, and creatively explores its possibilities.[11]

10. Etienne Wenger, *Communities of Practice: Learning, Meaning, and Identity* (New York: Cambridge University Press, 1998), p. 83.
11. Wenger, *Communities of Practice*, pp. 272-73.

The Christian Pragmatist and her students share to some degree an educational imagination and an associated repertoire; they inherit these from the Christian church. This commonality allows classroom discussions and activities to differ from what they would be in a Secular Divisionist's classroom or a Hermeneutic Mediator's classroom. Values, virtues, and other axiological concerns are neither held at bay nor merely engaged as a matter of mutual respect between individuals. Rather, they function as common motivations for everyone's participation in the course (students and teacher). The meanings and implications of the gospel are supposed to be felt and acknowledged in all the freedoms and constraints that serve Christian learning. In this framework, Christian teaching should not be simply a matter of injecting Christian faith into standard course content or teaching Christian perspectives alongside secular disciplines. That approach would be too accepting of the predominant secular model of education, and it would constrain the reach of the gospel in order to let disciplines be what they would be in the gospel's absence. When the Christian Pragmatist's imagination takes hold of the academic disciplines, they all become part of a grand narrative about a world that belongs to God, and the internal concerns of coursework become nested within the broader concern for faithful living.

This is not to say that the Christian Pragmatist's course is heavily scripted. Just as there are lots of ways to design an amusement park ride in order to produce thrills and serve the goal of fun and enjoyment, there are lots of ways to design classroom activities in order to serve the goal of Christian faithfulness. This book explores several possibilities, each with its own connection to traditional Christian practices. Such connections help configure various pedagogical constraints in such a way that the logic of traditional practices enters into the logic of an educational setting. Even though a Christian practice may have to be altered or adapted to fit the context of an academic course, the adaptation can still serve the same axiological function that the original practice served in its original context. The Christian Pragmatist has considerable freedom to judge which practices might fit a particular educational context and to decide how each practice might be implemented. In the final section of this chapter, I will describe my own pedagogical adaptation of the Christian contemplative device known as a prayer labyrinth.

Labyrinthine Courses

The metaphor of a journey is embedded within much discussion of either formal education or forms of Christian piety. An academic "course" is a path taken for learning; to take a "pilgrimage" is to travel to a place that has religious significance. Through these everyday allusions to specific, directed actions in space and time, we portray ourselves as travelers setting out on the walk or journey of life. We all know what it means to travel from here to there, and this meaning is part of our linguistic repertoire. When life becomes difficult to understand or to endure, it is natural to speak of confusion, exhaustion, or fear in terms of a meandering or tortuous path. Such a path — perhaps such a life — may in fact lie before us, and there might be no alternate route.

As a teacher of physics, I have seen students tire and stumble in their educational pursuits. Many have had to deal with only minor bumps and obstacles, but on occasion some have lagged so far behind that catching up has seemed impossible. Nevertheless, most students have needed passing grades in order to proceed along their chosen career paths. School is a real-life concern for such students, and I want to offer them all possible encouragement and guidance along the way. Since I work at a Christian college, I feel justified in assuming the role of Christian Pragmatist and offering the kinds of support that are found in the traditions of the church. Practices associated with the Christian prayer labyrinth seem to be a fitting resource.

For centuries, the prayer labyrinth has served as an emblematic representation of the journey of faith and has provided a physical template for "active contemplation" of life's predicaments. The labyrinth's single, winding path connects an outer perimeter with a central region, so that a walker's motion is first inward and then outward. The double movement recollects the death and resurrection signified in baptism and is intended to aid the transformation and renewal of persons. Labyrinth walks are also understood as small-scale re-enactments of pilgrimages to holy places. They proceed at a slow, contemplative pace and involve frequent stops for prayerful dedication of oneself to the Lord. As part of the repertoire of Christian practices, then, the labyrinth is a symbolic or metaphorical adaptation of other practices. I have attempted to take this adaptation one step further by inviting Christian students to engage in the traditional logic and function of prayer labyrinths as a way to sustain their strength, focus, and motivation for learning physics.

My pedagogical experiment took place in two courses that dealt with similar scientific ideas but served different audiences. One was populated by pre-service elementary school teachers, the other by students majoring in health sciences, including speech pathology and physical therapy. In each course we met three times per week for two hours at a time (there were fourteen weeks in the semester). The extended meeting time allowed us to move freely between lab work and lecture or discussion. In their lab activities, the students followed a workbook that I had written to facilitate a hands-on, inquiry-based approach to concept development. They were seated around tables in groups of three or four, and each group worked at its own pace, setting up experiments, fixing problems, and responding to the questions I had posed. As they did this, I circulated around the classroom and listened in on the discussions of each group. I was thereby able to observe each group's activities, detect individual difficulties, and offer strategic advice and encouragement. It was in this interactive, peer-oriented environment that I tried using the prayer labyrinth as a teaching tool.

The course workbook had a large diagram of the Chartres Cathedral's labyrinth on its cover. After I handed a workbook to each student on the first day of class, we took note of the labyrinth's structure and discussed traditional uses of prayer labyrinths. I suggested that, in lieu of walking a "real" labyrinth, the students might use their fingers or pencils to trace through the path pictured on their book covers. I then asked, "How could this exercise be an aid to your learning in this course?" Most students saw no point in it. I even sensed that some thought my suggestion silly or childish. Nevertheless, I asked them all to consider my reasons for finding pragmatic value in the labyrinth metaphor. This introductory discussion was a first step in building trust with these students, most of whom eventually became willing to engage with the labyrinth theme to some degree or another.

I required all students to turn in daily journals describing their learning experiences. They had to reflect on the activities and ideas developed in class, and they were invited both to ask physics-related questions and to compare their academic journey to a walk in a prayer labyrinth. Were they unsure whether they would find their way through the course material? Did they feel like they were running into walls or hitting too many sharp turns? Were they unable to see how physics was at all relevant to their college major or their career goals? Were they stepping along an unfamiliar path with no goal or payoff in sight, but still able to put hope and trust in the structure of the course? Could they conceive of this structure, this course, the curriculum for their major, and these very college years as God's way of guiding them and transforming them? As these questions suggest, I attempted to let the metaphor of the prayer labyrinth operate at different levels. The course itself could be thought of as a small-scale labyrinth, with its own twists and turns and difficult stretches. Or, on a larger scale, it could be seen as just a single step in the labyrinthine journey by which a young student grows into adulthood and follows a vocational path. In stating an expectation that journal entries might address these different levels, I intended to encourage students to draw upon, exercise, and expand our shared imagination.

The course-as-labyrinth analogy captured our imaginations in several ways throughout the semester. Some students made study guides out of the printed labyrinth image, writing key words from each day of class into the open stretches of the winding path. At the end of the semester, they were able to review the conceptual development of the course by tracing the labyrinth with their fingers. Perhaps more importantly, the labyrinth helped the class develop a way of speaking openly about attitudes, expectations, successes, and frustrations related to the course. Student journals were sprinkled with allusions to the twists and turns of the assigned work, the uphill slog of learning, the feeling of being lost, and the need to rely on others for guidance. In this last regard, students often reflected on how they had to trust me to lead them, to be patient with them, and to be familiar with the territory. This sort of journal entry was useful to me as a reminder of my pedagogical responsibility, and it prompted me to offer in-kind encouragement by way of the labyrinth metaphor. In one of the course handouts I wrote,

> When you're in the labyrinth, it is almost impossible to see precisely how all of the twists and turns will lead you to where you want to be. The point is to participate fully at each step, and then to repeat the journey often enough that the steps become familiar.

The metaphor enabled me to offer this kind of "coaching" more naturally and more frequently than I had done in any other course. Students seemed to respond more trustingly than usual when I would say, "I know this is hard and unsettling, but this one little step will get you where you need to go," or, "You don't see it now, but soon we'll be on an easy stretch." This coaching posture emerged as the most effective way to give students the freedom to explore concepts and make mistakes. They came to trust that I would not punish them, abandon them, or waste their time. Their trust in me was something to lean on, a constraint that gave them freedom. The point here is that the labyrinth was not simply a static emblem of life's journey, but was dynamically involved in shaping the teacher's and the students' abilities to communicate in qualitative and affective modes.

As part of our course repertoire, the metaphor of the labyrinth provided a resource that we used to structure our thinking. It was an important part of our "reflective infrastructure" in both interactive conversation and individual contemplation. A few students echoed the contemplative piety of traditional labyrinth-walking by tracing through their printed labyrinth images at particular times. Some did this as a preparatory exercise just before class started. At least one found it to be a useful "retreat" during class, a way to rest and refocus when mental exhaustion set in. I used the labyrinth image as a tool for reminding myself of each student who had become — at least for a semester — a very central part of my life. On the first day of class, I asked the students to enter their names in the labyrinth appearing on the cover of my copy of the course workbook. I would often take this book home with me, along with the journals submitted in class, in order to prepare for our next class meeting. I frequently began this preparation by tracing through the winding path of student names, reflecting upon the progress each one was making in class, and offering prayers for those I knew to be facing hard times. Of course, these different kinds of individual reflection had implications for the whole group. One student's preparatory reflection before class gave her an emotional steadiness that affected the tone and tenor of our lab activities and discussion. Another student's momentary, contemplative retreat enabled her to regain a capacity to concentrate on our collective work. Reflecting on individual student situations increased my thoughtfulness in preparing for class and aided my ability to respond wisely to various classroom situations. At one point during the semester, I was struck by the sense of community that the labyrinth theme had begun to instill, and I shared the following thoughts in a course handout:

> Perhaps we can use our labyrinth image to remind us not only of our individual journeys, but also of our fellow travelers. It can remind us to ask for help when we need it, and also to lend a hand when someone else is having difficulty. It can even remind us to pray for one another. Do not expect to learn physics on your own. Plan to rely upon and to help your peers as you work together on in-class activities, homework, and preparation for tests. It is worth noting that one purpose of the

prayer labyrinth in Chartres Cathedral was to symbolize the ritual pilgrimage to Chartres that many medieval Christians made. That pilgrimage was a group effort, perhaps closer to what we see in Chaucer's *The Canterbury Tales* than to what is portrayed in Bunyan's *Pilgrim's Progress.*

The commemorative role of the labyrinth at Chartres is suggestive of another function of the printed pattern on our books. There were times when our labyrinth images functioned as icons, directing our consciousness to the big picture, the ultimate concerns of Christian faith. In a way they provided a portal between the internal and the external interests of the class. I could stand beside a lab table of a group that was struggling with conceptual difficulties or interpersonal tensions and, while talking things through, point to (or sometimes just glance at) the labyrinth image on one of our books. "Can we step back and think about this in a new way?" I could ask. Such cues were, of course, manipulative to some extent, though I never detected resentment in the students. In the end, every teacher uses some form of manipulation to capture and maintain students' attention (the lure of the roller coaster is a case in point). For my own pedagogical purposes, I thought it valuable to alert students to the possibility of the big story breaking into our little classroom. Prior to the course, I had recognized that this kind of cueing might be useful, and wrote the following in one of my first-day handouts:

> Maybe you remember this scene from the movie *Pirates of the Caribbean:* The pirate Hector Barbossa confronts his prisoner with the stark reality of her predicament. A whole new dimension of the story is revealed when he steps into the moonlight and exclaims, "You best start believing in ghost stories, Miss Turner. You're in one!" The image on the front of our course booklet might not exactly reveal anything, but it can still serve to remind us that what we're doing in this physics course is part of a much bigger story. That story includes the material world of science, but it also goes far beyond that. It's the story — the good news — of the Lord Jesus Christ, and of the Holy Spirit who remains with us in the here and now. We best start remembering that we're in that story, and that even in this course we are playing the roles to which we've been called.

Duly warned, most students were ready to acknowledge the broader dimensions of their learning context. Things normally left unattended beyond the margins of awareness came to be glimpsed through the lens of the labyrinth. Though they happened only intermittently, our peripheral glimpses were evidence that an open path existed between the internal and external interests of Christian education. The supposedly rigid boundary constructed by Secular Divisionists proved to be porous, or perhaps merely imaginary. Indeed, our own educational imagination was unconstrained by it, and we never took note of having crossed it. Such was our freedom to explore. We were open to discovery, and not only discovery of a scientific sort. The following journal entry was submitted by a student who had made a habit of using labyrinth-themed metaphors to describe her struggle to maintain patience and fortitude in our course. Here she emerges with expressions of surprise as she sees a reward at the end of the curricular tunnel:

> Today's lesson came as a relief. To finally see how all that we learned related to the video we watched was an "Aha" moment of sorts. Everything fit together, and it all pointed to the big picture. In life, it is also great to have these "Aha" moments, especially when it comes to our prayer life. We pray for wisdom daily, and God grants us this prayer piece by piece even if we do not realize it. At long last, though, we finally see the big picture. The "Aha" moment comes upon us, and we stand in awe of God's graciousness and the complexity of this world and His wisdom. If we had been given all the information for electricity and generators at the beginning, we would have been overwhelmed and lost in confusion — and God's wisdom is too much to bear all at once, too. Instead, we learn tidbits everyday, and this is the best way for us to learn so that we can fully understand and not be overwhelmed.[12]

Perhaps it is appropriate that this passage does not refer explicitly to the physical structures and experiences of the labyrinth. For a labyrinth is not an end in itself but a means to an end, or a tool, and as such it rightly yields the spotlight to the central Christian themes it is supposed to reinforce — namely, prayer, patience, wisdom, and grace. Had this student not already walked through lengthy stretches of difficult scientific terrain, and had she not developed the practice of reflecting on the journey, I think she would not have become so cognizant of the virtues of simple, patient attentiveness. The fact that she could share these thoughts with me at all is an affir-

---

12. Journal entry submitted on 5 November 2008 by Calvin College student Jessica Wilcoxson. Used with permission.

mation of my attempt to cultivate trust and encourage contemplative practices through use of the labyrinth theme. As the journal entry suggests, the pedagogy of a Christian Pragmatist opens itself to reflecting on the blind corners, endurance tests, and general vagaries of life and learning. It can be seen as a labyrinthine pedagogy, following a circuitous, inward movement into disciplinary details and re-emerging into a broader arena in which those details find their ultimate importance.

Christian Practices and Technical Courses: Making Integral Connections

Kurt C. Schaefer

Introduction: "Integration" in a "Technical" Course

A number of my colleagues who teach in the traditional liberal arts are also thinking carefully about the relationships among teaching, learning, and Christian practices. In my conversations with them, the word "restoring" often comes to mind. They express the intention of engaging in practices in order to restore to their students in their professions something that has been lost or sidelined. Often the disposition or capacity being restored has been diminished as a result of the influence of modernism. A colleague in literature draws on a long history of Christian practice in charitable reading to inform his classroom's practices for approaching literature; a colleague in foreign languages draws on the tradition of Christian hospitality to strangers and foreigners to shape her students' study of foreign languages; a colleague in philosophy draws on monastic practices surrounding liturgies of the hours to breathe new life into meditative reflections on philosophical texts.

I face a different challenge. I teach courses that many would view as "technical," courses in areas for which there is virtually no pre-modern history upon which to draw. I teach a professional discipline to which others might point as a vanguard in modernism's triumph over traditional, good practices.[1] I teach econometrics in an economics program, a sub-

---

1. This criticism has come in several flavors, from both within and without the discipline. Alasdair MacIntyre provides the classic current account of modernism's tendency to erode practices and virtues (*After Virtue: A Study in Moral Theory*, 3rd ed. [Notre Dame: University of Notre Dame Press, 2007]). For the work of practicing economists that explic-

discipline that emerged after the mid-twentieth century and quickly rose to dominate practice in the profession,[2] a profession which itself only emerged as distinct from philosophy in the middle of the prior century.[3]

If you've ever wondered how economists make forecasts about the economy, or how they anticipate the effects and costs of policy proposals, or how they can claim to know what would have happened if a particular thing had *not* happened, the answer usually is that some econometricians have been at work modeling the situation, then collecting and analyzing some relevant data, then reporting on the results. The discipline of econometrics is a combination of economic theory, data handling, statistics, and computer programming. Virtually everything in these fields — and in many other fields beyond econometrics — emerged during the modern era, and emerged without any obvious connection to traditional Christian practices. To many people, these disciplines would appear to be "technical" in the most literal sense: their courses seem to be about learning mere technique, technique that is done correctly or incorrectly, not virtuously or

---

itly ties this general tendency of modernism to the details of their own profession, from an explicitly Christian viewpoint, see Anthony M. C. Waterman, "Is 'Political Economy' Really a Christian Heresy?" *Faith and Economics* 51 (Spring 2008): 31-56; Charles K. Wilber, "Can a Christian Be an Economist?" *Faith and Economics* 47/48 (Spring/Fall 2006): 59-86; John P. Tiemstra et al., *Reforming Economics: Calvinist Studies on Methods and Institutions* (Lewiston, N.Y.: Edwin Mellen Press, 1990); Alan Storkey, *Transforming Economics* (London: SPCK Publishing, 1986); "Symposium: Two Approaches to Fashioning a Christian Perspective on the Liberal Market Order," ed. Edd S. Noell, *Faith and Economics* 44 (Fall 2004): 39-92; "Symposium: Values, Empirical Analysis, and Finding Possible Consensus on the Moral Ecology of Markets," ed. Edd S. Noell, *Faith and Economics* 49 (Spring 2007): 1-43; James A. Marcum, "Contemporary Philosophy of Science and Neoclassical Economics: An Opportunity for Christian Economists?" *Faith and Economics* 42 (Fall 2003): 4-16; John P. Tiemstra, "What Should Christian Economists Do? Doing Economics, But Differently," *Association of Christian Economists Bulletin* 23 (Spring 1994): 3-8; and Laurence R. Iannaccone, Derek Neal, Peter Boettke, and Deirdre McCloskey, "The Economics of Religion: A Symposium," *Faith and Economics* 46 (Fall 2005): 1-23. See also Robert Nelson, *Economics as Religion: From Samuelson to Chicago and Beyond* (University Park: Pennsylvania State University Press, 2002); and, for a refreshing break from the others, Deirdre N. McCloskey, *Bourgeois Dignity: Why Economics Can't Explain the Modern World* (Chicago: University of Chicago Press, 2010).

2. See, for example, "The Rise of Mathematics and Econometrics," Chapter 4 in E. Ray Canterbery, *The Making of Economics*, 4th ed., vol. 2 (Hackensack, N.J.: World Scientific Publishing Company, 2009).

3. Among the many sources considering the process, see John B. Davis, Alain Marciano, and Jochen Runde, *The Elgar Companion to Economics and Philosophy*, Part One (Northhampton, Mass.: Edward Elgar Publishing, 2004).

unvirtuously. And fascination with technique — the unreflective application of process to pursue control and indulgence — is taken to be at the
heart of modernism's attack on traditional virtue and practices.

I often meet people who apply this interpretive grid not only to
econometrics but to all of the discipline of economics. They express the
belief that the discipline of economics is defined by what it studies. "It's
about the money." But that has never been the case. Economists usually
think of their discipline as being about *studying human choices*.[4] Much of
economists' work concerns choices that have to do with goods and services, but, as popular books like *Freakonomics*[5] have demonstrated, the
profession studies all sorts of human choices and their consequences.

Because of that, the discipline's methods are ambidextrous. Economics can be (and in the last fifty years generally has been) quite mathematical. At the same time, economics has traditionally also been grounded in
the study of philosophy and history, and many of the greats of the profession — Mill, Smith, and Marx, for example — are still read and claimed by
both economists and philosophers.[6]

I teach courses at both ends of this methodological spectrum —
econometrics and the history of economic thought — and I have published in each. Unfortunately, though the profession is ambidextrous in
approach, many individual economists are not, and the education of
economists increasingly emphasizes one over the other. The fact that both
econometrics and the history of economic thought exist as legitimate
subfields within economics leads even many economists to promote a
mental specialization: let the historians of thought reflect on things like
the role of practices in learning, and let the econometricians drill students
in proofs and rote technique. In fact, it is now rare that a graduate program offers, let alone requires, coursework in the history of economic

---

4. Witness the mantra in the first chapters of virtually all introductory economics
textbooks: Economics studies the ways by which cultures choose what to make, how to make
it, and for whom it will be made. See, for example, William J. Baumol and Alan S. Blinder,
Economics: Principles and Policy, 9 (Mason, Ohio: South-Western, 2003), Chapter 2; N. Gregory Mankiw, *Essentials of Economics*, 5 (Mason, Ohio: South-Western, 2009), pp. 4-6; and
Robert H. Frank and Ben S. Bernanke, *Principles of Economics*, 3 (Boston: McGraw-Hill,
2007), Chapter One. Witness also the framing of political economy as *public choice* following
the work of Tversky, Posner, and others.

5. Steven D. Levitt and Stephen J. Dubner, *Freakonomics: A Rogue Economist Explores
the Hidden Side of Everything* (New York: HarperPerennial, 2009).

6. Robert B. Ekelund Jr. and Robert F. Hebert, *A History of Economic Theory and
Method*, 5 (Long Grove, Ill.: Waveland Press, Inc., 2007), Chapters 5-11.

thought.[7] This presents a challenge for teachers who believe that these areas are complements, not substitutes for one another. Textbooks and curricula gradually accommodate to the mental habits of the profession, and as time passes, the "standard" econometrics course has less and less history and reflection, more and more technique.[8]

Interpreting Well: Christian Practices and Epistemic Virtues, Ontology, and Praxis

For my part in the project that led to this book, I decided to take up this challenge by considering how to organize my econometrics course around a set of traditional Christian practices that seemed most clearly complementary to the core of the work of econometricians. I wanted to think through a process by which a teacher could form an integral, natural, faithful connection between the distinctives of a particular "technical" class and a set of Christian practices that are fitting for the study of those distinctives. I was hoping to match Christian practices to this particular class in such a way that students would see a comfortable, organic connection; I did not want them to hear me saying something like "this fall we are going to organize our study of econometrics around the practice of sleeping on nail beds," leaving them to wonder what ascetic sleep has to do with econometrics.

As I have suggested, econometrics might at first look like a course only about technique. "Here is how we gather the data; here is how we enter data into databases; here is how we use software to calculate summary statistics from the data; here is how we write up a technical paper about those summaries. . . ." But at its heart, econometrics is about piecing together a credible, faithful explanation of events from information that is fragmentary, for which the investigator did not control the data-generating process, from which a number of credible inferences could be drawn.[9] Econo-

---

7. Ted Gayer, "Graduate Studies in the History of Economics Thought," *History of Political Economy,* annual supplement to Volume 34 (2002): 35-61. Gayer says, "Almost no Ph.D. programs require HET as part of their core curriculum, and a relatively limited number of programs offer field courses (or even electives) in HET" (p. 35).

8. See A. Francisco Louc, *The Years of High Econometrics: A Short History of the Generation that Reinvented Economics* (London: Routledge, 2007).

9. See W. James Bradley and Kurt C. Schaefer, *The Uses and Misuses of Data and Models: The Mathematization of the Human Sciences* (Thousand Oaks, Calif.: Sage, 1998), Chapter 7.

metrics is less like a laboratory science and more like a crime-scene investigation.

So, thinking of econometrics as an exercise in learning mere technique would be like thinking that all training in detective work is about mere technique: "Here is how we turn on the siren; here is how we gather the fingerprints; here is how we type a crime report. . . ." Instead, learning about detective work is, at its core, learning about standards for claiming to have demonstrated that something is true. So it, and econometrics, are fundamentally training in epistemic or interpretive practices. Detective work, like econometrics, is the art and science of reconstructing a true account of things, using evidence that is partial, complex, often somewhat corrupted, and not the result of a controlled experiment. The detective comes upon the information, information she did not create, and she must develop ways to make credible inferences while disciplining her own biases and blind spots. She must be faithful to the (unknown) events she is reconstructing, and construct a defensible account of things while still remaining open to new information and alternative framings of the evidence. Her work is never "objective" in the pure sense, and her data never truly speak for themselves. Yet there should also be no room in her profession for advocacy of a pre-determined point of view. So her work is never appropriately thought of as merely technical in the sense of an algorithmic process that generates guaranteed, self-evident conclusions; techniques exist only to serve, discipline, clarify, and support the bigger project of meeting standards for warranted truth claims — of engaging in epistemic practices aimed at truth. This bigger project requires more competences — one could even say "virtues" — than training in mere technique can provide. It is just this sort of attitude — the disposition that technique is the servant of and finds its fulfillment in epistemic considerations — that is the essence of being a good econometrician. Although competence in technique is essential, nurturing and maintaining an epistemological attitude is the main difference between training a good econometrician and producing a mediocre one.

So econometrics is not fundamentally an exercise in mathematical or programming techniques; it is an exercise in the art and science of knowing what we can know, and why we can know it. Whereas the Christian tradition might have limited direct, influential connection to the finer technical points of mathematical technique and statistical analysis, questions of knowing are at the very core of most religious traditions, and have a long and rich history in the Christian tradition. So my work in rethinking my econometrics course began with this consideration: *What are the Christian practices that have traditionally been associated with knowing well, and how might those practices become central to an econometrics course?*

Let me pause briefly to let that last paragraph sink in. I am suggesting that all sorts of "technical" courses and fields — not just econometrics — should consider a new and different way of pursuing integrity between what is done as professionals and what is lived as orthodox believers. That new and different way is unlike approaches that rely heavily on considering ethical issues or critiquing presuppositions; instead, I have begun by asking what my profession actually *is,* and then have asked how *knowledge practices* are related to this thing that is my profession.

So we return to the central question: What are the Christian practices that have traditionally been associated with knowing well, and how might those practices become central to an econometrics course? It is fair to say that there is no single Christian epistemic tradition. I relied on a good deal of simplification in my approach to the topic, simplification that I hope will still be faithful to the core of the traditions from which I attempted to draw. I began with two fundamental simplifications that set the basic course of my work. First, I work within the Reformed tradition of historic Christianity, and, without unnecessarily ignoring the insights and wisdom available elsewhere, I wanted to maintain faithfulness to that particular instantiation of the Christian tradition. Second, partly because it is a hallmark of that Reformed tradition, I wanted to tie my work as closely as possible to the Christian scriptures, including the Reformed tradition of interpretive practices especially concerned with understanding those scriptures.[10] Perhaps those epistemic practices that have proven to be help-

---

10. Let me clarify that last sentence a bit for those who already have some exposure to the Reformed tradition and the elements of it that are directly concerned with epistemology, since I need to distance myself from some of that work's more restricted definition of "Reformed epistemology." During the past forty years, the phrase "Reformed epistemology" has taken on a new, technical, limited meaning in some circles, due largely to the work of Alvin Plantinga (along with William Alston and Nicholas Wolterstorff). In this more recent conversation, "Reformed epistemology" indicates the position that belief in God is "properly basic," and does not necessarily require an argument for or sensory evidence of God's existence. This view is taken to be an extension of the discussion among the classical religious reformers of the 1500s concerning the relationship between faith and reason, grace and nature — hence the appellation "Reformed epistemology." This recent discussion primarily concerns fundamental, epistemological questions surrounding the *existence* of God. See Alvin Plantinga, *God and Other Minds: A Study of the Rational Justification of Belief in God* (Ithaca, N.Y.: Cornell University Press, 1967); Nicholas Wolterstorff, *Reason within the*

ful in knowing well will lead us toward analogous practices that can help establish good epistemic habits for knowing the world around us. If, as the Reformed tradition has emphasized, God speaks to us through "two books" — the Book of Nature and the Book of Scripture — then perhaps the interpretive disciplines that help us read Scripture well could also be relevant to helping us understand nature (and culture) well.

This analogical "simplification" leads to new forms of complexity. Whereas there are historic practices, emerging from the Reformed tradition, related to studying and understanding the Scriptures, that same tradition makes a soft distinction between *special revelation* and *general revelation*. Special revelation is the self-revelation of God in the Scriptures and, especially, in the life of Jesus; general revelation is God's self-revelation found throughout the creation, including most of the study matter of economics.[11] While the two are revelations of the same God, and therefore never ultimately contradict one another, the methods of study can appropriately be quite different between the two, and we would expect that the two might tend to answer very different sorts of questions. For example, the Belgic Confession (Article 5) receives the books of the Bible "for the regulation, foundation, and confirmation *of our faith*" (emphasis added); Article 7 indicates that "whatsoever man ought to believe unto salvation . . . is *sufficiently* taught therein [the Scriptures]." The confession only claims "sufficiency," and claims that only on issues of salvation; there is no claim that the Scriptures teach comprehensively or exhaustively or self-evidently, even in areas of faith, let alone in matters of understanding the world around us.[12]

Bounds of Religion (Grand Rapids: Wm. B. Eerdmans, 1976); *Faith and Rationality,* ed. Alvin Plantinga and Nicholas Wolterstorff (South Bend: University of Notre Dame Press, 1983); William P. Alston, *Perceiving God: The Epistemology of Religious Experience* (Ithaca, N.Y.: Cornell University Press, 1991); Alvin Plantinga, *Warranted Christian Belief* (Oxford: Oxford University Press, 2000); and Alvin Plantinga, "Reason and Belief in God," Chapter 2 in *Faith and Rationality.*

11. See, for example, The Belgic Confession, 1561, Article 2, or Herman Bavinck, *Reformed Dogmatics,* vol. 1 (Grand Rapids: Baker Academic, 2003), chapters 10-11, especially pp. 340-43.

12. This is balanced by the view that, in contrast to some elements of late-medieval church thinking, the Scriptures are the essential "spectacles" that work to rectify the noetic effects of the fall into sin. "Just as old bleary-eyed men and those with weak vision, if you thrust before them a beautiful volume, even if they recognize it to be some sort of writing, yet can scarcely construe two words, but with the aid of spectacles will begin to read distinctly; so Scripture, gathering up the otherwise confused knowledge of God in our minds,

So I needed to be clear that my work as a teacher involved thinking about how traditional Christian *practices,* habits of life and discernment that have proven useful in epistemic issues surrounding the special revelation, might also complement one particular way of studying one particular element of the general revelation. Unfortunately, keeping this distinction is not as straightforward as one might hope. Let me first attempt a three-paragraph summary of the main distinctives of a traditionally Reformed approach to epistemic issues in reading the special revelation.

First, a few definitions. *Hermeneutics* is, in general, a set of rules or guidelines for interpreting the Scriptures — the principles in play, the field of study of interpretation (and not the content of the interpretation itself). It is both an art and a science, involving grammatical analysis, vocabulary study, literary stylistic and genre considerations, historical/cultural analysis, and the place of one text in an entire corpus. *Exegesis* is the process of then using those principles to lead out the truth that exists in the Scriptures, an interpretation of a particular passage. *Homiletics* is the application of the exegesis of that ancient text to the here and now, often in a sermon. This style of logic — revelation to abstraction to application — is itself a hermeneutic principle that does not arise from revelation and should be subject to review. But its virtue is that, in conjunction with other good practices like disciplined attentiveness and communal reading, this practice can help develop particular habits of heart and mind, the sorts of habits that help discipline one's tendency to misunderstand the intent and meaning of the Scriptures. One does the exegesis first in a principled fashion, rather than rushing to "relevance," and one considers the text to be multifaceted, requiring study from several angles.[13]

Throughout the process, one's view of the nature of inspiration of the text matters. A reader who considers the words on the page to be literal, dictated words of the Almighty faces a different interpretive task from the reader who thinks the text is the record of the subjective religious experience of a particular, distant tribe. The Reformed tradition has held[14] that the text is *both* fully the word of God and fully the word of humans; writers were used by the Holy Spirit in an organic way, not dictated to in a way

having dispersed our dullness, clearly shows us the true God" (John Calvin, *Institutes of the Christian Religion,* Bk. I, VII).

13. See Louis Berkhof, *Principles of Biblical Interpretation* (Grand Rapids: Baker, 1950), pp. 48ff., 174ff.; and John Cooper, *A Cause for Division? Women in Office and the Unity of the Church* (Grand Rapids: CRC Publications, 1991), p. 29.

14. For example, see Bavinck, *Reformed Dogmatics,* vol. 1, pp. 428-48.

that denies the history and character of the human author, yet not merely "inspired" in the same way that, say, Mozart's compositions were. Thus grammar, translation issues, literary form, genre, and historical/cultural context all become fully legitimate considerations in interpreting a text. And, perhaps most characteristic of the Reformed tradition, the correct theological placement of a text within the larger corpus of revelation is an important element of interpretation; as much as is possible, Scripture should interpret Scripture.

Finally, in this tradition there is a complex relationship between the present, individual interpreter, the interpretive community, and the long history of prior interpretation. It is, after all, the *Reformed* tradition, tied to the sixteenth-century split in the Christian church that involved the contested relationship between the contemporary interpreter and prior tradition. The Reformers might be stereotyped as people who had little respect for other opinions, least of all traditional opinions, advocating an individualistic free-for-all on epistemic issues. But that would not be accurate. It is fairer to say that they intended an Augustinian reform to *restore* or harvest earlier traditions of Christian epistemic practice, some of which had been altered by medieval Scholasticism. Just as the original revelation did not involve direct divine dictation, neither should a contemporary individual necessarily presume divine authority for his or her interpretation of the text. Furthermore, whereas the Scriptures speak with authority on those things that must be known for salvation, they do not necessarily speak, as we have seen earlier, on other topics.[15] Our understanding of revelation is not necessarily automatic, but may require further explanation (and certainly a moment-by-moment dependence on the teaching of the Holy Spirit, who inspired the original writers[16]), partly because language, time, culture, practices, and tradition stand between us and the Scriptures. Thus, while the Reformers rejected the view that the Bible should be entrusted not to the average person but only to trained clergy who are trustworthy, they did not mean by this that *everything* in revelation is straightforward,

15. The Belgic Confession, for example, indicates that revelation teaches only two essential things in a clear and perfect way: things necessary for God to be glorified and for us to be saved.

16. Thus Calvin, preaching on 1 Timothy 3:8-10: "When we come to hear the sermon or to take up the Bible, we must not have the foolish arrogance of thinking that we shall easily understand everything we hear or read. But we must come with reverence, we must wait entirely upon God, knowing that we need to be taught by his Holy Spirit, and that without him we cannot understand anything that is shown to us in his Word."

clear, or obvious.[17] They therefore bound themselves to confessions —
transcultural statements of faith developed through an unhurried process
of discernment — and to practices. The Christian faith is, for them, the
faith of the church, which is *received* by individuals, not constructed by
them. Thus Christian epistemic practice must always take place in the larger
context of other Christians, coming from a variety of perspectives, discerning together what is being revealed in the text and in the world — not quite
a hermeneutic of suspicion, but a hermeneutic of humility concerning the
cultural blinders that each of us necessarily wears.

Translating Christian Practices of Interpretation for the "Technical" Classroom

Now how might one appropriate this epistemic tradition for the study of
econometrics (or, for that matter, for a wide range of disciplines whose interests are "technical")? What interpretive practices and epistemic virtues
in this tradition's engagement with special revelation might resonate with
the study of natural revelation and the sorts of things that economists usually study? Though I do not want to inappropriately transfer practices fit-
ted for some areas of study that would be out of place in others, it seems
reasonable to expect some resonance or congruence of practices across the
various kinds of revelation that Christians engage, appropriate to all our
works of interpretation. As a way of crystallizing and translating some of
the key features of Reformed hermeneutics, I adopted several keynotes that
have emerged as habits of life and discernment running through this Reformed tradition:

1. Our aim should be to *lead the truth out of* the revelation that surrounds
us. This habit emphasizes careful discernment, the kind of attentive faithfulness that sometimes — usually — must be unhurried and communal.
This habit demotes the premium commonly placed on giving a clever or
original interpretation for its own sake; work should be judged not by its
"eloquence" but by its integrity with the world as it exists. Students should
learn to demote the urge to find a result that is "striking" or surprising or
sensational. Many times I have sat in my office as students working on a

---

17. As Luther put it with characteristic brevity and punch, "The Bible was written for
people with heads upon their shoulders."

term paper sheepishly "admitted" that the results of a project are pretty much what was expected, as if that should be a cause for shame. In contrast to the common fare in professional journals, these habits of mind require that empirical projects should not be presented in such a way that novelty of result is overly prized.[18]

These practices also demote temporal efficiency. The rush to publish must be resisted, and results that are publishable but not fully warranted or trustworthy must be allowed more time to ripen, or else set aside. This implies that, as a part of training students to digest and reconsider and vet their research ideas and results, some classes should probably be organized as research colloquia in which students present preliminary work for critique, with multiple deadlines for partial completion of term projects.

These habits of mind also imply that standards for citing and organizing and evaluating and criticizing evidence should figure large in the course, much like the Christian tradition's standards for analyzing grammar, genre, and context when doing hermeneutics. As a consequence, I concluded that, at least in my circumstances, the commonplace practice of assigning enormous numbers of "practice" problems until methods are learned by rote is counterproductive; in my experience this practice is at odds with real mastery, much like an overemphasis on rote learning of Scripture and theology can have a deadening, prophylactic effect on deep appreciation. I have gradually become something of a homework minimalist, requiring that students do careful evaluative work concerning the data they use. A more common approach to empirical assignments accepts and distributes pre-digested data as a starting point from which students are required to do many, many "practice" problems, which have the effect of dulling their actual understanding of the problems they are completing, and of leading them to memorize a series of steps that are quickly forgotten. Fewer, better assignments instead encourage learning and retention of the process of discernment; this will always lead to a proper series of steps, and to an understanding of why that particular series of steps is appropriate in each particular situation. Thus assignments and class exercises and exams should be designed without time pressure, and

---

18. Fascination with novelty has been matched by a long and rich Christian conversation on the dangers of curiosity. For a good contemporary treatment, see Paul J. Griffiths, *Intellectual Appetite: A Theological Grammar* (Washington, D.C.: Catholic University of America Press, 2009); see also Josef Pieper, *Leisure: The Basis of Culture* (South Bend: St. Augustine's Press, 1998); Thomas Aquinas, *Summa Theologica*, Question 167 ("Can the vice of curiosity regard intellective knowledge?").

should expect and require that students think broadly about the context of the situation they are modeling.[19]

Finally, these habits drawn from Christian epistemic practices concerning our responsibility to lead the truth out of the revelation that surrounds us also imply a different attitude toward expectations for the length of term papers involving empirical projects. The assignment's statement about length should be taken as a suggestion about the breadth of the project as it is being planned. Students should try to choose a topic that can probably be done well in the suggested number of pages, neither too broad nor too narrow. This is inevitably a guess. If the eventual paper is shorter or longer, that is irrelevant to the question of whether the project was faithful to the realities it is considering.

2. There may be more fundamental parallels between considerations of grammar, translation, literary form/genre, and historical/cultural context in Reformed hermeneutics and empirical work in economics. In my profession, we are usually working with secondary data sources rather than instigating the collection of original data. This is not altogether unlike the difference between interpreting a text written by others and writing one's own literature. Reformed hermeneutics is all about interpreting texts that are distant in time, place, and culture, interpreting a message that the reader did not generate — a secondary data source, as it were. So faithful econometrics, like the Reformed emphasis on grammar, form, and context, should involve familiarity with the peculiarities of any particular data set under study — its origin, its blind spots, the research agendas that may have shaped its collection, and a detailed knowledge of the original situation of which these data form an imperfect abstraction. This discipline is very frequently ignored among economists; convenient data are pressed into uses for which they were not designed. In fact, a significant part of the professional repertoire of a working econometrician consists of statistical strategies for making do with rough proxies and mismeasurements of the realities that are not directly available for measurement. While this can be an extremely useful set of skills, if not carefully disciplined it can lead to unfaithfulness to the truth of things in the world.

19. Of course, students may eventually find themselves in professional situations in which time pressure cannot be avoided. But the way to prepare for such situations is to patiently, slowly develop good practices that will become automatic and reflexive under time pressure. The football guard instinctively responds to changes under pressure on the field only because he has patiently run drills in a situation that was unhurried.

3. The Reformers emphasized the primacy of the entire Scriptures in interpreting any particular section of the Scriptures, a practice they termed "the analogy of Scripture."[20] The rest of what we know from revelation should guide our work in any particular circumstance. In my case, this involves being aware of and, where appropriate, bowing to the work of others in the area under study. I came to believe that this requires, as much as is possible, that students do their work in conversation with other published work in the same area, even when doing homework assignments, as a way of building proper habits.

4. We should limit our inferences to things about which the revelation is clearly speaking. When revelation shouts, we should shout; when it only whispers, we must not overstate our case. In econometrics, this requires that I spend a good deal more time delving into the details of inference, especially the uses and abuses of statistical tests of significance, than is done in the standard course. We should also organize the class sessions in such a way that students develop the habit of instinctively, publicly using this standard to evaluate the things they see and hear in the course. For example, I spent a good deal of classroom time reworking published articles, using the data of the original authors, so that students could see, evaluate, and where necessary correct the inferential work of others. I also gave a prize ("The Sophist Award") to the student who excelled at catching me making mistakes of inference in the class.

5. Our work should be done openly in the context of conversation with others who will bring different perspectives to the revelation under study. This is an echo of the Reformed "hermeneutic of humility" regarding epistemic claims, and it also resonates with several of the habits of mind I have developed in the preceding points.

To summarize, I set out to construct an econometrics course that would prize commonplace but true findings above sensational but questionable ones; that would be unrushed in its pace and not rigid in its apprenticeship to the profession's ways of knowing; that would contemplate the particu-

---

20. Thus, for example, the Westminster Confession, I ix: "The infallible rule of interpretation of scripture is the scripture itself; and therefore, when there is a question about the true and full sense of any scripture, it must be searched and known by other places that speak more clearly."

larities of situations rather than running over them roughshod; that would be intentional rather than casual in its uses of statistical methods; and that would engage the work of other scholars rather than encouraging students to do their work in isolation.

My Experiment

My duty was to try to shape my curriculum by these distinctives, and to adopt classroom practices and habits consistent with them. I also wanted these practices to be, as much as possible, resonant with traditional Christian practices that are *not* directly related to epistemic issues — practices like hospitality, simplicity, liturgical calendars and schedules, fasting, prayer, meditation, study, solitude, submission, service, confession, worship, feasting, and alms-giving. Yet I wanted to adopt these Christian practices not arbitrarily, but because specific ones were organically connected to the epistemic distinctives I was trying to form in my students.

In brief, on the basis of the considerations outlined thus far, I concluded that my econometrics course should be built around *conversation* rather than lecturing. That meant *extending the conversation as widely as possible* by using published articles and their data rather than "pre-cooked" data and exercises from textbooks, *evaluating standards for evidence* rather than taking the evidence as given while emphasizing the statistical manipulation of that evidence, and *practicing humility in stating our results*, holding each other accountable to never go beyond claims that are legitimately warranted by the work we have done. The practices that I found myself drawing on most directly were *hospitality* (because it is a prerequisite for honest conversation), *simplicity* (because it serves humility, and because exercising care in evaluating evidence requires that one do fewer repetitive exercises than the standard econometrics course), *meditation* (because careful evaluation of evidence requires that one hover over it for extended periods of time and view it from a variety of angles), and an open attitude toward *confession* (because there are so many ways to go astray when doing econometrics — one needs to double-check many things, and cultivate an open atmosphere in which one's first conclusion is not taken as necessarily correct).

All econometrics courses with which I am familiar take the following approach. A teacher stands before the class, doing proofs on a blackboard or explaining how to do the advanced statistics that econometrics involves.

Then students are assigned problem sets, consisting either of doing proofs or of using statistical software to complete exercises that analyze data sets provided by the textbook. There is always a single, correct answer, and if one follows the procedure in the textbook, one arrives at that answer — and generally is publicly praised for quickly coming to that correct solution, rather than engaging the issues we have identified in this chapter. For a term project, students may write a paper that ties together several of these classroom topics, using a data set provided by the text or perhaps a new one retrieved from the Internet. This is the culture to which I wanted to bring something fresh from the traditions of Christian practices.

There is no denying that any good econometrics course must contain a big dose of "standard" material that must be mastered, so I chose a standard econometrics textbook (though one that tends to emphasize original research and taking a critical attitude toward one's data), and supplemented it with several readings and articles that laid out the main epistemic traps that come up when doing empirical work. These readings generally drew on the history of ideas in econometrics, along with the more common (and more fun) literature that discusses the possibility of "lying with statistics."

Because of a scheduling peculiarity, I was blessed with a small class — just four students for the term. With the students' approval, we met in my office for class rather than in one of the classrooms. I always prepared some refreshments, and each student chose a tea mug from my shelf that became theirs for the term. I tried to raise each day's material in conversation, providing printed handouts at the end of class each day that documented the more technical elements of the day's work so that during our time together we could spend our energies developing the ideas as conversationally and intuitively as was possible. We prayed together, both about "life matters" that we shared with each other and about the formation of our work in class. We limited ourselves to a few empirical studies per chapter, so that we could spend time investigating the details surrounding the data under study in each case. Most of those exercises were drawn not from textbook data sets but from published articles, for which I had, as often as was possible, reconstructed the original data on which the article was based. In some cases we corresponded with the original authors about choices they made in doing their work. We were sometimes doing Internet searches on the spot to investigate details of particular situations, or redoing statistical results in the classroom, using a paper's original data but investigating them from an angle different than the approach taken by the original author. We also frequently split up empirical problems into parts, assigned a different part of each problem to each person, did those parts on our own outside of class, then brought them together for each other's review and evaluation at the next class, as an exercise in maintaining humility and a gently critical attitude toward our own findings.

Most of these practices are not quite direct appropriations of traditional Christian practices. For example, in practicing confession I did not literally use a liturgy of confession, and I did not pronounce absolution over student assignments! But I did try to keep before the class the notion, the principle, that in doing our work we were echoing the fundamental practices at play in the Christian tradition. We may not have literally confessed sins to each other, but we did work to maintain an atmosphere of open talk about choices taken and mistakes made, accountability to each other and to the situations we were studying, and pliable willingness to acknowledge weaknesses and learn from each other. In humbly submitting our empirical work to each other for peer review, and acknowledging the missteps we took in analyzing data, we were acting out a Christian practice. In limiting our "diet" of study problems, and completing them critically and in conversation, we were acting out a Christian practice. In welcoming each other and each other's ideas while eating and drinking, we were acting out a Christian practice. In attending with care to the revelation before us, we were acting out a Christian practice.

I can imagine a number of ways in which this approach to the course might be evaluated. On our campus, like most campuses, our default evaluation of courses relies on confidential student evaluations. The teaching evaluations from this course were quite appreciative, both concerning the material learned and the way in which it was learned. I happened to have a very bright group of students who are all bound for graduate work, but I believe that the approach taken in this course would, relative to the way in which such courses are normally taught, tend to raise the likelihood that weaker students would succeed. I was especially happy to have a conversation with one of the students several months later, after he and a student colleague from the class attended a large professional economics conference that was attended by professional econometricians as well as undergraduates and graduate students. The conference consisted of professional sessions at which faculty members presented econometric work in progress. My student reported that, based on his conversations with other students at the conference, our class had actually covered quite a bit more material than similar classes at other schools seemed to cover, and that he understood the material at a deeper level than other students seemed to grasp it.

The particular shape of Christian practices in "technical" courses will vary from course to course, but I think the basic approach taken for this course can serve as a useful framework. First, consider carefully the deep resonances that exist between the Christian tradition and the essence of the course's subject. In my case, econometrics is fundamentally about knowing well, and the Christian tradition has developed practices relevant to knowing well. Second, think carefully about the similarities and differences between the details of your course and the resonances it finds in the Christian tradition. Third, seek to shape the curriculum and classroom practices around the resonances and similarities you have discerned. And fourth, evaluate the propriety of your analysis and the effectiveness of your strategy, with the aim of seeking natural, organic consonance between your teaching and Christian practices.

Recruiting Students' Imaginations:
Prospects and Pitfalls of Practices

David I. Smith

As the conversations that led to and accompanied many of the chapters in this volume unfolded, a familiar-sounding concern raised its head more than once. The attentive reader will find its traces here and there in the preceding essays. Sometimes it appeared as a simple question to someone who had tried to introduce a Christian practice into their class: Did students get it? Or, more anxiously: When you introduced an unfamiliar set of practices, did students resist? Did they think it was weird? Is this more like church than higher education? At other times it came as a cautionary anecdote: even though we spent time at the start of the semester discussing theological perspectives, at the end some students claimed to have perceived no Christian dimension to the course. Occasionally colleagues rather than students were the target: How did your department react? Was this a hard sell? Whatever the specific guise under which it arose, a recurring underlying concern was whether introducing some form of Christian practice not commonly encountered in the classroom would lead students or colleagues to either bewilderment or resentment, distracting from learning or perhaps undermining the professor's need to be liked, understood, or at least perceived as sane.

This book is an extended effort to persuade colleagues that there is something in the connection between practices and learning that is worthy of serious consideration. Rather than offer an extended theoretical account of why practices are important and what they have to do with learning (several of those already exist and are cited in multiple places in earlier chapters), we have chosen to paint pictures of attempts to rethink and re-enact our classes in the light of Christian practices. If colleagues are not persuaded by this point that there is something to the enterprise, further argument is likely to be superfluous. This final chapter will focus on anxieties about the reactions and experiences of students, suggesting some possible pitfalls and cautious remedies. It would be nice to be able to offer an original, comprehensive, and sure-fire recipe for avoiding student indifference or opposition and making Christian practices reliably carry the day in every classroom, but that's not how teaching works, and so I am going to have to content myself with rather less. My aim in what follows is simply to identify some ways in which effort might strategically be applied in order to reduce possible frictions.

Imagination and Practices

Various accounts of the nature of social practices offer the observation that there is an important relationship between the contours of practices and the particular form of imagination that sustains them and is sustained by them.[1] Imagination here does not mean fantasy, or even creativity — it refers to a particular way of making sense of the world, a construal of what it is that we are doing together and why.[2] Alasdair MacIntyre, for instance, whose account of practices has achieved near-canonical status, couches discussion of the imagination informing practices in terms of the narratives that frame our sense of identity and purpose and make practice possible: "I can only answer the question 'What am I to do?' if I can answer the prior question 'Of what story or stories do I find myself a part?'"[3] Craig Dykstra, applying MacIntyre's account to Christian education, notes that as we grow into Christian practices, "what is always at stake is *intelligible* action, action imbued with discernment and imagination, with understanding, purpose, and meaning."[4] Miroslav Volf argues that "Christian

---

1. There are, of course, some differences of emphasis concerning the balance here — the degree to which imagination works on practices and the degree to which it is a by-product of immersion in them. For present purposes, the main thing is to note that both processes are in play.

2. Compare Philip D. Kenneson, "Gathering: Worship, Imagination, and Formation," in *The Blackwell Companion to Christian Ethics,* ed. Stanley Hauerwas and Sam Wells (Oxford: Blackwell Publishers, 2004), pp. 53-67.

3. Alasdair C. MacIntyre, *After Virtue: A Study in Moral Theory,* 3rd ed. (Notre Dame: University of Notre Dame Press, 2007), p. 216.

4. Craig Dykstra, *Growing in the Life of Faith: Education and Christian Practices,* 2nd ed. (Louisville: Westminster John Knox Press, 2005), p. 72.

practices are such that a Christian normative vision is part and parcel of what these practices are; and Christian beliefs are such that informing Christian practices is part and parcel of what these beliefs do. Practices are essentially belief-shaped, and beliefs are essentially practice-shaping."[5] In a rather different context, Etienne Wenger's account of how groups gathered around a common enterprise develop into communities of practice emphasizes that coming to partake of a shared imagination, a shared way of construing the joint enterprise and the tasks and roles surrounding it, is a key way of belonging.[6] Not sharing this construal is one way of not fitting in. In various ways, these and other authors point to how the complex of elements that make up "practices" includes the things we tell ourselves and one another about just what we are engaged in and for what purposes.

This substrate of imagination does not float independently of the actual moves that we make. To draw a little further from Wenger's account, which has the merit for present purposes of being focused on how learning situations work, participation over time in a particular emerging or established community of practice generates a particular "identity of participation" — a sense of self, a sense of appropriate roles and possible moves that is associated with this group and setting. As interactions take place around common tasks, and meanings are negotiated in the process ("No, do it this way"; "I didn't mean it like that"; "Didn't you get my e-mail?" "Ask Jim how he wants it done"), a gradual process of alignment takes place. We become attuned to one another's expectations and sensitivities, to what we mean by certain terms and gestures, to the boundaries that need to be observed, the explicit and implicit goals and priorities being pursued. What start as single behaviors and events become shared repertoire, a familiar set of moves and symbols that provide the kind of continuity and stable frame of reference necessary to focus on getting things done, rather than constantly renegotiating the parameters of interaction. There is something both enabling and comforting about having a well-functioning repertoire in place.[7]

This process is not hard to observe within individual classrooms.

---

5. Miroslav Volf, "Theology for a Way of Life," in *Practicing Theology: Beliefs and Practices in Christian Life,* ed. Miroslav Volf and Dorothy C. Bass (Grand Rapids: Wm. B. Eerdmans, 2002), p. 254.

6. Etienne Wenger, *Communities of Practice: Learning, Meaning, and Identity* (Cambridge: Cambridge University Press, 1999), pp. 51-57, 152-56, 175-78.

7. This does not necessarily imply harmony; in order to resist and be obstructive, one also needs to have acquired some understanding of community norms and expectations.

The early part of a school year or a semester commonly includes an emphasis on setting expectations and procedures that fades as time progresses. Students at this point are learning not only subject matter but also how to work with this teacher and this particular group of peers, what the priorities will be, and how the affective, social, and moral contours of this group will play out. This professor wants homework on Fridays and sent by e-mail; this one wants it in a physical drop-box on Tuesdays. This classmate talks too much; that one might be a useful source of help. Sitting this way in the chairs here is more comfortable; doing the assigned reading will not matter much in this class because the teacher repeats it all in lecture form anyway. And so on. Despite the common habit of spending the first day of class reading out syllabi and stating expectations, much of this process is not primarily a matter of explicitly stated rules. From the patterns of interaction themselves there gradually emerges a repertoire consisting not only of stated expectations but also of less explicitly articulated norms surrounding matters such as grades; styles of greeting; who speaks when, to whom, and about what; signals that trigger note-taking; in-jokes; modes of attacking others' ideas; and so on *ad infinitum*.

While this process to some degree gets renegotiated with each new teacher or class, this local negotiation takes place within the parameters of broader repertoires established by institutions and disciplines. Students imagine their school in particular ways; perhaps, for instance, it is perceived as quite an academic place where it is hard to get good grades, or as a "party school," or as very traditional in its approach. This imagination is generated and sustained by existing repertoires within the institution, and by participants' ways of talking about them, and it also conditions how fresh encounters with more localized repertoires will be interpreted. Whether a particular class is imagined to be an "easy" class requiring little serious attention will depend in part on wider perceptions of norms at the institution as a whole and of the discipline in particular (perhaps German is, for instance, perceived as somehow inherently harder than Spanish, or physics as inherently more weighty or valid than art). Similarly, past experience of classes within a particular discipline leaves students coming to a new class with a construal of "what we do in this kind of class" already formed, and this will be both generated and compounded by the subject cultures that shape norms and expectations within particular disciplines. There are certain things one does and does not do in science classes, or in English classes; there are certain things that make one fit a given learner's profile of a "good" math teacher. These things may or may not consist of publicly established or defensible parameters of "best practice" — they might have as much to do with past experience of the personal strengths, weaknesses, philosophies, and quirks of past individual teachers, and with the uncritically (or ideologically) inhabited rhythms of "how we do things" in a given department or guild. They may equally be influenced by sources outside of schools altogether — media representations, for instance, or peer narratives of classrooms in subjects of which the student so far has little experience.

Making Moves That Count

Given all of this, it is not that surprising if students sometimes react negatively when shared points of reference are disrupted. Students typically have a considerable stake in the navigability of classroom repertoire, given the usual relationships between mastering the expected student roles, the granting of teacher approval, and the achievement of personal success. In other words, they have learned or are still learning how to survive or get ahead in the current system of practice, and disruptions carry potential cost. To be sure, a repertoire is not a fixed thing; it contains an ongoing measure of ambiguity that allows meanings to be played with and renegotiated over time. However, it also becomes resistant to radical change; new moves that are too different from past moves may fail to count as part of the repertoire (much as picking up the ball and running with it fails to count as a move in soccer). Such moves are likely to be received as disruptions of the jointly constructed enterprise.

Students need to be able to construct a picture of their education such that the actions in which they are involved as students make sense as teaching and learning. Present behaviors stand in relation to an imagined personal and social history of practice, and behaviors that fall outside the perceived parameters risk failing to be construed as teaching and learning. This may have little to do with whether they are actually capable of promoting learning, resting more on what we are used to learning looking like. For instance, students who have a history of learning a second language through worksheets and grammar explanations may need help perceiving a class period spent conducting conversation in the target language as really amounting to "doing work." Although the activity might actually be doing more to foster their process of language acquisition than a class spent writing worksheet exercises, it can be perceived as a less serious act of teaching and learning if the account of learning within which it makes sense is not made clear.

Imagination affects not only the identification of particular behaviors as belonging or not belonging to the repertoire of teaching and learning, but also the ways that particular tasks are experienced and how meaning is assigned to them. Wenger uses this example:

> Two stonecutters . . . are asked what they are doing. One responds: "I am cutting this stone in a perfectly square shape." The other responds: "I am building a cathedral." Both answers are correct and meaningful, but they reflect different relations to the world. The difference between these answers does not imply that one is a better stonecutter than the other, as far as holding the chisel is concerned. At the level of engagement, they may well be doing exactly the same thing. But it does suggest that their experiences of what they are doing and their sense of self in doing it are rather different. This difference is a function of imagination. As a result, they may be learning very different things from the same activity.[8]

Not only whether the activity counts as learning, but also the kind of thing that is being learned depends, Wenger claims, on imagination. Neither practice nor learning from practice is simply a matter of actions; each is also a matter of what these actions come to count as.

Pressures on a Practices-Oriented Pedagogy

This returns us to the opening concern. Indifference and resentment may arise when teachers introduce practices that disrupt existing repertoire, and when students do not become able to imagine the disruption as a valid instance of the kind of learning for which the group has gathered. There is a mismatch between repertoire and imagination. This suggests a number of pressure points likely to require attention when efforts are made to connect pedagogy to Christian practices.

First there is the matter of prior experience of the practices themselves, and its effects on how their importance is imagined. On the one hand, where students are also part of churches, Christian youth groups, and other forms of Christian community, the familiarity of such spiritual

---

8. Wenger, *Communities of Practice*, p. 176.

practices as are present in those other contexts may increase their plausibility when they are introduced in learning settings; these practices can then serve as fruitful bridges between these multiple memberships. On the other hand, such familiarity is far from guaranteed. Even in churches, many historic Christian practices may be unfamiliar to congregants, perhaps due, for instance, to the dominance in some settings of an individualistic, ahistorical approach to faith. Dykstra notes that while his list of characteristic Christian practices seems at first sight very ordinary, containing as it does entries like worshiping, interpreting the Scriptures, forgiving, serving, suffering with, and so on, nevertheless "most of the practices on this simple list are, for most of us, most of the time, relatively untried."[9] Thus in most cases, even in Christian institutions and with Christian students, one cannot assume rich prior experience with traditional Christian practices. This lack of experiential familiarity may go together with an understanding of faith and spiritual growth mostly focused on individual inner experience and/or voluntaristic activism. There may also, in some Christian instances, be prejudice against the liturgical, or even simply the old — a graduate student recently turned in to me a book review of a volume dealing with historic Christian practices, and mentioned that he had at first been disinclined to read the book at all; someone had told him that it didn't sound very interesting, since it was about old ideas. As, for instance, Ashley Woodiwiss notes in his chapter in this volume, if this layer of student imagination regarding Christian practices is not addressed in some way, then accessing the learning potential and formational possibilities of those practices may be a challenge. Students may need specific help brokering the boundaries and connections between the academic setting, their own conception and experience of Christianity, and elements of the wider Christian tradition.

Second, there is the question of how the relationship between practice and learning is imagined. If Christian practices are imagined as belonging solely to a realm of private spiritual experience and individual life-

---

9. Dykstra, *Growing in the Life of Faith*, p. 54. Dykstra goes on to argue, "Our situation requires planned and systematic education in these practices. Such education must never be detached from participation in the practices; it is not satisfactory simply to describe and analyze them from afar. Nonetheless, education must order this participation in such a way that all the practices are engaged in meaningfully and with understanding at increasingly broader and more complex levels. And that presupposes systematic and comprehensive education in the history and wider reaches of the practices, as well as in the interpretation and criticism of the reasons and values embedded in the practices" (pp. 73-74).

style choice, their connection to wider learning processes, overall formation of the learner, and the shaping of particular kinds of learning community is likely to seem obscure, even eccentric. Students (and perhaps their teachers) may need help understanding how particular practices can function as forms of learning and forms of dwelling together. They may need help seeing practices not only as things that can be learned *about,* as further pieces of information about the world, but as structures that when *indwelt* bring their own forms of learning and growth that may not be accessible outside of that indwelling. Given the images of learning fostered by many of the characteristic repertoires of the modern academy, images commonly tied to distanced processing of impersonal information or autonomous criticism of ideas, it may not be immediately intuitive to understand bodily participation in the rhythms of practice as potentially carrying within itself a kind of learning. Pointing out that this may be a culturally induced myopia does not automatically remove the inertia present in such shared imagination. Participation in practices may require teachers and students to acquire new vocabulary for describing aspects of their own educational activity and growth. Rebecca Konyndyk DeYoung's chapter in this volume explores how new vocabulary alongside new enacted experiences of practice can create significant learning. Christian teachers and students need not only Christian perspectives on the theories and information in play; they need Christian ways of practicing learning accompanied by fitting ways of imagining, naming, and embracing that process.

Third, disciplinary subcultures and discipline-based expectations concerning the "normal" shape of learning may make connections with Christian practices less plausible if it does not seem possible to construe the practice concerned as embodying a form of learning appropriate in some way to the specific subject matter at hand. The chapters in this volume cover a range in this regard. Some explore what may be relatively easily understood connections, such as joining practices of charitable reading to engagement with literary texts, the giving of testimony to a psychology class, or acts of hospitality to a nutrition course. Others see less immediately intuitive connections, such as those suggested between physics education and prayer labyrinths in Matthew Walhout's chapter. In all cases, to one degree or another, it is likely to be necessary to plan strategies for helping students (and colleagues!) see plausible connections between the practices proposed and what they imagine to be involved in progressing in the discipline at hand. This may not always mean finding some specific connection with the content of the discipline; but even in cases where the benefits are more in terms of formation of the self who is learning the discipline, the relevance of this kind of formation may need to be negotiated.

Fourth, the very act of articulating to students the relationship between classroom practices and learning goals draws to the fore the challenge of actually achieving plausible conformity between imagination and repertoire. If I am going to claim to students that I have particular goals for how they will grow during my class, then the practices that I engage in and help to shape within the learning community should be plausibly interpretable as leading to such growth. If, for instance, I claim to centrally value creativity, then the shape of class discussion, the room layout, the grading practices, and the design of assignments should not communicate a primary concern for accurate transmission and reproduction of predefined information. The concepts and images that we work with should fairly describe what we actually do and its likely outcomes; otherwise, they become self-deception. This (like all of the others thus far) is a fairly basic point, but it is all too easy to end up preaching one set of goals while relying on an unexamined repertoire that in fact points in a different direction.

As teachers we often inherit both poorly articulated aspirations for students in a given course and unexamined classroom practices, and there is no guarantee that there will be much congruence between the two. Adding a Christian frame to the mix may fail to resonate as a way of picturing the actual lived repertoire. This can create a plausibility gap, fostering a feeling that the focus on Christian practice is an awkward intrusion into the learning setting. If, for example, I frame a world language course with talk about the Christian practice of hospitality to the stranger,[10] and then teach using mainly language exercises focused on consumer transactions, or focus learners' speech mainly on talking about themselves and their own experiences and interests, or justify hard work to students primarily in terms of various forms of personal gain to be achieved, there will be a mismatch between proposed imagination and actual repertoire. The talk of hospitality will either ring hollow or be adopted only as an ideological cover, with students learning to imitate me in saying one

---

10. I have discussed framing world language education in terms of the Christian practice of hospitality to the stranger in a number of publications, including, principally, David I. Smith and Barbara Carvill, *The Gift of the Stranger* (Grand Rapids: Wm. B. Eerdmans, 2000); and David I. Smith, *Learning from the Stranger* (Grand Rapids: Wm. B. Eerdmans, 2009).

thing, doing another, and feeling more righteous in the process.[11] In such a case, the talk of hospitality has been adopted as a label, but not as a construal — I can label a jar of honey with the word *salsa;* it is much harder to reasonably construe it as salsa while eating it. The temptation in an academic context (noted, for example, by Glenn Sanders in his chapter) to drift from actual practices to merely talking about practices may also come into play here.

There is some caution needed at this point. Amy Plantinga Pauw notes two sides of an inevitable tension when she writes, on the one hand, that "a community's beliefs become more credible to them as they engage in practices congruent with those beliefs," and, on the other hand, that "beliefs often put up a certain resistance to our current desires and practices, and may at times interrogate or even temporarily disband them. . . . Reductive approaches correlate beliefs and practices more directly than religious experience warrants, and thus have a hard time accounting for persistent gaps between belief and practice."[12] Hypocrisy is not to be sought, yet, especially in an educational setting, proposing or claiming a watertight fit between belief and practice implies more control over our beliefs and practices than we in fact possess, and risks promoting self-deception as we ignore the cracks. The gaps between belief and practice should be neither ignored nor denied. If we see ourselves not as providing sealed packages of coherent belief and practice, but as inviting students into the struggle to align our beliefs and our practices, then the search for consistency and the need for ongoing critique and critical thinking can both be honored. Our ways of naming Christian practices in relation to a wider Christian imagination need to be able to function with integrity as ways of construing what we are actually doing together in the classroom, and we (teachers *and* students) need honest ways of naming and engaging with the ongoing gaps.

---

11. I discuss this in more detail, with suggestions regarding the contours of a language classroom repertoire consistent with hospitality to the stranger, in David I. Smith, "Hospitality, Language Pedagogy, and Communities of Practice," *Journal of Christianity and Foreign Languages* 12 (2011): 29-44.

12. Amy Plantinga Pauw, "Attending to the Gaps between Beliefs and Practices," in *Practicing Theology: Beliefs and Practices in Christian Life,* ed. Miroslav Wolf and Dorothy C. Bass (Grand Rapids: Wm. B. Eerdmans, 2002), pp. 36-37.

From Requiring Behaviors to Recruiting Imaginations

I suggest that these forms of congruence — between practices talk and the subjective experience of learning, and between imagination and actual repertoire — will not be best achieved through some of our most common strategies for communicating intent. A speech at the start of the semester about the importance that Christian practices will have for the course, a call to arms in the course syllabus, or even a module in the opening week of the semester on a Christian way of framing the discipline might all have something to offer. However, none of them seem by themselves well-fitted to bringing about the kind of gradual alignment and ongoing renegotiation of repertoire and imagination that characterize a successful community of practice. The path that we are exploring in this volume requires, I suggest, both a continuing attentiveness to classroom repertoire (Are the moves we make together honestly consistent with the Christian practices that we are hoping to espouse?) and an equally ongoing attentiveness to how our actions together are being framed and understood (Are students being helped to see the moves we are making as instances of a Christian practice of learning, or to see how they fall short?).

Teaching in a manner shaped by Christian practices involves not only requiring behaviors but recruiting imaginations. This may take place in a variety of ways — some of those suggested in essays in this volume include the use of visual cues in course materials, reminders in ongoing teacher responses to student journals, regular interaction with past practitioners who have reflected on the Christian practice concerned, noting of thematic connections between practices and course content, use of overt liturgical rhythms and references, renaming of course components, and simple prayer for students by name. Whatever the particular strategies adopted, engaging pedagogically with Christian practices seems likely to be at its most formative when there is an ongoing interaction between action and imagination, so that ways of seeing learning emerge from the participatory experience of engaging in new repertoires even as those repertoires are named and queried in ways that make them visible as attempts at Christian practice. This means getting beyond simple dichotomies between believing and doing, faith and learning, content and pedagogy. If the vital relationship between revising repertoire and recruiting imagination is not attended to, then perhaps things will be only as they should be if resistance, bafflement, and resentment turn out to be our lot.

David I. Smith

Practicing Together

All of this implies that Christian practices are not techniques, not something we do *to* students while we stand outside and above the process (falsely implying both our mastery and their status as objects). They are rather something that we do *with* students, something that we seek to indwell together. They are also something that we do with other teachers and members of our institutions, a journey best sustained amid a community of colleagues actively attending to their communal formation as practitioners of Christian learning. As Dykstra puts it,

> To learn these practices and learn in the context of them, we need others who are competent in these practices to help us: to be our models, mentors, teachers, and partners in practice. We need people who will include us in these practices as they themselves are engaged in them, and who will show us how to do what the practices require. We also need them to explain to us what these practices mean, what the reasons, understandings, insights, and values embedded in them are. And we need them to lure us and press us beyond our current understandings of and competence in these practices, to the point where we together may extend and deepen the practices themselves.[13]

This, of course, demands a significant degree of self-involvement on the part of the teacher, as all of those involved in the projects reported in this volume discovered. This is not a path for teachers wishing to remain in the role of distanced technician, lone wolf, or articulate conveyor of expertise,[14] or even for those seeking to rely on their personal sincerity, enthusiasm, and care for students. Carolyne Call, for instance, describes very clearly the realization that she needed to be sustained by participation in Christian practices as much as her students did, and that it was those prac-

---

13. Dykstra, *Growing in the Life of Faith*, pp. 72-73.

14. A pedagogy rooted in Christian practices is thus at profound odds with the sense of self captured by Gordon Johnston in the metaphor of teacher-cosmonauts who prefer to orbit alone in the cold reaches of intellectual space around whichever subject has fascinated them, "regularly descending from their cool zeroing around the subject to engage others in conversation about it and, as far as they are able, explain its relevance to the grounded." See Gordon Johnston, "Poetry and Professing," in *Gladly Learn, Gladly Teach: Living Out One's Calling in the Twenty-First Century Academy,* ed. John Marson Dunaway (Macon, Ga.: Mercer University Press, 2005), p. 15.

tices more than individual willpower that provided the matrix that made Christian teaching and learning possible.

Given this depth of demand on the teacher, it is perhaps best to end with a reminder that part of the point of Christian practices is to provide Spirit-inhabited ways of living with our failings. Practices are not theories. They have to be grown into in the living rather than plotted cleanly ahead of time. We have sought to illustrate how Christian practices can become fruitful ways of living and learning with our students. None of this is to be imagined as a new method guaranteeing success and applause if the steps are followed in the right order, the package that will (at last!) deliver real Christian education. It is, rather, an attempt to find a form of life as educators and learners that resonates with God's ways with the world in Christ, and to urge afresh that Christian learning must be considerably more than learning about Christian ideas. Miroslav Volf contends that "at the heart of every good theology lies not simply a plausible intellectual vision but more importantly a compelling account of a way of life," adding that "theology is therefore best done from within the pursuit of this way of life."[15] I suspect that something very similar could be said about Christian teaching and learning, and can in the end only recommend the pursuit.

15. Volf, "Theology for a Way of Life," in *Practicing Theology*, p. 247.

Contributors

Carolyne Call is Director of the Office for Civic and Social Engagement, Saint Mary's College, Notre Dame, Indiana, and is also ordained in the United Church of Christ. Her research interests include conditions promoting intellectual safety in higher education classrooms.

Rebecca Konyndyk DeYoung is professor of philosophy at Calvin College. She has published articles on various virtues and vices in the thought of Thomas Aquinas; her most recent work focuses on the seven capital vices in the Christian tradition. Her books include *Glittering Vices: A New Look at the Seven Deadly Sins and Their Remedies* (Brazos, 2009) and *Aquinas's Ethics: Metaphysical Foundations, Theological Context, and Moral Theory* (University of Notre Dame Press, 2009), co-authored with Christina Van Dyke and Colleen McCluskey.

Paul J. Griffiths holds the Warren Chair of Catholic Theology at Duke Divinity School. He works in philosophical theology. His most recent book is *Intellectual Appetite: A Theological Grammar* (Catholic University of America Press, 2009). His next is a commentary on the Latin text of the Song of Songs, due to appear from Brazos Press in 2011.

Glenn E. Sanders is professor of history and Chair of the Division of Behavioral and Social Sciences at Oklahoma Baptist University, Shawnee, Oklahoma. His interests include student moral formation through the study of the liberal arts.

Kurt C. Schaefer is professor of economics at Calvin College. He is also a student in the Master of Divinity program at Calvin Theological Seminary. He has directed semester programs in Budapest and London and the Calvin College Center for Social Research, and is the author (with W. James Bradley) of *The Uses and Misuses of Data and Models: The Mathematization of the Human Sciences* (Sage, 1998).

David I. Smith is Director of the Kuyers Institute for Christian Teaching and Learning and professor of German at Calvin College. He serves as editor of the *Journal of Education and Christian Belief* and of the *Journal of Christianity and Foreign Languages*. His most recent book is *Learning from the Stranger: Christian Faith and Cultural Diversity* (Eerdmans, 2009).

James K. A. Smith is professor of philosophy at Calvin College, where he also serves in the department of congregational and ministry studies and as a research fellow of the Calvin Institute of Christian Worship. His most recent books include *Desiring the Kingdom: Worship, Worldview, and Cultural Formation* (Baker Academic, 2009) and *Thinking in Tongues: Pentecostal Contributions to Christian Philosophy* (Eerdmans, 2010).

Matthew Walhout is professor of physics and dean for research and scholarship at Calvin College. In his laboratory research, he uses laser light to trap atoms and to study their behavior at extremely low temperatures. He has taught all levels of undergraduate physics, as well as courses on the history and philosophy of science.

Matthew Walters is a Calvin College graduate who worked as a student research assistant for the MEALS project in his senior year. His interest in this project springs from his work in and study of sustainable and ethical food systems.

Julie A. P. Walton is professor of health and exercise science in the Department of Kinesiology at Calvin College, where she teaches nutrition and exercise physiology. She is past president of the Christian Society for Kinesiology and Leisure Studies.

Ashley Woodiwiss holds the Grady Patterson Chair of Politics at Erskine College in Due West, South Carolina. He also directs the John Drummond Center for Statesmanship. His research interests include civic engagement, democratic theory, and political theology.